The
Struggle for
Black Equality
1954-1980

CONSULTING EDITOR

ERIC FONER

_____

American Century Series

HILL AND WANG · NEW YORK

A division of Farrar, Straus and Giroux

The

Struggle for

Black Equality

1954-1980

——

Harvard

Sitkoff

Copyright © 1981 by Harvard Sitkoff
Published simultaneously in Canada by
McGraw-Hill Ryerson Ltd., Toronto
Printed in the United States of America
Designed by Constance Fogler
First printing, 1981
Second printing, 1981
Library of Congress Cataloging in Publication Data
Sitkoff, Harvard.
The struggle for black equality, 1954–1980.
(American century series)
Bibliography: p.   Includes index.
    1. Afro-Americans—Civil rights.
2. United States—Race relations.   I. Title.
E185.615.S57   1981   323.1'196073   81-6536   AACR2
ISBN 0-8090-8925-4   ISBN 0-8090-0144-6   (pbk.)

FOR EVELYN

PREFACE

This book is concerned with one of the most significant developments in American history: the struggle for racial equality and justice waged between 1954 and 1980. It is designed primarily to provide a succinct narrative and interpretation of the civil-rights movement. I have, accordingly, written neither a comprehensive nor a scholarly account of the struggle. Important developments before 1954 are merely sketched; many events, organizations, and individuals that merit discussion are omitted; and topics that warrant definitive treatment are dealt with concisely. To help the reader who wishes to pursue a particular aspect of the struggle more fully, I have appended a bibliographical essay. The works listed there are also the source for all the quotations included in this account.

Some may consider it presumptuous to publish a historical analysis and synthesis of so recent and controversial a subject. The limited perspective of time, the many archival sources still closed, the scarcity of solidly researched monographs, and the inherent biases of most contemporary attempts to record and evaluate the bewildering rush of events from the pathbreaking *Brown* decision of 1954 through the crescendo of violence in the late 1960s combine to make the writing of a history of the modern struggle a hazardous task. This volume is sure to be revised as perspectives change and as more information becomes available. Nevertheless, I hope it will be of use to future historians. I am confident it will aid readers in the 1980s to develop an informed understanding of the recent past and to come to some preliminary conclusions and evaluations about the enduring significance of the struggle.

The facts of history, of course, do not speak for themselves. Any effort to describe and explain requires judgment; and no historian can entirely escape his basic beliefs. Honesty, however, dictates that a historian consider and test all the evidence according to the canons of the craft, guard against personal biases, avoid forcing the past into preconceived notions, and inform the reader of the author's viewpoint. My perspective derives from association and identification with the movement in the early sixties. I believed then that the struggle was confronting the United States with an issue that had undermined the nation's democratic institutions for nearly two hundred years, and that morality, justice, and a due concern for the future well-being of our society necessitated an end to racial inequality. This I still believe. Moreover, given the rapidity with which the popular media have relegated the civil-rights battles to the scrap heap of inattention and indifference, I felt compelled to write of the strivings and sufferings of these battles to make real the promise of democracy. I want the reader to encounter the anguish and hope, the violence and passion, the joy and sorrow that the fighters for freedom experienced. My attempt to recapture the drama of the era, as well as my value judgments, will certainly provoke disagreement. Good. At the very least, the writing of history ought to stimulate debate and further inquiry.

My effort to tell the story of the actions and consequences of the black struggle for equality, like the movement itself, has truly been a collective effort. Although a small part of the book derives from archival research and my own participation in some of the events narrated, this synthesis would not have been possible without the pioneering efforts of those historians, journalists, political scientists, sociologists, and memoirists who have written on aspects of this topic. Their personal accounts and scholarly studies, discussed in the bibliographical essay, underpin this book. My intellectual debt to them is enormous. I owe much, in addition, to the many important substantive and stylistic suggestions offered by my editor, Eric Foner, and my publisher, Arthur Wang. They made the manuscript much better in every way than it would otherwise have been. I am also indebted to many of my students and friends in the movement, too numerous to name individually, who shared with me their questions and observations, and sharpened my perception of the black struggle. As always, the encouragement and inspiration of William Chafe and William Leuchtenburg have been invaluable. The flaws of content, expression, and interpretation that remain are mine alone.

The final words are for my wife Evelyn, who was always there when needed, and to whom I dedicate this book.

H.S.

CONTENTS

The
Struggle for
Black Equality
1954-1980

ONE

Up from Slavery

Nourished by anger, revolutions are born of hope. They are the offspring of belief and bitterness, of faith in the attainment of one's goals and indignation at the limited rate and extent of change. Rarely in history are the two stirrings confluent in a sufficient force to generate an effective, radical social movement. They were in black America by the 1960s.

During the last decade of the nineteenth century, however, few Afro-Americans struggled for racial equality with much optimism. Their efforts to continue the campaign against Jim Crow initiated by the black abolitionists failed to stem the rising crest of white racism after Reconstruction. Largely bereft of white allies, blacks fought on the defensive, trying to hold their limited gains. They lost each battle. Congress permitted the white South to reduce blacks to a state of peonage, to disregard their civil rights, and to disenfranchise them by force, intimidation, and statute. So did the Supreme Court. Writing into the

Constitution its own beliefs in the inferiority of blacks, the late-nineteenth-century high court tightened every possible shackle confining the ex-slaves. Most American scholars cheered this legal counterrevolution which effectively nullified the Fourteenth and Fifteenth Amendments. It exemplified their teachings of inherent and irremediable racial differences, and of the folly of governmental tampering with local folkways. Whether appealing to scriptural or scientific evidence, to Darwinism, the gospel of Anglo-Saxonism, or the new interest in eugenics, a generation of clergymen, editors, and educators propounded the intellectual rationalizations for white supremacy.

Not surprisingly, most white Americans at the beginning of the twentieth century believed that, for the good of all, the naturally superior whites should rule over the baser races. They heard or read little to the contrary. The Southern Way had become the American Way. Even the most humanitarian reformers concerned with racial injustice counseled gradualism rather than immediacy. Northern liberals preached the necessity of deferring citizenship for blacks until the freedmen were ready for it; they emphasized the long-term gains to be derived from education, religion, and economic uplift and denigrated strategies predicated on agitation, force, or political activity.

This total acquiescence by government officials and Northern public opinion gave the white South all the permission it needed to institutionalize its white-supremacist beliefs. First came disenfranchisement, accomplished in the 1880s mainly through fraud and force. All the Southern states felt emboldened in the next two decades to follow the lead of the 1890 Mississippi state constitutional convention in officially adopting such disenfranchising techniques as poll taxes, "grandfather clauses," literacy and "good character" tests, and white primaries. Black voter registration plummeted 96 percent in Louisiana between 1896 and 1900. The number of Afro-Americans permitted to vote in the new century hovered around 3,500 in Alabama, which had an adult black population of nearly 300,000; and in

Mississippi, with an even larger black population fewer than a thousand blacks voted.

Political impotency bore on every aspect of Afro-American life. Unable to participate in the enactment or enforcement of the law, Southern blacks became increasingly vulnerable to physical assault and murder. Over a thousand were lynched between 1900 and 1915. No records exist to tally the number beaten or tortured. Nor can one describe adequately the terror of living with a constant fear of barbarity and violence, of having your security subject to the whim of those who despise you, of having no recourse to police or courts.

The Southern states, in addition, adopted a host of statutes methodically outlawing everything "interracial." These new segregation laws expressed the white South's all-encompassing belief in the inequality of blacks. Most Southern states now formally required Negroes and whites to be born separately in segregated hospitals; to live their lives as separately as possible in segregated schools, public accommodations, and places of work and recreation; and, presumably, to dwell in the next life separately in segregated funeral homes and cemeteries. The rapid proliferation of Jim Crow laws inspired an irrational competition among Southern legislators to erect ever more and higher barriers between the races. "White" and "Colored" signs sprouted everywhere and on everything. Atlanta mandated Jim Crow Bibles in its courtrooms. Alabama forbade Negroes to play checkers with whites. New Orleans segregated its prostitutes, and Oklahoma, its telephone booths. The lawmakers of Florida and North Carolina saw to it that white students would never touch textbooks used by blacks. Such edicts, branding blacks with an indelible mark of inferiority, could not but demean the spirit of Afro-Americans.

Jim Crow, furthermore, easily led to gross inequities in the distribution of public monies for education and civic services. The eleven Southern states in 1916 spent an average of $10.32 per white public-school student, and only $2.89 per black pupil.

There was one hospital bed available for every 139 American whites in the 1920s, but only one for every 1,941 blacks. And that was not all. Southern governments victimized blacks by bestial convict-leasing and chain-gang practices, and confined them to serfdom on the lowest rung of the economic ladder, doing all they could to implement the view of James K. Vardaman, who became Governor of Mississippi in 1904, that "God Almighty had created the Negro for a menial."

And blacks could do little to alter the situation or even to protest loudly. More than 90 percent of the nearly ten million Afro-Americans in 1910 lived in the South, three-quarters of them in rural areas, the vast majority working a white man's land, with a white man's mule and a white man's credit. Theirs was an oppressive, closed society, designed to thwart black advancement and encourage black subservience. All political and economic power remained vested in whites determined to maintain the status quo, however many black lives it cost. Daily facing grinding poverty, physical helplessness, and all the banal crudities of existence under an open, professed, and boasting racism, many blacks grew fatalistic and hopeless. Segregation and discrimination came to seem permanent, immutable, an inevitable condition of life, and the majority of Southern blacks succumbed to the new racial order.

But not all. Some protested by migrating. Between 1890 and 1910, nearly two hundred thousand Southern blacks fled to the North. Others returned to Africa or established autonomous black communities in the West. A few, mostly members of the tiny, Northern black elite, continued the struggle they had inherited from the black abolitionists and from the inspiring vision of equal rights nourished by the Civil War and Reconstruction. They spoke out for racial justice in such organizations as the Afro-American Council, Monroe Trotter's National Equal Rights League, Ida B. Wells's Antilynching League, and the Niagara Movement. Yet few blacks heard their pleas, and fewer whites heeded their demands. These small civil-rights groups of the early twentieth century, lacking adequate finances, political leverage, influential white allies, access to the major institutions shaping public opinion and policy, and the support of large numbers of blacks, could do virtually nothing to alter the course of American life and thought.

The ascendancy of Booker T. Washington at the turn of the century epitomized both the widespread despair of blacks and the powerlessness of the handful of blacks actively fighting against racial injustice. Although he worked covertly to diminish disenfranchisement and Jim Crow, Washington publicly and repeatedly emphasized the necessity of accommodation, con-, ciliation, and gradualism. Again and again he deprecated political and protest activity aimed at the immediate attainment of civil rights for blacks. "The best course to pursue in regard to civil rights," he often lectured to blacks, "is to let it alone; let it alone and it will settle itself." Thus, when the British author H. G. Wells criticized Jim Crow while on a visit to the United States, Washington answered back: "The only answer to it is for colored men to be patient, to make themselves competent, to do good work, to give no occasion against us." Primarily a spokesman for the leadership of the emerging black middle class, he counseled all blacks to lift themselves up by their own bootstraps. Too few, however, even had boots, and in the years before his death in 1915, Washington's nostrums failed abysmally to alleviate the plight of blacks.

The National Association for the Advancement of Colored People, organized in 1910, fared no better. Declaring its purposes to be "to promote equality of rights and eradicate caste or race prejudice . . . to advance the interests of colored citizens; to secure for them impartial suffrage; and to increase their opportunities for securing justice in the courts, education for their children, employment according to their ability; and complete equality before the law," the interracial NAACP relied on litigation and agitation as the chief means to those ends. Despite two victories at the Supreme Court, which declared unconstitutional the grandfather clause and city ordinances mandating residential segregation, the association's goals remained an impossible dream during its first quarter of a century. It could not destroy the edifice of discrimination, lessen the rampant prejudice everywhere in the nation, or deter the mushrooming ghettoization of blacks. Because of continuing white indifference and black impotency, the NAACP could do nothing to affect the racial policies of Southern governments or to compel the necessary corrective actions by the national government.

Indeed, no black leader or organization or strategy could stem the tide of discrimination and segregation in the first third of the twentieth century. Powerlessness fostered frustrations. Defeat bred disillusionment. Blacks in the 1920s squabbled among themselves more than they assailed their oppressors.

Certain harbingers of change nonetheless appeared. Most stemmed from the mass migration of blacks to the cities and to the North. Between 1910 and 1920 the "Great Migration" brought more than half a million blacks northward, and another three-quarters of a million blacks fled from the boll weevil and the lynch mob in the 1920s. Many who followed the North Star looking for the Promised Land found hell instead: educational and residential segregation, dilapidated housing milked by white slumlords, discrimination by labor unions and employers, brutality by white policemen, and liquor and narcotics the only means of escape. Yet, for most, the Northern urban ghetto meant surcease from permanent tenantry, poverty, disease, and ignorance, and the first step into the mainstream of the industrial labor force.

Northern Negroes, unlike their Southern brethren, could also vote. In 1928, for the first time in the century, an Afro-American was elected to Congress. Other blacks won local offices in Chicago, Cleveland, Detroit, New York City, and Philadelphia, and Negro votes in those cities became a factor in determining election results. Politically, the Negro slowly began to command attention. The bonds of hopelessness of the rigid caste system of the Black Belt less and less characterized all of black America.

Hope sprouted also from the seeds of spiritual emancipation planted by the literary movement of the 1920s that Afro-Americans labeled the Harlem Renaissance, the Black Renaissance, and the New Negro Movement. Whether celebrating the racial chauvinism of blacks, the identification of Afro-Americans with Africa, or decrying lynchings and discrimination, Negro poets and novelists sought to free themselves from white symbols and images and to write in their own idiom. By focusing white America's attention on blacks, by awakening the pride of Afro-Americans in their race and folk traditions, and by militant protests and demands for civil rights, the New Negro articulated the consciousness of the possibility of change brought about by migration.

So did the NAACP. Led by W. E. B. Du Bois, the brilliant black editor of its monthly journal, *The Crisis,* the NAACP publicized the hostility of organized labor to blacks, railed against disenfranchisement, and demanded that Congress enact an anti-lynching bill. Despite repeated rebuffs, the NAACP kept aloft the banners of racial equality, and gradually gained adherents among blacks and whites in the cities of the North. Most important, its tactic of complaining loudly and insistently at each manifestation of racism slowly eroded the myth that Southern whites and black accommodators had forged: that blacks were content, even happy, with the status quo; that they did not consider the rights and duties of citizenship vital to black interests; and that they preferred the separation of the races to association with whites.

And so did Marcus Garvey's movement for racial pride and self-determination. Despite his Universal Negro Improvement Association's labeling of Du Bois and the NAACP as worse enemies of the Afro-American than the Ku Klux Klan and its denunciation of all programs promoting interracialism as plots against blacks, Garvey convinced millions of blacks to believe in their ability to shape their destiny. A master showman, Garvey dramatized the extreme plight of Afro-Americans and the desperate necessity of change. An intuitive psychologist, he radicalized the powerless by instilling in them a sense of their potential power. And as a persuasive teacher, the Jamaican leader convinced masses of Negroes that white racism and not black failings explained their lowly status.

In the 1930s, these stirrings began for the first time to inner-vate significantly the struggle for black equality. The proponents of civil rights no longer stood alone. They fought alongside radicals pressing for class unity unhampered by racial divisions, labor leaders wanting strong unions, ethnic and political minorities desiring greater security for themselves from a strong central government that would protect constitutional rights, and liberals battling Southern opponents of the New Deal. A growing number of black-rights organizations also benefited from the new ideological consensus emerging in the academic community. It undermined racism by emphasizing the influence of environment on peoples rather than innate characteristics. It stressed the damage done to individuals by prejudice and the costs to the nation of discrimination. It demolished the stereotype of the Afro-American as a contented buffoon. Intellectually, white supremacy was now on the defensive.

Most of all, the New Deal's unprecedented substantive and symbolic aid to blacks stimulated hope for racial changes. With some success, the New Deal insisted on equality of treatment in its relief programs. President Franklin D. Roosevelt appointed over a hundred blacks to administrative posts, and the number of Afro-American federal employees tripled in the Depression decade. The Roosevelt Administration began the desegregation of federal rest rooms, cafeterias, and secretarial pools. A host of government publications and conferences made explicit the federal government's responsibility for issues of human rights. Never before, moreover, had a First Lady and so many high-level government officials been associated so closely with civil-

rights groups. On a wide variety of racial issues, the most prominent whites in the nation had started to make legitimate the
aspirations of blacks. This was especially true of Roosevelt's
appointees to the Supreme Court. Their decisions in the late
1930s increasingly made the Afro-American less a *freedman*
and more a *free man.*

Nevertheless, the basic conditions of life for most blacks
barely changed in the thirties. Civil rights had begun to emerge
as a major national concern but disenfranchisement and discrimination remained the rule, and the "job ceiling" kept blacks in
the lowest-paid positions. The majority of whites, enslaved by
fear, ignorance, and prejudice, favored neither desegregation
nor equal opportunities for blacks. And most blacks, still
plagued by poverty and powerlessness, could not yet battle for
full citizenship or rebel against the inequities destroying them.

That changed, however, during the Second World War and
the years immediately after. The ideological character of the war
and the government's need for the loyalty and manpower of all
Americans stimulated blacks to demand a better deal. Many
responded with a militancy never before seen in black communities. Membership in the NAACP multiplied nearly ten times, to
a half a million. The Congress of Racial Equality, organized in
1942, experimented with nonviolent direct action to challenge
Jim Crow; and A. Philip Randolph attempted to build his
March-on-Washington Committee into an all-black mass protest
movement. In 1941, his threat of a massive black march on
Washington, combined with the growth of the Afro-American
vote and the exigencies of the defense effort, led Roosevelt to
issue Executive Order 8802. The first Presidential directive on
race since Reconstruction, it established the President's Committee on Fair Employment Practices and prohibited discriminatory employment practices by unions and companies with
government contracts or engaged in war-related work. The
FEPC and the desperate labor shortage caused by the draft
and booming war production resulted in some two million blacks

gaining employment in defense plants and another two hundred thousand entering the federal civil service. By 1945, black membership in labor unions had doubled to 1,250,000.

Still other barriers crumbled during the war. The army integrated its officer-training program and the marines and navy opened their ranks to blacks for a variety of duties other than messmen. Liberals repeatedly emphasized that the practices of white supremacy impeded the war effort and brought into disrepute the stated war aims of the United States. And over seven hundred thousand blacks pulled up stakes in the South to find a new home outside Dixie. By the end of the war, blacks had gained enough from the expansion in jobs and income, from service in the armed forces, and from the massive urbanization of the black population to be able to launch an aggressive assault on racist practices.

But they did not. In part, the Second World War stifled black protest. While discrimination in defense employment and in the armed services had stimulated militancy early in the war, the prolonged involvement of the United States in what it viewed as a war for survival dampened that militancy. Winning the war as speedily as possible with the least possible loss of American lives overrode all other concerns. Few took kindly to anything that threatened that goal, such as a war against racism at home. The nation demanded unity not division, consensus not conflict. Accordingly, few black leaders after 1942 flirted with any tactic or strategy that might remotely be considered to harm the war effort, and the belligerence of blacks dramatically decreased. The race riots in 1943, particularly in Detroit and Harlem, further frightened the black leadership, causing it to concentrate on reducing black assertive behavior of any kind. "Good Conduct" campaigns and the control of racial rumors took precedence over actively combatting segregation and discrimination. A poll by the Pittsburgh *Courier* in the midst of the war showed 71 percent of Afro-Americans opposed to a March on Washington to protest discrimination, a sharp turn from the mood of 1941. So did the fact that every major civil-rights spokesman and Negro newspaper denounced A. Philip Randolph's 1943 call for civil disobedience against Jim Crow schools and railroads, and that CORE's efforts to involve large numbers of blacks in militant direct action came to naught. Thus, while the war brought revolutionary changes in American life that would eventually make possible a successful black campaign for racial justice, in the short run it hampered the growth of mass black protest.

Also in part, the very steps taken toward racial justice after a half a century of deteriorating race relations beguiled civil-rights leaders. They chose, in the words of a popular song of the day, "to accentuate the positive, eliminate the negative." With pride they ballyhooed the increasing number of "Negro firsts," listing the advances made by individual blacks and the race. Their loud cheers for Jackie Robinson's crossing the color line and his quick rise to star status in major-league baseball drowned out their quiet grumbling at the black Brooklyn Dodger not being allowed to stay in the same hotels as his white teammates and at the overwhelming extent of segregation remaining throughout professional and amateur sports. They made far more of the awards and honors accorded Dr. Julian Perry, the renowned black scientist, than of the news of firebombing of his home by whites who would not accept the presence of a black scientist in their neighborhood. Indeed, while Afro-American spokesmen confidently counted on the benefits to be derived from the migration of blacks northward, the white trek to the suburbs of the North became an exodus. At the close of the 1950s, whites outnumbered blacks in the suburbs by a ratio of more than thirty-five to one. A new color line, just as effective as the old, still kept the United States two nations—separate and unequal.

The Negro press, similarly, went to great lengths to publicize the jump in the number of blacks registered to vote in the South, from 250,000 in 1940 to over a million in 1950, but downplayed the fact that three out of four adult blacks in Dixie still could not vote. Headlines trumpeted the election of blacks to the governing councils of Richmond and Nashville in 1948 and 1951. Yet hundreds of counties deprived blacks of any voice in government whatsoever, and blacks throughout the South remained politically powerless. In scores of articles and speeches, moreover, the leadership of civil-rights organizations played up the Negro vote in the North as the "balance of power," and credited it with providing the margin of victory for Harry Truman in 1948. After the election, however, President Truman refused to press Congress to enact civil-rights legislation and did nothing to implement the Supreme Court's 1950 decision against segregation in interstate commerce. Nevertheless, the NAACP's balance sheet in race relations that year, after an impressive compilation of black strides toward the mainstream of American life, concluded optimistically: "Some might call these mere straws in the wind, but they do indicate the direction in which the wind is blowing."

The widespread anticipation of even greater progress in race relations further subdued black anger. Virtually every basic change in American society gave blacks hope that discrimination and segregation would soon be overcome. None was more important than the elephantine growth of the American economy. The Gross National Product rose from $206 billion in 1940 to $285 billion in 1950, and then to nearly $400 billion in 1955. The number of civilian jobs increased from 54 million at the end of World War II to 60 million in 1950, to 63 million in 1955. Personal expenditures leaped in these same years from $122 million to $195 million to $257 million. This spectacular rate of economic growth made possible an increasing income for blacks, their entry into industries and labor unions previously closed to blacks, and a gain in occupational status as the constant shortage of workers necessitated a slackening of restrictive promotion policies. The huge enlargement of the economy, moreover, meant that the advancement of blacks did not have to come at the expense of whites, thus undermining perhaps the most powerful source of white resistance to black progress.

The effect of economic changes on race relations was particularly marked in the South. The rapid industrialization of Dixie since 1940 ended the dominance of the cotton culture. With it went the need for a vast black underclass of unskilled laborers. Power began to shift from rural areas to the cities, and from tradition-oriented landed families to the new officers and professionals in absentee-owned corporations. Industrialization also accelerated urbanization and the migration to the South of millions of white-collar employees and their families who had little stake in the perpetuation of the rural color-caste system. The "New South," many prophesied, would be far more concerned with profits and economic expansion than with outdated racial mores.

In addition, changes in the economy radically affected black migration. The mechanization of cotton production pushed blacks off the farms and the lure of jobs pulled them to the cities. Over a million would leave the South in the 1940s, and another million and a half in the fifties. This mass migration fundamentally altered the configuration of the race problem. It became national in scope. No longer affecting only one region, it could not now be left in the hands of Southern whites. It also both modified the objective conditions of life for blacks and changed their perceptions of goals and tactics. Freed from the confines of a rigid caste system and subject to urban formative experiences, blacks developed new norms and beliefs. Aggression could be turned against one's oppressor rather than against one's self, more employment and educational opportunities could be secured, and political power could be mobilized. The promise of a better world in the next one would not suffice. The urban black would not wait for his rewards until the afterlife, and enfranchisement promised all in this life that religion did in the next. The New Deal and the Second World War, moreover, had corroded the doctrines of localism and decentralization which had blocked all hope for a federal effort to guarantee blacks either civil rights or economic opportunity.

The new prominence of the United States as a world power further presaged black advancement. During World War II, millions of Americans became aware for the first time of the danger of racism to national security. Japan focused on the United States' racist treatment of nonwhites as the core of its propaganda campaign to win the loyalty of the colored peoples of China, India, and Latin America. Each lynching, race riot, and manifestation of Jim Crow during the war was publicized by the Axis as proof of the hypocrisy of President Franklin Roosevelt's Four Freedoms. The costs of racism went even higher during the Cold War. The Soviet Union continuously undercut American appeals to the nations of Africa and Asia by highlighting the ill treatment of blacks in the United States. Rarely in the first two decades after the Second World War did a plea for civil rights before the Supreme Court, on the floor of Congress, or emanating from the White House, fail to emphasize the point that white racism adversely affected our relations with the rest of the world. The rapid growth of independence movements among the world's colored peoples had special significance for Afro-Americans. They proved the feasibility of change and the vulnerability of white supremacy, while at the same time aiding Afro-Americans to see themselves as members of a world majority rather than as a hopelessly outnumbered American minority.

The decline in intellectual respectability of racist ideas also convinced blacks that the winds of change blew their way. The excesses of Nazism and the decline of Western imperialism combined with internal developments in various academic disciplines to discredit the pseudo-scientific rationalizations once popularly accepted as the basis for white supremacy. Books and essays attacking racial injustice and inequality, epitomized by Gunnar Myrdal's *An American Dilemma,* dominated discourse on the subject. Racial egalitarianism became a major theme in the nation's media and educational systems. And every public-opinion poll and attitude survey after the start of World War II underlined white America's increasing recognition of the harm done to blacks by racism.

These fundamental transpositions made it easy to believe that continued progress would be automatic. At most, just a bit more legal action or political pressure would suffice to usher in a new era in race relations. The demise of Jim Crow would necessitate neither struggle nor sacrifice, neither radical strategies nor disruptive tactics. This faith, obviating the need for mass black direct action, also reflected the conservative American mood after World War II. After more than a decade of rapid, bewildering change, and exhausting battles against the Great Depression and the Axis, the vast majority wanted surcease. Most Americans yearned for stability. They desired harmony. Few had any tolerance for revolutionary proposals, in civil rights or anything else. Fewer looked kindly on any policies likely to promote domestic conflict.

White supremacists, moreover, played on the obsessive American fear of Communism to discredit the civil-rights cause. They claimed repeatedly that agitation against Jim Crow sowed dissension among the American people, the primary Communist objective in the emerging Cold War. The leading spokesmen of the South constantly pointed to Communist support of the civil-rights movement. Segregationists missed no opportunity to link the black struggle with Communist ideology and subversion. In the heyday of red-baiting after World War II, these tactics worked. Most civil-rights groups avoided direct action. Their leadership opted for a conservative posture to avoid even a hint of radicalism. When a small interracial band of pacifists and socialists from the Congress of Racial Equality and the Fellowship of Reconciliation journeyed throughout the upper South to test compliance of a Supreme Court ruling against segregation in interstate travel, the Negro press barely reported the news, and other civil-rights organizations shunned the 1947 Journey of

Reconciliation. The following year they opposed A. Philip Randolph's call for civil disobedience to protest Jim Crow in the armed forces. With undue haste, the civil-rights leadership condemned the pro-Soviet remarks of Paul Robeson, a controversial black singer and actor, and disassociated themselves from the Marxist stance of W. E. B. Du Bois. The fear of McCarthyism so inhibited blacks that they failed to use the Korean War as a lever for racial reform, as they had World War II. At mid-century, direct action had ceased being a tactic in the quest for racial justice.

That suited the NAACP hierarchy. Never entirely at ease with the black mass actions during the New Deal and early war years, the NAACP became less a protest organization and more an agency of litigation and lobbying after World War II. No longer fearing that competition from more combative black groups would overshadow the NAACP, its branches in the South concentrated on voter registration, while those in the North endeavored to secure fair-employment and fair-housing ordinances. By 1953, twelve states and thirty cities had adopted fair-employment laws of varying effectiveness. Median black-family income rose from $1,614 to $2,338 between 1947 and 1952. As a percentage of median white-family income, black earnings jumped from 41 percent in 1940 to 51 percent in 1949, and to 57 percent in 1952. That year, nearly 40 percent of blacks were engaged in professional, white-collar, skilled, and semi-skilled work, double the proportion of 1940. The life expectancy of blacks increased from 53.1 years in 1940 to 61.7 years in 1953, compared to 64.2 and 69.6 for whites, and the proportion of black families owning their homes went from 25 percent to 30 percent in the forties. Meanwhile, the proportion of blacks aged five to nineteen enrolled in school leaped from 60 percent in 1930 to 68.4 percent in 1940, to 74.8 percent in 1950. That figure still lagged behind the 79.3 percent of whites in school, but the gap had narrowed dramatically. And the number of blacks in college had soared from about 27,000 in 1930 to over 113,000 in 1950.

Such gains apparently justified the NAACP's approach and secured its hegemony in race relations. The national office and legal staff at midcentury marshaled all their resources for a courtroom assault on *de jure* school segregation. Many blacks believed integrated education to be the main route to racial equality. No other Afro-American protest group even put forth an alternative strategy of social change. By 1954, all the hopes of blacks rested on the success of the NAACP litigation. It had become an article of faith that a Supreme Court decision ruling school segregation unconstitutional would cause the quick death of Jim Crow in America.

The first major crack in the edifice of school segregation had come in 1938, when the NAACP won a Supreme Court ruling which held that an out-of-state scholarship to a black Missourian wishing to study law at the University of Missouri denied that student the equal protection of the laws guaranteed by the constitution. The Court declared that Missouri could not exclude blacks from its law school when it offered Afro-Americans only out-of-state tuition grants as an alternative. Hoping to make segregation so prohibitively expensive that the South would dismantle its biracial system because of the financial burden, the NAACP launched a series of suits seeking complete equality in facilities governed by the separate-but-equal rule. Then, emboldened by the strides made by blacks during the Second World War, the NAACP's Legal Defense and Education Fund, led by Thurgood Marshall, shifted from skirmishes on the inequality of separate facilities to a direct attack on segregation itself. Marshall hoped his strategy would force the Court to overrule *Plessy,* the 1896 opinion that declared segregation no infringement on civil rights if the states provided blacks with separate accommodations equal to those given to whites. Marshall's work resulted first in three unanimous decisions on a single day in 1950 which demolished the separate-but-equal façade. The high court struck down Jim Crow on railway dining cars in the South; it ruled that if a state chose not to establish an equal and separate school for blacks, then it could not segregate blacks within the white school; and, lastly, the tribunal so emphasized the importance of "intangible factors" in determining the equality of separate schools that separate-but-equal no longer seemed possible. Although the Supreme Court held that it was not necessary to reexamine *Plessy* to grant relief to the three black plaintiffs, the 1950 decisions made the end of segregated schooling for students at all levels a near-certainty.

In 1951, Marshall began to coordinate a series of lawsuits charging segregated education with being discriminatory per se, even if the facilities were equal. In Clarendon County, South Carolina, the NAACP sued in the name of several black school-children, and in Prince Edward County, Virginia, they represented black high-school students. In New Castle County, Delaware, and in the District of Columbia, Marshall filed suits on behalf of both elementary and high-school black students. And in Topeka, Kansas, the NAACP argued the case of Oliver Brown, who sought to enjoin enforcement of a state law that permitted cities to maintain segregated schools, which forced his eight-year-old daughter, Linda, to travel a mile by bus to reach a black school even though she lived only three blocks from an all-white elementary school. On December 9, 1952, the Supreme Court heard oral argument on all five cases, combined and docketed under the name of the petitioner listed first—Oliver Brown. Unexpectedly, the NAACP was aided by the Truman administration, which, in its last days, filed a brief as a friend of the Court arguing against the constitutionality of segregation.

The Supreme Court initially divided on the question of overturning *Plessy*. After several months of discussion, two justices changed their mind, creating a slim majority in favor of the NAACP's contention. Now the question became whether the justices in the minority could be likewise persuaded. To that end, the Court voted for a reargument. It asked the litigants to prepare answers to questions pertaining to the intentions of the framers of the Fourteenth Amendment, the power of the Court to abolish segregation in the schools, and, if the tribunal did have such a right and chose to exercise it, whether the Supreme Court could permit gradual desegregation or did it have to order an instant end to segregation. While the lawyers revised their briefs, Chief Justice Fred Vinson died suddenly in the summer of 1953. The new President, Dwight D. Eisenhower, appointed California Governor Earl Warren to fill the vacant post. Vinson had sought to avoid ruling on *Plessy*, and in all likelihood, two other justices would have voted with him, resulting in either a further postponement on the constitutionality of school segregation or a seriously split decision.

Following the reargument, which began on December 7 and lasted for three days, the nation waited for what most commentators predicted would be a historic decision. But for half a year the Court remained silent on this most celebrated case. Behind closed doors, the bickering and bargaining continued. A clear majority of the justices wanted to void segregation in the schools and to reverse *Plessy*. Two justices held out, and Warren kept postponing the decision, hoping he could gain their concurrence. Above all, the Chief Justice wanted the Court's ruling to be unanimous. Anything less on a social issue so sensitive, on a political question so explosive, would destroy the chance for full compliance by Southern whites. So, patiently, Warren beseeched and compromised. Finally, early in May, the two dissenters gave the Chief Justice their assent. He had won unanimity.

By Monday, May 17, 1954, the Supreme Court ruling on school segregation had been so overdue that many forgot its imminence. The morning's newspapers gave no hint that a decision would be announced. Most journalists in Washington speculated on the consequences of a French loss of Dien Bien Phu in Vietnam, on the outcome of the Army–McCarthy hearings, and on the chances for more rain. Even those reporters seated in the ornate chamber of the Supreme Court did not anticipate that the segregation decision would be announced when the Court convened at noon.

After forty minutes of routine business, the Chief Justice leaned forward and began to read: "I have for announcement the judgment and opinion of the Court in No. 1—*Oliver Brown et al. v. Board of Education of Topeka.*" Warren traced briefly the paths that led the cases to the Supreme Court and reviewed the history of the Fourteenth Amendment, finding it "inconclusive" in relation to school segregation because public education, particularly in the South, had barely developed in the 1860s. "Today," the Chief Justice continued, "education is perhaps the most important function of state and local governments." Since it is the key to opportunity and advancement in American life, public education "is a right which must be made available to all on equal terms." On this premise, he quickly came to the nub of the matter: "Does segregation of children in public schools solely on the basis of race, even though the physical facilities and other 'tangible' factors may be equal, deprive the children of the minority group of equal educational opportunities?"

Warren paused. "We believe that it does." Buttressed by a footnote citing several contemporary studies on the psychological effects of segregation, the former governor contended that the separation of black children "from others of similar age and qualifications solely because of their race generates a feeling of inferiority as to their status in the community that may affect their hearts and minds in a way unlikely ever to be undone." He ended in a rising voice. "We conclude that in the field of public education the doctrine of 'separate but equal' has no place. Separate educational facilities are inherently unequal. Therefore, we hold that the plaintiffs and others similarly situated for whom the actions have been brought are, by reason of the segregation complained of, deprived of the equal protection of the laws guaranteed by the Fourteenth Amendment." Nothing in American race relations would be the same again.

Blacks shouted hosannas as they heard the news. They hailed Marshall, the black lawyer who had used the white man's laws before an all-white Supreme Court to win a verdict voiding segregation. Their jubilant leaders vied in choosing superlatives to laud the decision. Euphoric blacks declared that just as the first Emancipation Proclamation abolished slavery, so this second proclamation of emancipation would end all Jim Crow. *Brown* would be the precedent for declaring unconstitutional any state-imposed or enforced segregation. Surely, most rhapsodized, a new day in race relations had dawned. *Brown* promised a truly equal education for black children in integrated classrooms throughout the nation. More, it offered the real beginning of a multiracial democratic society. *Brown* heightened the aspirations and expectations of Afro-Americans as nothing ever had before. Nearly a century after their professed freedom had been stalled, compromised, and stolen, blacks confidently anticipated being free and equal at last.

Little in the next year shook this faith. Few Dixie politicians rushed to echo Mississippi Senator James O. Eastland that the South "will not abide by nor obey this legislative decision by a political court." Most educators foresaw scant difficulty in putting the court ruling into effect. According to a *New York Times* survey of school officials, none thought "that the threats to abandon the public school system would be carried out. . . . No one expected any violence or any real crisis to develop." Several hundred school districts in the border states (Delaware, Kentucky, Maryland, Missouri, Oklahoma, and West Virginia) and in states with local option on segregation (Arizona, Kansas, New Mexico, and Wyoming) quickly and peacefully integrated their classrooms, as did the District of Columbia at President Eisenhower's direction.

Then, on May 31, 1955, the momentum stopped. Just fifty-four weeks after the Supreme Court had taken a giant stride toward the demise of Jim Crow, it stepped backward. Its implementation decision on the *Brown* ruling rejected the NAACP's plea to order instant and total school desegregation. The justices, instead, adopted the "go slow" approach advocated by the Justice Department and by the attorneys general of the Southern states. The Court assigned the responsibility for drawing up plans for desegregation to local school authorities and left it to local federal judges to determine the pace of desegregation, requiring only that a "prompt and reasonable start toward full compliance" be made and that desegregation proceed "with all deliberate speed." Acknowledging the potential for difficulties, moreover, the Supreme Court refused to set a deadline and authorized delays when necessary. For the first time, the Supreme Court had vindicated a constitutional right and then deferred its exercise.

However much the Warren Court foresaw the seemingly endless round of further litigation, procrastination, and obstruction this invited, circumstances dictated the decision for gradualism. It was the price of unanimity in *Brown v. Board of Education,* the compromise needed to keep two justices from dissenting. Warren deeply believed that a divided Court on so sensitive an issue "would have been catastrophic," that only a unanimous desegregation decision stood a chance of public support.

He accepted gradualism to allay the fears of those justices who worried that the Court's inability to enforce a momentous ruling would discredit the entire judicial process. The compromise also reflected the unpopularity of *Brown* in the South. Public-opinion polls showed more than 80 percent of white Southerners opposed to school desegregation, and the Supreme Court hoped to head off resistance to the law of the land by permitting the change to be slow and piecemeal. To order immediate school desegregation, the Court reckoned, would force most Southern politicians to take up the cudgels of defiance to federal authority, an action only a tiny minority had taken to date. Desperately, the Justices sought to contain the rebellion, since they could not even count on the other branches of the federal government.

No help would come from the White House. The President of the United States, Dwight D. Eisenhower, declined to join the battle against segregation. He refused to endorse or support the *Brown* ruling. Covetous of the votes of white Southerners and wedded to a restrictive view of Presidential authority, Eisenhower repeatedly stated that he would express neither "approbation nor disapproval" of *Brown v. Board of Education*. He lumped together those who demanded compliance with the Court decision and those who obstructed it, publicly denouncing "extremists on both sides." Expressive of his conservatism, the President remarked often: "I don't believe you can change the hearts of men with laws or decisions." To one of his aides, Eisenhower emphasized: "I am convinced that the Supreme Court decision set back progress in the South at least fifteen years. . . . It's all very well to talk about school integration—if you remember you may also be talking about social *dis*integration. Feelings are deep on this. . . . And the fellow who tries to tell me that you can do these things by force is just plain nuts."

Eisenhower preferred change as a result of education, rather than coercion. But he would not educate. The President rejected all pleas that he tour the South seeking compliance, or call a conference of Southern moderates, or appeal on television to the nation for understanding. He simply did not favor school desegregation, much as he had never approved desegregation of the armed forces. Eisenhower regretted he had ever appointed Earl Warren to the Supreme Court, calling it "the biggest damfool mistake I ever made." And the titular head of the Democratic Party, Adlai Stevenson, barely differed on this issue from his GOP rival. Stevenson asked that the white South be "given time and patience," rejected the idea of using federal troops to enforce court-ordered desegregation, and opposed all proposals that would bar federal aid to schools maintaining segregation.

To be sure, no danger existed in the mid-fifties that Congress would legislate to speed desegregation. A conservative coalition of Midwestern Republicans and Southern Democrats controlled both the House of Representatives and the Senate, guarding vigilantly against any federal infringement on states' rights. Not content merely to stonewall any move to support *Brown,* Southern congressmen mobilized in 1956 to fight against what Senator Richard Russell of Georgia termed "a flagrant abuse of judicial power" and what Virginia Senator Harry Byrd called "the most serious blow that has been struck against the rights of the states." On March 12, 1956, 101 members of Congress from the South signed a "Declaration of Constitutional Principles" asking their states to refuse to obey the desegregation order. Labeling *Brown* "unwarranted" and "contrary to the Constitution," the Southern manifesto proclaimed that the Supreme Court possessed no power to demand an end to segregation, that only a state, and not the federal government, can decide whether a school should be segregated or not, and that the states would be in the right in opposing the Court's order. The signatories further promised to try to reverse *Brown,* and to prevent the government from using force if it tried to carry out the Supreme Court decision.

The manifesto, along with Eisenhower's silence and the Supreme Court's paradoxical "deliberate speed" ruling, ushered in an era of massive resistance to the law of the land in the eleven states of the Old Confederacy. Defiance of the Court and the Constitution became the touchstone of Southern loyalty, the necessary proof of one's concern for the security of the white race. With the overwhelming support of the South's white press and pulpit, segregationist politicians resurrected John C. Calhoun's notions of "interposition" and "nullification" to rationalize their effort to thwart federal authority. Together they galvanized racist hatred to gain backing for every conceivable diehard tactic of opposition to *Brown.*

White supremacists first resorted to stalling, doing nothing until confronted with a federal-court injunction. This forced black parents and NAACP attorneys to initiate individual de-segregation suits in the more than two thousand Southern school districts. Usually, the black plaintiffs faced economic intimidation by the local white-power structure; often they risked physical harm; always, they encountered repeated postponements due to crowded court dockets and motions for delay by school authorities. After years of harassment to the plaintiffs, mounting legal costs to the NAACP, lost jobs and incalulable psychological damage to blacks due to threats and fear, school authorities would finally come up with a plan for the most limited, token desegregation.

Then black schoolchildren had to face the horrors of racist resistance. In one school district after another, segregationists staged the same drama: forcing young blacks to enter a school by passing rock-throwing white mobs and white pickets shouting "Nigger! Nigger! Nigger!"; persuading white teachers to ignore or persecute the black students; encouraging the children to torment and threaten their new black classmates. " 'If you come back to school, I'll cut your guts out!' could be heard in the halls," recalled a Tennessee high-school teacher. "Eggs smashed on their books, ink smeared on their clothes, in the lockers, knives flourished in their presence, nails tossed in their faces and spiked in their seats. Vulgar words constantly whispered in their ears." The harassment proved too much for some blacks. They reenrolled their children in segregated schools; they moved to other towns and states. But more and more blacks endured the hatred and persisted in their struggle for dignity and equality.

To frustrate such black courage, segregationists pressed for new laws to obstruct integration. "As long as we can legislate, we can segregate," said one white supremacist, and the Southern states rushed pell-mell to enact more than 450 laws and resolutions to prevent or limit school desgregation. Some acts required schools faced with desegregation orders to cease operation; others revoked the license of any teacher who taught mixed classes; still more amended compulsory-attendance laws, so that no child could be required to enroll in an integrated school, and provided for state payments of private-academy tuition, so that districts could abolish their public-school system rather than desegregate.

Of all the legislative tactics of massive resistance, none proved more successful than the pupil-placement law. Theoretically, it guaranteed each child "freedom of choice" in the selection of a school. Local authorities could not consider race in assigning pupils to particular schools. But they could accept or reject transfer applications on such criteria as, in the Georgia law, "the psychological qualification of the pupil," "the psychological effect upon the pupil of attendance at a particular school," and "the morals, conduct, health and personal standards of the pupil." Invariably, school boards assigned black and white children to different schools. In 1958, moreover, the Supreme Court upheld the constitutionality of the pupil-placement laws, which were nondiscriminatory at face value but which actually maintained school systems as rigidly segregated as those which the justices had struck down four years earlier.

To frustrate blacks further, most of the Southern states also passed measures to hound and harass the NAACP, which had almost singlehandedly carried the campaign for school desegregation. Various laws required the NAACP to make public its membership lists, made membership a cause for dismissal of public-school teachers and state employees, charged the association with committing "barratry" (the persistent instigation of lawsuits), and made it a crime for organizations to cause trouble by attacking local segregation ordinances. In time, the Supreme Court struck down all the anti-NAACP laws, but for several years the association was forced to divert energy, money, and talent away from the desegregation battle to the fight for its own survival.

Not content with legal measures of obstruction, hostile segregationists preached violent resistance. Virulent rabble-rousers,

often with the approval of the South's most respected spokesmen, stirred up the region's rural and low-income whites to
attack blacks insisting on their constitutional rights. The Ku
Klux Klan revived. Zealots across the South organized new
klaverns, donned their white hoods and robes, and burned
crosses to terrorize blacks. Too respectable to join the low-
status KKK, tens of thousands of middle-class whites rushed to
enroll in the White Citizens' Councils. They wore no masks but
proved just as determined as the Klan to defy *Brown* and enforce racial orthodoxy, by intimidation if possible and by insurrection if necessary. Together, the KKK, the Councils, and a
host of local vigilante committees brought riots and violent
demonstrations to the South at the start of the school year each
September.

Their lawless behavior, often directed at young children, out-
raged millions of Americans who did not live in the South.
Most Northerners cared little about school desegregation in
Dixie and considered the NAACP too militant. Nevertheless,
they were shocked at the news headlines of schools being dyna-
mite-bombed and the televised scenes of hate-filled white mobs
rampaging to preserve segregation. Time and again in the decade
ahead, such racist extremism would discredit the cause of the
white South and force a majority of otherwise unconcerned citizens to demand that the federal government act to preserve
order and enforce the law of the land. It happened first in
Little Rock.

A New South city, Little Rock appeared an unlikely battle-
ground in the fight over school desegregation. It had a racially
moderate mayor, congressman, and newspaper, and a governor
not known to be a race-baiter. Several other Arkansas communities had peacefully begun to desegregate, as had the state university, and, after a bit of stalling, Little Rock's school board
acceded to a federal court order to admit nine blacks to Central
High, a school with some two thousand white students, as the
first step toward integration. A model of gradualism and def-

erence to the whites of Little Rock, the desegregation process would take eight years to complete. Indeed, the only vocal opposition to it came from the local NAACP, which denounced the process as too token and too slow.

In 1957, however, the winds of resistance howled. A storm of racial demagoguery swept the South. Politicians seeking office shouted defiance of the Supreme Court and vied in pledging unyielding opposition to *Brown*. Some vowed they would go to jail rather than desegregate; some swore they would die rather than permit integration. Those who counseled moderation customarily came in second and, like George C. Wallace in Alabama, promised: "They outniggered me that time, but they'll never do it again." In Arkansas, Governor Orval Faubus believed he faced a difficult fight for reelection. No gubernatorial incumbent had won a third term in half a century. But he found the answer to his ambitions in the political climate. He would campaign as the preeminent defender of white supremacy. He would "outnigger" his racist opponents. He would obstruct the federal court order in Little Rock.

On September 2, the evening before Arkansas schools were to reopen, Faubus unexpectedly went on television to announce that it would "not be possible to restore or to maintain order if forcible integration is carried out tomorrow," despite the fact that no Little Rock officials then anticipated trouble. He ordered a National Guard contingent to defend Central High School. Ostensibly, their mission was to prevent violence. But when the nine black students sought to enter the school on September 3, the guardsmen barred their way. "Governor Faubus has placed this school off limits to Negroes," announced a National Guard spokesman, forcing the black children to retreat. Now knowing that the state troops had been instructed to prevent desegregation, the nine blacks stayed home the next day, waiting for another court order. It came immediately. The federal district court in Arkansas again insisted that desegregation begin and ordered the governor to show cause why he should not be enjoined from interfering with the school board's plan. When the black students prepared to enter Central High the following day, a milling crowd of angry whites shouted: "Niggers. Niggers. They're coming. Here they come!" The guardsmen once again turned back the blacks seeking to enroll in Central High School. The authority of the federal government and of a state had directly clashed. National attention now focused on President Eisenhower, who was constitutionally required to enforce the law of the land.

Eisenhower had no desire to do so. He had never offered leadership on racial matters. He considered *Brown* a mistake. His belief in the limits of federal power and his fondness for states' rights combined to make the President highly reluctant to intervene in Little Rock. "You cannot change people's hearts merely by laws," he told a press conference that week, adding a grave remark about the white South's concern for the "mongrelization of the race." The general believed Dixie ripe for Republicanism. He had won four Southern states in 1952, and five in 1956. Looking ahead to 1960, Eisenhower was determined to avoid any action that would reestablish the Democratic grip on the mass of white Southern voters. Purposefully, he would do nothing to rally public opinion behind desegregation. Yet he could not ignore Faubus's defiance of a federal court. To give the appearance of action without really acting, Eisenhower met with the governor on September 14. Both politicians talked truce and temporized.

On September 20, the federal district court repeated its order to the governor to stop interfering with school desegregation in Little Rock. Predicting bloodshed, Faubus withdrew the National Guard from Central High and left the state. However, several of the governor's henchmen, adept at mobilizing mob violence, remained in Little Rock. By early Monday morning, September 23, over a thousand shrieking white protesters surrounded the high school. Racists from across the South had flocked to the city to prevent the blacks from entering the school.

While white students sang "Two, four, six, eight, we ain't gonna integrate," the growing mob chanted "Niggers, keep away from our school. Go back to the jungle." Over and over the crowd reassured itself: "The niggers won't get in." Suddenly someone roared: "They've gone in!" "Oh, my God!" a woman cried. "The niggers are inside!" "They're in!" others screamed. "They're in!" "The niggers are in our school." Barely constrained by the local police, hysterical whites surged toward the school. Some began a new chant: "Come on out! Come on out!" Groups of white students exited from Central High to shouts of approval, stimulating louder importuning, and more white students left the school. The mayor, fearful of violence, ordered the nine blacks withdrawn.

That evening President Eisenhower appeared on television to denounce the "disgraceful occurrence" at Little Rock. Aware that Southern extremism had become worldwide news, he issued a proclamation directing those who had obstructed federal law "to cease and desist." But an even larger mob milled about Central High the next morning and school board officials dreaded inflaming the howling protesters by forcing the entry of the nine blacks. Eisenhower responded by federalizing the Arkansas National Guard and dispatching a thousand troops of the 101st Airborne Division to Little Rock. The next morning, with fixed bayonets, the paratroopers dispersed the crowd and led the black students into Central High School. Armed troops remained in the school for two months, escorting the nine blacks to their classes. Then the President replaced the paratroopers with federalized Arkansas guardsmen, who continued to patrol Central High for the rest of the year.

Southern extremism had forced Eisenhower's hand. Not to have acted, he ruefully told a Southern senator, would have been "tantamount to acquiescence in anarchy and the dissolution of the union." As a last resort he dispatched federal troops to uphold national supremacy, defend Presidential authority, and enforce the law of the land. In so doing, Eisenhower became the first President since Reconstruction to use armed troops in support of Negro rights. However unwittingly, the President's actions raised the expectations of blacks that the federal government would finally protect their civil rights, and dashed the hopes of segregationists that court orders could be obstructed through violence.

Also in 1957, Congress enacted civil-rights legislation for the first time since Reconstruction. This further bolstered black aspirations and eroded the confidence of white supremacists that they could indefinitely thwart all measures to aid the struggle for black equality. More a symbolic milestone than an act to end black disenfranchisement, Republican and Democratic strategists fashioned a voting-rights bill designed to secure their own political aims rather than to increase black registration. Nevertheless, after eighty-two years of inaction, caused by apathy, opposition to Negro rights, and unwillingness to overcome Southern resistance, both houses of Congress formally declared illegal the disenfranchisement of Afro-Americans.

Attorney General Herbert Brownell began early in 1956 to press President Eisenhower to propose a civil-rights bill. Whether or not Congress passed it, Brownell argued, such a proposal would highlight the North–South split in the Democratic Party and bolster the image of the party of Lincoln with Northern black voters. A former chairman of the Republican National Committee, Brownell attributed Thomas Dewey's defeat in 1948 to the candidate's poor showing in black districts. The Attorney General knew that, in 1956, blacks constituted about 5 percent of the voters in fourteen states which held 261 electoral votes; he calculated that they held a balance of power in seven states that cast 197 electoral ballots, as well as in some sixty congressional districts. Brownell also sensed the widespread dissatisfaction with the Democrats among blacks, who blamed the party of Byrd and Eastland for the massive resistance to desegregation. The opportunity now existed, he pleaded with the President, to end the black allegiance to the Democrats that had been firm since 1936.

Eisenhower demurred. He feared stirring the wrath of the white South. The President remonstrated that any civil-rights action by Congress would worsen an already tense racial situation and would retard progress much as had the desegregation decision by the Supreme Court. "I personally believe if you try to go too far too fast in laws in this delicate field that has involved the emotions of so many millions of Americans," he said at a press conference, "you are making a mistake." Eisenhower had his eyes on the votes of Southern whites resistant to change. He wanted to make the Republican Party of limited government the new home of conservative Southern states' righters and decided not to support any civil-rights legislation before the 1956 election. Democratic congressional leaders sighed with relief. The last thing they wanted on the eve of a Presidential contest was a divisive intra-party squabble on civil rights. Only studied silence on race could keep them from alienating either Northern blacks or Southern whites, two of the major components of the fragile coalition known as the national Democratic Party.

Immediately after the election, however, Eisenhower requested suffrage legislation and the Senate majority leader, Democrat Lyndon Johnson of Texas, agreed to work for its passage. Unwilling to accept continued Democratic stalling on civil rights, Harlem's congressman, Adam Clayton Powell, Jr., had bolted to Ike in 1956 and brought tens of thousands of black votes into the GOP column. The President had a substantially increased proportion of the black vote over 1952, winning black majorities in at least a score of cities. This caused many Republicans looking ahead to an even better record in black communities in 1960, especially Vice-President Richard Nixon, to press Eisenhower to support civil rights. At the same time, the popularity of Republicanism among Afro-Americans in 1956 frightened Northern Democrats. They were determined to win back the black votes the GOP had just gained; they believed that enacting civil-rights legislation was the only sure way to do it. Democratic liberals would no longer sacrifice their own political needs in deference to those of their Southern brethren. Johnson, meanwhile, sought both to hold the Democratic Party together and to foster his own Presidential aspirations. He thought he could do so by fashioning a moderate civil-rights act, one not odious enough to alienate his Southern backing yet significant enough to enable him to shed his reputation as a provincial Southern white supremacist.

The politics of expediency, not surprisingly, produced a compromise bill. The forces fighting for and against civil rights each gained a little and gave up a bit, as did Democrats and Republicans, liberals and conservatives, Northerners and Southerners. Steering a middle course between reform and reaction, Eisenhower and Johnson won enactment of a mild bill palatable to most. The 1957 civil-rights act authorized the Justice Department to seek injunctions against interference with the right to vote and established a Commission on Civil Rights empowered to investigate, appraise, and report. The law ignored the issue of segregation and barely reduced the resistance to black voting by Southern election officials or the intimidation tactics of vigilante groups opposed to black enfranchisement. Still, in the spirit of the times, most Afro-American spokesmen argued that a half loaf is better than no bread at all. Roy Wilkins of the NAACP, changing the metaphor, summed up the general attitude of the black leadership: "If you are digging a ditch with a teaspoon, and a man comes along and offers you a spade, there is something wrong with your head if you don't take it because he didn't offer you a bulldozer."

After three years of registration drives which added fewer than two hundred thousand blacks to the voting lists, an increase of just 3 percent, the NAACP again demanded suffrage legislation, and the dynamics of election-year politics again resulted in an emasculated civil-rights act. The 1960 palliative authorized the courts to appoint federal referees to safeguard voting rights and made it a federal offense to obstruct court orders by violent means. Too weak to have any real impact on Southern voting, the measure still signified the growing strength of the civil-rights alliance and the diminished power of the white South to thwart Congress from joining the executive and judicial branches in their first steps toward a "second Reconstruction."

All these initial, halting, partial moves by the federal government to assist the cause of black equality resulted in intensifying the struggle. They produced among blacks both soaring expectations that Jim Crow could soon be eliminated from American life and a growing rage toward all temporizing. Cumulatively they generated a determination that segregation and discrimination, however wrong and unconstitutional, would cease only when blacks themselves acted massively and militantly enough to guarantee that end.

By enacting civil-rights legislation for the first time since 1875, Congress did much to legitimatize black aspirations for first-class citizenship. The termination of a Southern filibuster after 125 hours in 1960 encouraged blacks to believe that racial justice could be attained within the constitutional framework. The two voting-rights acts inspired Afro-Americans to attempt to register and to insist on other rights. But the patent weakness of the measures convinced them that they still did not have effective political power and that their white allies could not be depended on. Legislation, moreover, needed to be implemented to produce real change, and neither the Justice Department nor the federal judges in the South evinced much enthusiasm to utilize the two laws to promote the prospects for black voting. In the 1960 elections, less than one in four eligible blacks could vote in the South. Disappointed, Afro-Americans also questioned the legislative tactics of the NAACP, which placed a premium on neither provoking the black masses nor embittering the white majority, and the preference of Roy Wilkins for a quiet, diplomatic campaign rather than "the kind that picks a fight with the sheriff and gets somebody's head beaten."

The crisis at Little Rock similarly engendered black faith and frustration. However belated, Eisenhower's decisive use of federal force to protect black rights inspired trust in the government and confidence that Southern extremism would not be tolerated. Bolstering such assurance, some 90 percent of the whites outside the South questioned in a Gallup poll stated that Eisenhower had been right in sending troops to Little Rock. Still further buoying blacks, the Supreme Court convened a special session in 1958 to deal with Little Rock and ruled that the threat of white violence could not justify a refusal to desegregate. "The constitutional rights of respondents," the Court declared, "are not to be sacrificed or yielded to violence and disorder. . . . Law and order are not here to be preserved by depriving the Negro children of their constitutional rights." But the Supreme Court could not transform its lofty aims into reality; most Northern whites lost interest after the crisis subsided; and President Eisenhower refused ever again to enforce the school-desegregation decision. In addition, the whites of Little Rock replaced moderate Congressman Brooks Hays with a militant segregationist and opted to close down all the public high schools rather than accept token integration. It would take two years and another federal-court edict to reopen them, and by 1964 still only 123 black children out of a total Afro-American registration of nearly seven thousand students would be attending desegregated schools in Little Rock. Arkansas whites, meanwhile, swept Faubus back into the statehouse by a landslide and kept reelecting him until he retired in 1967. Stung by such events, the leader of the desegregation struggle in Little Rock expressed the new mood of bitter determination seeping throughout black America: "We've got to decide whether it's going to be this generation or never."

More than anything else, however, *Brown v. Board of Educa-*

tion and its aftermath stimulated black hope and anguish. For much of the first half of the twentieth century, blacks had accepted the leadership of the NAACP in their struggle for equality and had followed the association in relying upon litigation and legislative lobbying to eradicate racism. When their patient support began to be rewarded, each small victory led to the desire for more and bigger triumphs, each advance into the mainstream of American life quickened their anticipation for greater progress. By 1954, many Afro-Americans believed that the overturning of *Plessy* in the school cases would rapidly undermine the whole Jim Crow system.

But it did not happen. "Colored" and "White" signs remained over drinking fountains and rest rooms from one end of the South to the other. Southern blacks could not sit down next to a white and be served a hamburger or a cup of coffee. Drivers continued to demand that blacks stay in the back of the bus. Worse, black children kept attending schools that were usually squalid and almost always segregated. In 1960, only one-sixth of one percent of the black students in the South went to a desegregated school. By 1964, just two percent of the black children in the South attended integrated schools, and none at all in the two Southern counties involved in the *Brown* decision.

Disenchantment thus tempered the euphoria with which blacks greeted the Supreme Court's ruling on May 17, 1954. *Brown v. Board of Education,* Eisenhower's employment of federal troops to curtail racist extremism, and the passage of two civil-rights bills undoubtedly prepared the way for a more massive and militant phase of the black struggle. They gave legitimacy to the quest for equality. Each raised the aspirations of blacks and inspired blacks to insist on the full rights of citizenship. The repeated heroism of the black men, women, and children engaged in the school-desegregation battle, moreover, broke the shackles from many chained black minds. Yet disenfranchisement and segregation remained the rule in the South. The White Citizens' Councils continued to flourish and dominate state governments. In the North, suburbanization encouraged the growth of a racially segmented society. Automation and recessions would lead to a tripling of black unemployment in the 1950s. Blacks no longer counted on automatic progress. Their reliance on legalism, on the NAACP, and on white politicians diminished. Anger and hope gave rise to a new sense of urgency. Bitterness mixed with confidence stimulated a yearning to widen the scope of the struggle. And an amalgam of impatience, indignation, and buoyancy readied the black struggle for new protest leaders and strategies.

TWO

The Cradle Rocks

Mrs. Rosa Parks said no. Her feet hurt. Politely yet firmly, the forty-two-year-old brown-skinned seamstress said no a second time. Some black passengers on the bus, fearful for Parks's safety, and their own, shook their heads; others exclaimed "Lawd, Lawds," expecting a violent reprisal. The driver, however, just sternly insisted again that she move back and give up her seat to a standing white man. That was the law. Yet Parks held fast. Weary after her long hard day of holiday-season work at the men's alteration shop of the Montgomery Fair department store, and not feeling well, she wanted to remain seated for the rest of her ride. On that fateful first of December 1955, Parks demurred again, defying the canons of white supremacy.

"Are you going to stand up?"

"No."

"Well, if you don't stand up, I'm going to have you arrested."

Parks paused. Although she considered herself in the vanguard of the struggle for racial justice—she served as secretary of the state NAACP and had recently returned from an integrated workshop on desegregation held at the Highlander Folk School in Tennessee—she had no intention of challenging the Jim Crow laws. Yet Parks believed "that the only way to let them know I felt I was being mistreated was to do just what I did—resist the order."

"Go on," she replied softly, deliberately, "and have me arrested."

The Black Panther publicist Eldridge Cleaver would later write about that moment: "Somewhere in the universe a gear in the machinery had shifted." At the next stop, Court Square, where slaves had once been auctioned, the driver summoned police to arrest Rosa Parks for violating the municipal ordinance mandating segregation on publicly owned vehicles. Martin Luther King, Jr., would describe this as the moment when Parks had been "tracked down by the *Zeitgeist*—the spirit of the times. . . . She was anchored to that seat by the accumulated indignities of days gone by and the boundless aspirations of generations yet unborn." More modestly, Parks recalled: "I felt it was just something I had to do."

So did other blacks. News of her defiance, circulated by the telephone network of Montgomery's black elite, transmitted a sudden surge of determination through the community, a resolve to do *something*. Many looked to E. D. Nixon for leadership. President of the Alabama NAACP and a veteran member of the Brotherhood of Sleeping Car Porters, Nixon had long sought to arouse black Montgomery to a mass protest of their mistreatment by whites. He hurried to the jail to post bond for his friend Rosa Parks. The former local head of the World War II March-on-Washington Movement, Nixon remained a disciple of A. Philip Randolph's tactics and strategy. He longed for an opportunity to organize black power and pressure through mass demonstrations. As Nixon drove Parks home, he searched for an appropriate form of direct action, maybe a strike, perhaps a boycott. He felt sure that the arrest of Rosa Parks was a cause blacks would rally around. "Mrs. Parks," he finally summoned the courage to blurt out, "this is the case we've been looking for. We can break this situation on the bus with your case." Both knew the risks: the possibility of violence to Parks, the certainty of losing her job. Yet both knew the time had come. "I'll go along with it," Parks primly answered. *Something* had to be done.

"This is what we've been waiting for!" Nixon almost shouted on the telephone to Jo Ann Robinson later that night. Mrs. Robinson, president of the Women's Political Council, the black counterpart to Montgomery's segregated League of Women Voters, agreed. Impatient with the deferential leadership of Montgomery's black ministers, Robinson's council that year had pressured white merchants into ending the segregation of public drinking fountains and the custom of not using the courtesy titles of Mrs. and Miss when billing black women. They had also forced the city to begin hiring black policemen and were demanding equal recreational facilities for black Montgomery. The council, moreover, earlier in the year, had been set to stage a boycott of the city's buses to protest the arrest of a woman who refused to give up her seat to a white. But the fact that the defendant was an unwed mother made the Women's Political Council draw back. Rosa Parks, however, was dignified, intelligent, respectable, and married. Nixon and Robinson agreed that she was the perfect symbol. They would attempt to organize a one-day bus boycott on the fifth of December to coincide with Mrs. Parks's trial.

Early the next morning, Nixon began calling Montgomery's black ministers, college professors, physicians, and civic spokesmen. "We have taken this type of thing too long already. I feel the time has come to boycott the buses," Nixon repeated to each. "Only through a boycott can we make it clear to the white folks that we will not accept this type of treatment any longer."

To his surprise, many of the elite Nixon telephoned accepted his invitation to meet that evening to plan a bus boycott. Most had previously exhibited little inclination to act in concert, and even less desire to act militantly. The nearly fifty representatives of black Montgomery, mostly ministers, who gathered in the Dexter Avenue Baptist Church agreed even more unexpectedly to deliver sermons on the proposed boycott to their congregations on Sunday, to ask Negro taxicab companies to transport blacks at bus-fare cost, to cap the boycott with a city-wide meeting, and to distribute the mimeographed leaflets written by Robinson which urged:

Don't ride the bus to work, to town, to school, or anyplace Monday, December 5.

Another Negro woman had been arrested and put in jail because she refused to give up her bus seat.

Don't ride the bus to work, to town, to school, or any where on Monday. If you work, take a cab, or share a ride, or walk.

Come to a mass Meeting, Monday, at 7:00 P.M., at the Holt Street Baptist Church for further instruction.

On Monday, December 5, in the city called the Cradle of the Confederacy, over 90 percent of the blacks who ordinarily rode the buses stayed off them. Blacks walked, joined car pools, drove wagons, rode mules. They did not ride the buses. The historic Montgomery bus boycott had begun. It would last 381 days. It would cost blacks nearly a quarter of a million dollars. Out of it would come a towering leader, a new kind of Southern black leadership, an effective strategy for social change, and a determined spirit that Jim Crow could be ended, that life could be better. Historians eventually would look back to Montgomery as the Cradle of the New Negro.

Nixon had pressing concerns that fifth of December. Following Mrs. Parks's brief trial, which expectedly resulted in a guilty verdict and a fine of ten dollars plus four dollars court costs,

Nixon met on the courthouse steps with several black ministers. He feared that without active leadership, specific goals, and a committed organization the boycott would fizzle and the mass meeting would fail. Nixon suggested that an ad hoc group continue to lead the boycott until the city and bus company agreed to hire Negro bus drivers in black neighborhoods, insist that all bus drivers treat black patrons more courteously, and adopt a first-come, first-served seating system. Nixon initially had no intention of attacking the segregation ordinance confining blacks to the back of the bus. He merely proposed that those blacks seated in the rear be allowed to keep their seats. Nixon also thought the name for the new organization ought to be the Citizens' Committee. But the Reverend Ralph D. Abernathy, the young pugnacious minister of the First Baptist Church, objected. The name sounded too much like the White Citizens' Council. Abernathy suggested, instead, the Montgomery Improvement Association, adding: "Brother Nixon, now you gon' serve as president, ain'tchya?" "No," Nixon shot back, "not unless'n you all don't accept my man."

Nixon had his reasons for declining. His job as a Pullman porter frequently kept him out of town. His lack of formal education inhibited him, and he considered himself too old to be an active leader. Too many black ministers would not work with him, a legacy of old conflicts and rivalries. What we need, Nixon went on, was an intelligent, respected minister, a dynamic orator, someone who could easily find another job if the boycott failed and the white community retaliated. He further suggested that a man new in the community would be less likely to be identified with any faction of Montgomery's bitterly divided black leadership or to be a lackey of the white establishment. Nixon might also have added that his ideal candidate needed to be extraordinarily brave or naïve to be identified publicly as the leader of such an uncertain, hazardous, quixotic venture. He recommended Martin Luther King, Jr. The others agreed.

At three in the afternoon, Montgomery's black leaders met

again, to prepare for the evening's mass rally. The old fears suddenly surfaced. How, some asked, could their involvement in the boycott be kept secret from the white community? Could they ban white reporters from the evening meeting? Could they forego public forums and circulate their plans by mimeographed pamphlets and word of mouth? Enraged, Nixon jumped from his seat. "What the hell you people talking 'bout? How you gonna have a mass meeting, gonna boycott a city bus line without the white folks knowing it?" We are acting like little boys, he continued, afraid to discuss our plans in the open, wanting to pass around papers secretly. Now is the time to decide. "You oughta make up your mind right now that you gon' either admit you are a grown man or concede to the fact that you are a bunch of scared boys." Silenced, the leaders rapidly agreed to an organizing committee, named the Montgomery Improvement Association (MIA), to lead a bus boycott until the city met the three demands proposed by Nixon.

Rufus Lewis quickly nominated Martin Luther King, Jr., to the MIA presidency and in a moment the motion carried. Stunned by the speed of the maneuver, King did not decline, although he had recently turned down the presidency of the local NAACP because of the press of his pastoral duties and the new obligations of fatherhood. He could not afford the luxury of second-guessing his decision. King had less than an hour before the evening mass meeting to prepare "the most decisive speech of my life."

At first glance, neither King nor the blacks of Montgomery appeared ready for what would come. The black community seemed complacent or cowed, and King hardly fitted the mold of a fiery freedom fighter who could arouse and lead. The son and grandson of pastors of Atlanta's prestigious Ebenezer Baptist Church, "Mike" King grew up on prosperous "sweet" Auburn Avenue—the capital of the black bourgeoisie. Largely shielded from the worst of white racism, he learned resentment of Jim Crow from his father. Such lessons were abstract in the main, mostly derivative, and young King ignored the embryonic civil-rights struggles in Atlanta, concerning himself instead with books, baseball, and girls. An avid student, he skipped two grades of high school and at fifteen enrolled at Morehouse College, a branch of the Atlanta University system. He dreamed of being a lawyer or a teacher. But his father insisted that he be a minister. King obeyed, and following his graduation in 1948, he entered Crozer Theological Seminary in Pennsylvania for his Bachelor of Divinity Degree.

King, one of six blacks in a student body of one hundred, happily immersed himself in the world of ideas, particularly the philosophy of Kant, Hegel, the religious existentialists, and Walter Rauschenbusch's social gospel. He finished first in his graduating class, earning a fellowship to pursue a doctorate. In 1951 King began his course of study of systematic theology at Boston University's School of Theology. His dissertation on the thought of Paul Tillich strengthened his intellectual bent of mind. While in Boston, King met Coretta Scott, a graduate of Antioch College who was studying voice at the New England Conservatory of Music. They were married in 1953. Each reinforced the other's desire to remain in the North and for King to pursue a career of religious scholarship. But family ties and an attractive job offer proved too strong a lure. "Finally we agreed," wrote King in his autobiography, "that, in spite of the disadvantages and inevitable sacrifices, our greatest service could be rendered in our native South. We came to the conclusion that we had something of a moral obligation to return—at least for a few years."

King arrived in Montgomery in September 1954, aged twenty-six, to serve as pastor of the Dexter Avenue Baptist Church. Many blacks, in awe and in derision, referred to it as "the big people's church." Its small but influential congregation, largely professionals and faculty members of Alabama State College, emanated a respectability and an aura of intellectualism that King highly prized. He still found the emotionalism of the traditional Negro church distasteful, and still believed in moderate, middle-class politics as the best path for Negro advancement. His sermons infrequently dwelt on current racial issues. At most, he gingerly admonished his congregation to register to vote and to support the efforts of the NAACP. Quite removed from the needs and spirit of the black rank-and-file, King served on the Alabama Human Relations Council, a genteel, paternalistic organization as elitist as it was ineffectual.

Montgomery's blatant white supremacy, however, jolted King. A virulent white racism enveloped the city. It dictated its laws and mores. It poisoned white minds and destroyed the bodies and souls of blacks. The shocking contrast with what King had earlier experienced in Atlanta and Boston produced in him both a growing sense of urgency to change the racial situation and a belief that change was possible. Even before the boycott began, he had started to discuss with Coretta the idea of a nonviolent resistance movement. He reread Gandhi and Thoreau on civil disobedience. He pondered the speeches he had heard on the application of Gandhian tactics to the race problem by Howard Thurman, dean of the Howard University chapel, and by A. J. Muste of the Fellowship of Reconciliation. He studied past examples of direct mass action. In December 1955, King had not yet arrived at a definitive philosophy or strategy for racial change. But his thoughts were in flux. At the least, as he told his wife on the eve of the boycott, the continued passive acceptance of evil could only perpetuate its existence.

Beneath the placid surface of the black community in Montgomery, many had quietly come to the same realization, with a similar resolve. For some, the moment of decision came with the coupling of the 1954 Supreme Court decision and the white vow to fight integration at any cost, or with the juxtaposition of the news of successful beginnings of school desegregation in various border cities and headlines telling of violent riots to thwart the law of the land. For others, who believed in the steady improvement in race relations, the moment of decision came with the August 1955 lynching of fourteen-year-old Emmett Till and the brazen appearance of White Citizens' Councils throughout the South. The absurdity of the fact that the days of the cotton South had ended while its racial practices continued aroused many. Blacks had become far more educated, industrialized, and urbanized than their parents' generation, yet they faced the same racial indignities. The black who had experienced integration in the armed services during the Korean War, or who had lived for a while without Jim Crow in the North, or who worked on the desegregated military bases just outside the city, still faced in Montgomery a near-total system of segregation and white supremacy. It was pervasive, cruel, and humiliating.

Twice daily, for most Montgomery blacks, the Jim Crow buses served as a constant reminder of how far toward freedom they still had to travel. Blacks had to pay the driver at the front of the bus and then enter through the door at the rear, however inclement the weather. They had to stand in the crowded back of the bus while seats were empty in the white-only front section. They could do little to constrain a vicious bus driver, no matter how abusive or violent he became. Then, in the last week of November 1955, the Interstate Commerce Commission banned racial segregation in all facilities and vehicles engaged in interstate transportation. On the first of December, Rosa Parks said no. Could they now do less? The trend of the law seemed unmistakable. The Parks incident had unified the black community, for a while at the least. Perhaps . . . Maybe . . . The time had come to force Montgomery to change.

When King returned for the evening rally, Montgomery blacks had filled every seat in the Holt Street Baptist Church and stood shoulder to shoulder in the blocks surrounding the church. More than four thousand stood outside to listen to the loudspeakers, demonstrating the commitment and solidarity they had shown by staying off the buses. Seemingly with one voice they sang "Onward Christian Soldiers." In unison they shouted that "like a mighty army" they would march against the citadel of Jim Crow. Impatiently and unanimously they voted to boycott the buses until they gained their three demands. Then the crowd grew silent. Dr. King began to speak.

King quietly recounted the arrest of Rosa Parks. Unemotionally, he reviewed the many injustices blacks had endured on Montgomery buses. The murmurs of "Amen" grew louder and King suddenly brought his audience to a fever pitch.

There comes a time when people get tired. We are here this evening to say to those who have mistreated us so long that we are tired—tired of being segregated and humiliated, tired of being kicked about by the brutal feet of oppression. We have no alternative but to protest. For many years, we have shown amazing patience. We have sometimes given our white brothers the feeling that we liked the way we were being treated. But we come here tonight to be saved from that patience that makes us patient with anything less than freedom and justice.

"We are impatient for justice"—King moderated his tone— "but we will protest with love. There will be no violence on our part." He preached persuasion, not coercion. He dwelt on the transforming power of love. "Love must be our regulating ideal. . . . If we fail to do this our protest will end up as a meaningless drama on the stage of history, and its memory will be shrouded with the ugly garments of shame." "Let no man pull you so low as to make you hate him," he quoted Booker T. Washington. The "Amens" swelled again. "If you will protest courageously"—King built to a crescendo—"and yet with dignity and Christian love, when the history books are written in future generations, the historians will have to pause and say 'There lived a great people—a black people—who injected new meaning and dignity into the veins of civilization.' This is our challenge and our overwhelming responsibility." The thousands listening roared their approval. Again and again they shouted their joyful determination. King had crystalized their feelings.

He had articulated their mood and exalted their vision. The time had come.

White Montgomery at first ridiculed the boycott. Disdainful whites thought the fractious Negro leadership would be unable to maintain a semblance of unity, much less be competent to deal efficiently with the complicated day-to-day operations of a city-wide boycott. They scorned the black masses as too apathetic, too cowardly, to stay to a course of sacrifice. A little stalling, a bit of pressure, a few threats would surely end this folly. "Our niggers," the contemptuous assumed, "will soon tire out and start climbing back on the buses." Secretly, some blacks also feared the collapse of the boycott if it went on too long. Memory made them doubt the perseverance of the troops and the fortitude of their leaders. They hoped for a speedy settlement. After all, the doubtful black Montgomerians sought to reassure themselves, none of their three moderate demands struck directly at segregation, and their fares accounted for 75 percent of the Montgomery City Line revenue.

After three days of almost total black boycott, King met with Mayor W. A. Gayle, his commissioners, and the attorneys for the bus company. Logic and reasonableness, King optimistically believed, would prevail. He could not have been more wrong. There would be no compromise. The whites spurned King's proposals. They would not accept anything that might suggest a black victory for fear that it would stimulate additional demands. They drew the line. To underscore their adamancy, the city fathers threatened legal action unless the black cab companies again began to charge the prescribed minimum fares for taxis.

Disheartened, King returned to confer with the MIA. He now realized that the matter was one of power, not reason, that "no one gives up his privileges without strong resistance." Far more than courtesy and comfort were involved in the bus issue, moreover, for "the underlying purpose of segregation was to oppress and exploit the segregated, not simply to keep [people] apart."

A chastened MIA turned to the organization of car pools to replace the black taxis. Over a hundred and fifty blacks volunteered their automobiles at a mass rally that evening. Within several days forty-eight dispatch and forty-two collection stations were operating with what the local White Citizens' Council groused was "military precision." The boycott continued. Black Montgomery stayed off the buses. Most rode in the car pool; some hitched or bicycled; many just walked. As one elderly black woman expressed it: "My feets is tired, but my soul is rested." And another, when offered a ride so she would not have to walk: "I'm not walking for myself. I'm walking for my children and my grandchildren." The days of the boycott became weeks and then months.

The white community, no longer deriding the boycott, felt its impact. After two months, the downtown merchants claimed that they had lost a million dollars in sales due to the restricted travel of blacks. The boycott cut into the bus company's income some 65 percent, forcing it to raise fares and trim schedules. Its huge losses mounted daily. At the end of January, Mayor Gayle announced a "get-tough" policy. "We have pussyfooted around on this boycott long enough." He went on television to denounce the boycott as a campaign to stir up racial strife and its leaders as "a group of Negro radicals who have split asunder the fine relationships which have existed between the Negro and white people for generations." He warned Montgomery that the blacks sought to end segregation, that "what they are after is the destruction of our social fabric." It is time to be honest and frank, Gayle concluded: "The white people are firm in their convictions that they do not care whether the Negroes ever ride a city bus again if it means that the social fabric of our community is to be destroyed so that Negroes will start riding the buses again."

An official policy of harassment began. The mayor and his commissioners ceremoniously took out memberships in the

White Citizens' Council. Some blacks prominent in the boycott lost their jobs; many others were threatened with dismissal. Car-pool drivers faced warnings that their licenses would be revoked and their insurance policies cancelled. Many were fined on trumped-up charges of speeding. Indiscriminate arrests for imaginary violations followed. The old fears resurfaced. The car pool lost many of its volunteers. Some blacks climbed back on the rear of the buses. Four days of retaliation by white Montgomery had brought the boycott to the brink of collapse. Then two policemen arrested King for speeding.

His jailing revitalized the movement. It rekindled that spark of dynamic determination that had existed at the start of the crusade. Hundreds rushed to the jail to protest, and the police gave in, releasing King on bond. Several days later, as King addressed an MIA rally: "Let us keep moving with the even greater faith that God is with us in the struggle," a dynamite bomb shattered the front of his house. Quickly he left the meeting to return home. When he arrived, several hundred angry blacks, armed with guns, knives, rods, and rocks, surrounded his house. After assuring himself that no harm had come to his wife and baby, King stepped out on his porch. Now a volatile crowd of more than a thousand blacks milled in front of the house. "Don't get panicky," King raised his arms. "Get rid of your weapons"—he quieted the crowd. "We are not advocating violence. We want to love our enemies. We must love our white brothers no matter what they do to us." He spoke of forgiveness and promise. "I did not start this boycott. I was asked by you to serve as your spokesman. I want it to be known the length and breadth of the land that if I am stopped, our work will not stop, for what we are doing is right. What we are doing is just and God is with us."

This moment—Lerone Bennett, Jr., a biographer of King and a historian of the movement, would write—"changed the course of the protest and made King a living symbol. He and other members of the boycott directorate had spoken before of love and forgiveness. But now, *seeing the idea in action*, fleshed out by pain, paid for by anguish, millions were touched, if not converted. The parable of the porch went out now over the wires of the news media and King's name became a token for almost all American Negroes." As the nation watched, subsequent events solidified King's reputation as the preeminent leader of black nonviolent protest and wholly transformed the bus boycott for limited demands into a religious offensive against segregation and discrimination.

On February 21, 1956, city officials obtained indictments against King and some one hundred other leading boycott participants on charges of violating a 1921 law forbidding hindrance to a business without "just cause or legal excuse." "In this state," the indictment read, "we are committed to segregation by custom and law; we intend to maintain it." Instead of fearing jail, of seeking to avoid arrest, the black leaders of Montgomery hurried to the police station to surrender. E. D. Nixon arrived first. "You are looking for me? Here I am." Hundreds of blacks gathered outside the station to applaud the leaders as they entered one by one. King, visiting his parents in Atlanta, declined their advice that he not jeopardize his life by returning, and rushed to the Montgomery jail. The photograph of him with a numbered plaque hanging from his neck captured national and international attention. Statements in support of the boycott, as well as cash contributions, poured in from all over the world.

At a mass meeting the next evening, the indicted black leaders marched between thousands of cheering men, women, and children who overflowed the street outside the Dexter Avenue Baptist Church. Women held their babies to touch these men of courage. Inside, hundreds more chanted, and shouted, and prayed, and pledged themselves to "passive resistance," to shun the buses and "walk with God." They learned a new song, to the tune of the spiritual "Give Me That Old-Time Religion," whose four stanzas proclaimed the essential elements of their struggle: protest, unity, nonviolence, and equality.

> *We are moving on to vict'ry*
> *With hope and dignity.*
>
> *We shall all stand together*
> *Till every one is free.*
>
> *We know love is the watchword*
> *For peace and liberty*
>
> *Black and white, all our brothers*
> *To live in harmony.*

They sang "O lift me up and let me stand on higher ground," and then grew quiet to listen to King, as the television cameras ground away.

"We are not struggling merely for the rights of Negroes," the Baptist minister began, "but for all the people of Montgomery, black and white. We are determined to make America a better place for all people." The protest, said King, was not against a single incident but over things that "go deep down into the archives of history."

We have known humiliation, we have known abusive language, we have been plunged into the abyss of oppression. And we decided to rise up only with the weapon of protest. It is one of the greatest glories of America that we have the right to protest.

There are those who would try to make of this a hate campaign. This is not a war between the white and the Negro but a conflict between justice and injustice. This is bigger than the Negro race revolting against the white. We are seeking to improve not the Negro of Montgomery but the whole of Montgomery.

If we are arrested every day, if we are exploited every day, if we are trampled over every day, don't ever let anyone pull you so low as to hate them. We must use the weapon of love. We must have compassion and understanding for those who hate us. We must realize so many people are taught to hate us that they are not totally responsible for their hate. But we stand in life at midnight, we are always on the threshold of a new dawn.

A month later, King went on trial as the first of the indicted defendants. Again, with TV cameramen and reporters crowding into the city, Montgomery was seen by the world. For four days, a parade of twenty-eight witnesses summoned by the defense offered testimony that, despite the certain legal victory of the Montgomery city fathers, showed them to be morally bankrupt. One by one the witnesses recounted tales of being spat upon, cursed, beaten, and shot at by white bus drivers. These were their "just causes" for hindering the business of the bus company. Nevertheless, the judge found King guilty, ordered him to pay $1,000 in fines, and released him on bond pending appeal. One middle-aged woman rushed to King: "My heart and my pocketbook are at your disposal"—while on the lawn outside the courthouse Montgomery blacks sang their response: "We ain't gonna ride the buses no more." They didn't.

On June 4, a three-judge federal district court handed down its ruling in the case brought by four Montgomery black women to end bus segregation in the city. "We hold that the statutes requiring segregation of the white and colored races on a common carrier," the majority declared, "violate the due process and equal protection of the law clauses of the Fourteenth Amendment." The order enjoined the mayor from enforcing racial segregation on the buses, but stayed the effect of the decision until Montgomery officials appealed the case to the Supreme Court. Fearing the worst from the high court, white leaders in Alabama again fought the boycott with vengeance. The state outlawed the NAACP as a foreign corporation that had failed to register; accused it of "causing irreparable injury to the property and civil rights of residents," a reference to its role in handling the federal suit against Montgomery; and fined the association $100,000 for refusing to surrender its membership lists. Concurrently, Montgomery obtained an indictment against the MIA on charges of operating a business—the car-pool— without a license.

"You know the people are getting tired," King confided to his wife. "If the city officials get this injunction against the car pools—and they will get it—I am afraid our people will go back to the buses." The blacks of Montgomery had become dependent on the MIA station wagons and the volunteer automobiles. Their loss would be incalculable; the boycott without them inconceivable. On November 13, King appeared before the same local judge who had previously found the MIA leaders guilty of hindering a business enterprise. At his lowest ebb since the boycott began, King awaited the crushing ruling. As if providentially, at that terrible moment for King, a reporter handed him a note. It read: "The United States Supreme Court today affirmed a decision of a special three-judge U.S. District Court in declaring Alabama's state and local laws requiring segregation on buses unconstitutional." That ruling came, said King, "as a joyous daybreak to end the long night of enforced segregation in public transportation." Another black in the courtroom shouted: "God Almighty has spoken from Washington, D.C." The Montgomery judge, as expected, granted the city's request for an injunction—but it no longer mattered.

The next night, nearly ten thousand blacks convened to end the boycott officially. The Reverend Robert Graetz, the sole white in the MIA hierarchy, rose to read the scripture according to Paul to the meeting: "When I was a child, I spoke as a child, I understood as a child, I thought as a child. . . ." He could not go on. "There was a vast uproar," reported Lerone Bennett. "All over the floor now, men and women were on their feet, waving handkerchiefs and weeping." Belatedly, haltingly, Graetz ended the sentence: "But when I became a man, I put away childish things." Not since the Civil War had the Southern black rank-and-file protested so visibly and volubly for equality. Their numbers and courage would point the way for countless other blacks to assert their rights militantly. That was the meaning of the 381-day struggle.

On this same night, the Ku Klux Klan, hooded and gowned, appeared in black Montgomery. A procession of forty vehicles drove slowly through the black neighborhoods. In the past, such demonstrations had petrified the black community. They had caused panicked blacks to flee and hide. On the evening of November 13, 1956, most of black Montgomery reacted as if the Klan were truly invisible. No one ran away or dimmed their lights. Some blacks followed the Klan procession, applauding, laughing, and jeering. Dumbstruck, the KKK terminated its effort at intimidation and slunk away into the night. That, too, was the meaning of the Montgomery bus boycott. "A once fear-ridden people had been transformed," King would later write of the blacks who openly defied Montgomery statutes used to try to destroy the protest campaign. "Those who had previously trembled before the law were now proud to be arrested for the cause of freedom."

Shortly before 6 a.m. on December 21, 1956, King and his aides boarded a Montgomery bus and sat in the front, black next to white. Droves of news reporters and cameramen recorded the historic event, proclaiming its significance throughout the world. "For the first time in this 'cradle of the Confederacy' all the Negroes entered buses through the front door," *The New York Times* reported. "They sat in the first empty seats they saw, in the front of buses and in the rear. They did not get up to give a white passenger a seat. And whites sat with Negroes." The 381-day struggle which began as a hope for simple courtesy and convenience ended as a major triumph for desegregation. And, King added: "The skies did not fall when integrated buses finally traveled the streets of Montgomery."

In preparation for this day, King in the preceding weeks had schooled blacks in the techniques and philosophy of nonviolent resistance. The Montgomery movement had been explicitly Christian. King had quoted Jesus, not Gandhi. The tactics of the MIA had been patterned on previous examples of black protest, not on Thoreau's "Civil Disobedience." The fervor with which the MIA practiced passive resistance sprang from the religious fundamentalism of the Black Belt. Its strategy flowed from the pragmatic recognition that black violence in the Deep South, where whites held a preponderance of force and power, would be self-defeating, even suicidal. The heart and soul of the movement—noncooperation with evil, coupled with love and forgiveness—simply exemplified the Southern blacks' faith in their church and in their leaders' orthodox gospel of avoiding armed conflict.

King, however, began to construct a new ideational framework based on Gandhian precepts of nonviolence during the "laboratory institute periods" held nightly in the churches to acquaint blacks with "some of the things that might be expected," on the soon to be integrated Montgomery City Bus Lines. Films of Gandhi's resistance movement were shown regularly to black congregations. Demonstrations of nonviolence were accompanied by references to the Mahatma. Songs and skits emphasized the success of passive resistance in India. A leaflet given out in every black church urged the bus protesters to "read, study and memorize" seventeen rules, among them: "Pray for guidance and commit yourself to complete nonviolence in word and action as you enter the bus. . . . Be loving enough to absorb evil and understanding enough to turn an enemy into a friend. . . . If cursed, do not curse back. If pushed, do not push back. If struck, do not strike back, but evidence love and goodwill at all times. . . . If another person is being molested, do not arise to go to his defense, but pray for the oppressor and use moral and spiritual force to carry on the struggle for justice. . . . Do not be afraid to experiment with new and creative techniques for achieving reconciliation and social change. . . . If you feel you cannot take it, walk for another week or two."

King's advanced education in philosophy, quite likely, led him to articulate the thrust of the movement in grand, conceptual terms. It suited the habits of his mind. His training in systematic theology had left him with an appetite for transcendent ideas, for theoretical constructs. He considered himself a thinker, not only a preacher, and he wanted others to view him in the same way. Larding his speeches with such terms as *ahimsa* and *sobornost,* discoursing on the distinctions between *agape, eros,* and *philia* seemed a sound way of assuring his status as a solon. This new idiom in the black revolt, moreover, was accentuated in press reports of King as the *new* Afro-American leader, or the leader of the *New* Negro. Journalistic accounts emphasized the uniqueness of King's Gandhian approach to the race problem. They succeeded in differentiating him from leaders of the NAACP and the ministerial hierarchy of the black church.

The influence of Bayard Rustin and Reverend Glenn E. Smiley furthered King's turning to Gandhi. Both had come to Montgomery in February 1956 to assist the MIA. They stayed, became indispensable to King, and prodded him to articulate the bus boycott as a manifestation of nonviolent passive resistance. Rustin, the black executive secretary of the War Resisters' League, and Smiley, a white field secretary for the Fellowship of Reconciliation (FOR), were both pacifist disciples of the Mahatma and of A. J. Muste, and they took every opportunity to reinforce King's understanding of *Satyagrapha.* Both, as well, were thoroughly familiar with the wartime experiences of the March-on-Washington Movement and the Congress of Racial Equality (CORE). They recalled A. Philip Randolph's insistence on the need for broad, organized, militant mass action, rather than polite pleading, to achieve racial equality, and CORE's adoption of Gandhian nonviolence to the race problem. With their assistance, King developed an ideology of disciplined, nonviolent direct action by the black masses.

King's neo-Gandhian persuasion fit the needs of the American South in the mid-twentieth century. It offered something to nearly all in an especially palatable way. King had learned in the crucible of the boycott that this form of black protest weakened the white community's resolve, unity, and readiness to retaliate with violence. It placed blame on the impersonal system of segregation, not on individual segregationists; it played on the whites' growing feeling of guilt; it forced whites to confront the plight of blacks, while assuaging the white fear of bloody reprisals. King also continually emphasized that the achievement of the movement's goals would result not in victory for blacks alone but in triumph for all Americans. He clothed the consequences of racial change in the garb of reconciliation and the creation of a beloved community. At the least, this disarming message from a man of God minimized virulent white opposition and made the inevitable appear a bit more acceptable.

Simultaneously, King's words energized the black community, dispelling its feelings of helplessness, insignificance, and powerlessness. He sensed the untapped wellsprings of black hostility. He understood how the resentment of white supremacy had been kept in check by a Christian tradition tabooing hatred and by an awesome fear of white violence. So King transformed the immoral into the moral: "To accept passively an unjust system is to cooperate with that system; thereby the oppressed become as evil as the oppressor. Noncooperation with evil is as much a moral obligation as is cooperation with good." He equated apathy, not protest against the existing racial order, with sin. He bestowed legitimacy on aggression against racism, redefining it as Christian love. Moreover, by lessening the likelihood of white vengeance, by decreasing the dangers to black protesters, King increased the probability of black militancy. The possibility of violent reactions by whites remained, and King made a virtue of it by exalting black suffering as redemptive, heroic, the highest manifestation of Christianity and the surest path to triumph. Unearned suffering, he preached, amplified the self-esteem of blacks much as knowing that they were part of a larger movement, a mass movement, gave them a sense of strength they had not possessed individually.

King's exhortations and the example of the successful bus boycott accelerated the movement of the black struggle from the courtroom to the streets. Together, they ushered in an age of open confrontation with a regnant racism by inspiring large numbers of blacks to fight for their own freedom and by forging the precepts of nonviolent direct action into a weapon congenial to Southern blacks and admired by many whites. This also was the significance of the Montgomery campaign. In the years ahead, it would encourage tens of thousands of blacks to march under King's banner and to court beatings, jailings, even death, certain in the faith that their martyrdom would hasten the victory of their cause, firm in their belief that "we shall overcome."

Martin Luther King's emergence as a worldwide symbol of Afro-American determination was yet another enduring consequence of the Montgomery bus boycott. He became one of the nation's most sought-after speakers, and the willing recipient of a flood of honors and awards; there were innumerable magazine stories and newspaper interviews, radio and television broadcasts by and about him. King traveled widely, recounting the story of the boycott to audiences large and small, North and South, black and white. His rhetoric, his philosophy, the fact of his success in Montgomery, vaulted him to the forefront of black leadership. He was the new hope. He appeared to have a following as broadly representative and as deeply loyal as any Afro-American had ever had. Other leaders, black and white, took note. The Democratic National Committee invited him to appear before the platform committee of the 1956 convention. The following year, he and Ralph Abernathy conferred for over two hours with Vice-President Richard M. Nixon. In 1958 he met with President Eisenhower at the White House. Along with Dr. Ralph Bunche and Adam Clayton Powell, Jr., King attended the 1957 independence ceremonies of Ghana. In addition, that year, King began to coordinate his strategies with those of A. Philip Randolph and Roy Wilkins of the NAACP.

On the day of the third anniversary of the Supreme Court decision outlawing school segregation, King spoke to the huge crowd assembled before the Lincoln Memorial. The occasion was the 1957 Prayer Pilgrimage to Washington. Over thirty thousand participants from thirty-three states attended to demonstrate black unity, to protest white violence in the South and "the crippling of the NAACP," and to mobilize support for pending civil-rights legislation. Wilkins, Powell, Mordecai Johnson, and several black ministers associated with King gave preliminary speeches. Then, to climax the pilgrimage, Randolph, presiding over the conference, introduced Dr. King. The crowd's reception of King, and his placement in the program, made clear his preeminence in the civil-rights movement.

He assailed the White House as "too silent and apathetic" and Congress as "too stagnant and hypocritical" in the realm of race relations. He demanded that the federal government aggressively enforce desegregation, that white sympathizers advance beyond "quasi-liberalism" to a positive commitment to the black cause, and that black community leaders act unequivocally to inspire their people. Then, evoking the familiar "Amens" and chants in unison, he pointed to the one certain solution to black needs: "Give us the ballot," his strong voice sang out.

Give us the ballot and we will no longer have to worry the federal government about our basic rights. . . . Give us the ballot and we will no longer plead to the federal government for passage of an anti-lynching law. Give us the ballot and we will no longer plead—we will write the proper laws on the books. Give us the ballot and we will fill the legislature with men of goodwill. Give us the ballot and we will get the people judges who will do 'justly and love mercy.' Give us the ballot and we will quietly, lawfully, and nonviolently, without rancor or bitterness, implement the May 17, 1954, decision of the Supreme Court. . . . Give us the ballot and we will transform the salient misdeeds of the bloodthirsty mobs into the calculated good deeds of orderly citizens.

The "Amens" swelled and King exhorted the throng to return to their homes to fight for civil rights in the spirit of Montgomery: "We must meet hate with love, physical force with soul force."

The bus boycott also led to the organizing of black clergymen throughout the South into a cadre of protest leaders. The Southern Christian Leadership Conference (SCLC) sprang directly out of the Montgomery movement. Indeed, even before the successful termination of the Montgomery crusade, black ministers in other cities began to plan similar campaigns of noncooperation. After visiting King in the winter of 1956, the Reverend Charles K. Steele returned home to Tallahassee, Florida, to organize a bus boycott. He formed an Inter-Civic Council, modeled on the MIA. After desegregating the buses in Tallahassee, the council followed King's new emphasis on the ballot and in three years more than quadrupled the twelve hundred blacks that had been registered to vote in 1956. In Alabama, clergymen Joseph E. Lowery of Mobile and Fred L. Shuttlesworth met with King throughout 1956 to plan the bus boycotts in their respective cities. In nearby Tuskegee, blacks led by C. G. Gomillion, who also regularly conferred with King, boycotted white merchants to fight disenfranchisement. In Georgia, the Montgomery experience produced bus boycotts in Atlanta and Savannah. "Thank you, Montgomery," said Atlanta's Reverend William Holmes Borders after desegregation. "Thank you, Martin Luther King, Jr."

King recognized the need to capitalize on this momentum. With Steele and Shuttlesworth, he issued a call for civil-rights-minded clergymen to convene in Atlanta on January 10–11, 1957. Sixty blacks from ten states, almost all preachers, agreed on the necessity of a coordinating force for their various movements. They named themselves the Southern Conference on Transportation and Nonviolent Integration and urged Afro-Americans "to assert their human dignity" by refusing "further cooperation with evil." A month later, nearly a hundred black ministers attended the formal organization of the conference in New Orleans. They elected King president and Abernathy treasurer, and tried several different names before calling themselves the Southern Christian Leadership Conference. In its first official declaration, the SCLC called upon blacks "to understand that nonviolence is not a symbol of weakness or cowardice, but as Jesus demonstrated, nonviolent resistance transforms weakness into strength and breeds courage in the face of danger." Until the founding of the SCLC, the struggle for racial equality had been largely the domain of a Northern elite oriented primarily toward legal action. Now the Southern black church would become preeminent in leading black resistance to white oppression, and they would do so by preaching the virtues of massive nonviolent protest. More than anything else, this crucial consequence of the Montgomery bus boycott eventually would ignite a civil-rights revolution.

But not in the next three years. The SCLC accomplished little and failed to spark the mass, direct-action movement needed to alter the South. Blacks scored few victories for desegregation. Indeed, momentum shifted to those in the white South who defiantly said *Never* to black calls and court orders for integration. The second half of the fifties was the high tide of white massive resistance, of white reaction and repression. Authorities in Alabama had Autherine Lucy permanently expelled after she had won a federal court order admitting her to the University of Alabama in 1956. The university would remain segregated for seven more years. Governor Orval Faubus closed the schools in Little Rock, and Virginia officials disbanded the public educational system of Prince Edwards County rather than comply with desegregation. The KKK waxed and the White Citizens'

Councils flourished. Crosses were burned; black churches, homes, and schools were bombed. The Southern Regional Council tabulated over two hundred acts of violence against black protesters and their allies from 1955 to 1959. The NAACP struggled just to survive. It channeled its energies and resources primarily into the effort to thwart the scores of Southern laws passed to outlaw the association directly or to hamstring its ability to function effectively. The civil-rights offensive envisioned by King seemed to many in the late 1950s more like a retreat before the forces of racism.

Not surprisingly, King's strategy of nonviolent resistance struck many blacks as unproductive, even unbearable. Some considered it debasing; others questioned what fundamental conditions it could change; many simply tired of turning the other cheek. In 1959, the dismissal of Robert Williams as head of the Monroe, North Carolina, NAACP rocked the association's fiftieth annual convention. Earlier in the year, Williams had organized some fifty blacks into a gun club. Armed and drilled, they repelled with gunfire a group of Klansmen threatening the home of an NAACP official. Williams then publicly advocated defensive guerilla warfare by blacks and called for the formation of rifle clubs throughout the South. The NAACP hierarchy defended the dismissal of Williams, but the deep rumblings of discontent by delegates served notice that proponents of civil rights would not indefinitely adhere to nonviolence if it proved fruitless. Near the end of the year, a two-hour television documentary, "The Hate That Hate Produced," shocked the nation with its portrayal of the Black Muslims, nearly a hundred thousand strong, rejecting Christianity and integration. These angry blacks warned that "an eye for an eye and a tooth for a tooth" was the only way to settle racial differences.

Yet other blacks, mainly the young, demonstrated an impatient hopefulness. They took heart from the legal and legislative victories of the NAACP. The desegregation efforts of the federal government, however irresolute, buoyed them. They knew that national and international politics made it imperative for Washington to deal with the racial problem. They sensed that the economic, educational, and demographic changes swirling about them foretold the crumbling of the old racial order. Montgomery had made them proud and confident. They read and reread FOR's widely circulated comic book *Martin Luther King and the Montgomery Story* and King's *Stride Toward Freedom: The Montgomery Story*. They dreamed of their opportunity to act.

Returning from a nonviolent action workshop in 1958, Barbara Ann Posey decided to act. A member of the Oklahoma City NAACP Youth Council, Posey organized a sit-in which resulted in the desegregation of five stores. The idea spread to the Youth Councils in Tulsa and Stillwater, and then across the state line to NAACP youth in Wichita and Kansas City, Kansas. King and Rustin organized a Youth March for Integrated Schools that brought nearly nine thousand young blacks to Washington, D.C. The following year, the March drew twenty-five thousand. Two thousand attended a Pilgrimage of Prayer for Public Schools in Richmond, Virginia, the first such large demonstration in the Deep South to decry "massive resistance" to school desegregation. Black students in Charlotte, North Carolina, protested being barred from state ceremonies which welcomed whites, while their counterparts in Marion, South Carolina, desegregated an ice-cream stand after a successful boycott. Also in 1959, CORE members in Miami, Florida, sat-in at a W. T. Grant's lunch counter and started a drive to desegregate the beaches of that resort city. None of these actions attracted national press coverage. None led to new organizations or leaders. None sparked a nationwide movement.

Yet together they revealed a new mood of restiveness, compounded of hope and anger. The charismatic young preacher who imparted a more moral and militant quality to the movement and the nonviolent, direct action campaign by the mass of ordinary black Montgomerians that rocked the Cradle of the

Confederacy had together made an extraordinary impression on Afro-Americans, especially black middle-class youth. They yearned to take to the streets. They bitterly decried the lack of racial progress in the late 1950s, yet optimistically believed that by using the strategy fashioned by Martin Luther King in Montgomery they could topple Jim Crow, quickly and throughout the South. King's prediction to the annual convention of the Fellowship of Reconciliation in mid-1959 that the coming years would witness mounting black "direct action against injustice without waiting for other agencies to act" defined their propensity. His thundering peroration to the FOR—"We will not obey unjust laws or submit to unjust practices"—adumbrated their cause.

THREE

More Than a Hamburger

"We don't serve Negros." This common retort, like the daily indignity of having to board a Jim Crow bus, stung and humiliated blacks seeking to eat in Dixie's restaurants and lunch counters. Such segregation was usually a matter of custom or tradition; sometimes it was required by statute or city ordinance; in either event, blacks throughout the South and the border states could not sit down and eat alongside white diners.

"We don't serve Negroes here," the waitress responded to Joseph McNeill on January 31, 1960, at the bus terminal in Greensboro, North Carolina. He had heard it before. It always hurt. Now it particularly rankled. That night in his dormitory at North Carolina Agricultural and Technical College, McNeill emotionally recounted the incident to his roommate, Ezell Blair, Jr., and fellow freshmen Franklin McCain and David Richmond. The four young men often sat together for hours discussing the racial situation. They all resented the snail's pace of desegregation in the South. The countless subterfuges employed by the Greensboro school board to evade the *Brown* decision especially angered them. They were not content to wait forever for the courts and the white South to grant them rights they felt were their due. They had frequently expressed their desire to act. The moment had arrived.

"We've talked about it long enough, let's do something." "But what can we do?" Suddenly the room grew quiet. No one spoke. Then McNeill answered his own question: "Let's have a boycott. We should go in and ask to be served and sit there until they do." They decided to go to the local Woolworth store and request service at the lunch counter. "We'll stay until we get served." "Well, you know that might be weeks, that might be months," Blair wondered aloud. "That might be never." But they were determined. They gave one another courage. All agreed "that's just the chance we'll have to take."

The next afternoon the four freshmen walked into the downtown Greensboro five-and-dime store. They bought some school supplies, then took seats at the lunch counter, and asked for coffee and doughnuts. "I'm sorry," came the anticipated reply of the waitress, "we don't serve colored in here." "I beg to disagree with you," Blair responded politely, showing the receipts for their purchases. "We've in fact already been served; you've already served us at a counter only two feet from here." Dumbfounded, the waitress hurried off to get her manager. "Fellas," he tried kindly, "you know this is just not the way we do business. Why don't you go on back to your campus?" The students explained what they called their "passive demand for service" and promised to remain until they could eat where they sat. By then, other customers in the store had crowded around the lunch counter. One white woman patted them on the back, saying, "Ah, you should have done it ten years ago. It's a good thing I think you're doing." "Nasty, dirty niggers," other whites rasped, "you know you don't belong here at the lunch counter." A black dishwasher, fearful of losing her job and of what might happen to the young blacks, reprimanded them: "That's why we can't get anyplace today, because of people like you, rabble-rousers, troublemakers. . . . This counter is reserved for white people, it always has been, and you are well aware of that. So why don't you go on out and stop making trouble?" The four students would not be moved. They remained seated until the store closed, and vowed to repeat their demand the next day.

By the time they returned to their campus, a local radio station had flashed the news. Word spread. The college was a beehive of activity. The four students now knew they were not alone. That evening they met with about fifty student leaders and formed the Student Executive Committee for Justice. They voted to continue the boycott "until we get served," and agreed on ground rules for new volunteers. The protesters would remain passive, never raise their voices, never indulge in name-calling. Their movement would be one of nonviolence and Christian love.

On Tuesday, February 2, twenty-three A & T students and four black women from Bennett College sat-in with Blair, McCain, McNeill, and Richmond at the Woolworth lunch counter. None was served. They just sat. Wednesday morning the students occupied sixty-three of the sixty-six lunch-counter seats. On Thursday, they were joined by three white students from the Woman's College of the University of North Carolina campus in Greensboro and scores of sympathizers from A & T and Bennett. They overflowed Woolworth's and began to sit-in at the lunch counter in the S. H. Kress store down the street. Greensboro became national news. Over three hundred young blacks demonstrated on Friday. Even more jammed Greensboro's lunch counters the next day. City officials, seeking to end the protest, decided that the time had come to negotiate. Although not a single black had received a cup of coffee at the lunch counters, nearly 1,600 students, flushed with victory, attended a mass rally Saturday night. They would cease demonstrating to allow an agreement to be settled.

But, as would happen time and again all over the South, the white leadership of Greensboro, unable to gauge the depth of black determination, was unwilling to compromise. Whites resisted all pleas for change. They insisted on preserving the status quo. So pressure had to be applied anew. On April 1, the sit-ins resumed. White officials now offered the blacks a plan for partial desegregation of the lunch counters. The Student Executive Committee for Justice rejected the offer. Tokenism was no longer acceptable. Greensboro merchants and officials tried another tack, arresting forty-five students on trespass charges on April 21. This enraged the already fired-up black community of Greensboro, provoking a massive boycott of targeted variety stores. After profits had dropped by more than one-third, Greensboro's white leaders grudgingly acceded. Six months after the four freshmen sat-in at Woolworth's, Greensboro blacks could sit down at a lunch counter and be served a cup of coffee.

Greensboro, moreover, inspired sit-ins all over the South. The actions taken by Blair, McCain, McNeill, and Richmond initiated the student phase of the black struggle. The Greensboro "Coffee Party" made direct action the vogue. By April 1960 the tactic had spread to seventy-eight Southern and border communities; some two thousand students had been arrested. A year later, both figures had nearly doubled. In September 1961, the Southern Regional Council estimated that at least 70,000 blacks and whites had actively participated in the massive wave of sit-ins against unjust laws and practices. The American racial situation would never be the same. The lunch counters in Greensboro had joined the buses of Montgomery, Gandhi's salt marshes, and Thoreau's Walden Pond as focal points in the quest for justice through nonviolent civil disobedience.

First within North Carolina, then to neighboring states, the spark ignited in Greensboro spread like a brushfire. On February 8, 1960, sit-ins began in Durham and Winston-Salem. "We want to put justice in their business," explained the chairman of the student movement from Winston-Salem Teachers College. "We believe it is morally wrong, as well as un-Christian, to maintain segregated facilities. We will continue to use the non-violent approach because we believe non-violence is not the weapon of the weak and the coward; it is the weapon of the strong and the brave." The students' articulation of their dissatisfaction, however, initially produced only resistance from white officials. In both cities it would take the arrests of students, the mobilization of the adult community, boycotts by blacks, and the support of white faculty and students from Duke University and Wake Forest College before desegregated lunch-counter service would begin.

On Tuesday, February 9, about 150 black students from Johnson C. Smith University began sit-ins against white-only eating facilities in Charlotte. "It's a manifestation of the unrest among this generation of students. It comes from their desire to dramatize the injustices of the Negro's position," stated one divinity student. "It is part of their feeling about the schools, the vote—civil rights in general." Another student leader expounded on the demonstrations as a "means of expressing something that has been in our hearts for a long time." Again, arrests and a "Don't buy where you can't eat" campaign had to precede desegregation in Charlotte.

Two days after the protest began in that city, students in High Point and Raleigh, and in Portsmouth, Virginia, voiced their impatience at the slow progress toward racial equality. Without leadership, planning, or organization, high-school students staged sit-ins in High Point and Portsmouth. Sporadic violence followed. The Portsmouth police turned their dogs loose on the young blacks. "Our struggle is not an easy one," their spokesman said, "but we know we are not alone and we plan to continue in accordance with our common ideal: equality for all through non-violent action." A news broadcast reported that black students at Shaw University and St. Augustine College in Raleigh would not follow the Greensboro example. That sparked the rebellion of black young people there to do just that. Dissatisfaction with the racial situation in this capital city ran high. Not a single Raleigh public school had yet started to desegregate. Not a single black operated a bus. To enjoy an evening out, black students had to enter the local movie theater, owned by the mayor, through a "colored" side door, sit in the "owl's nest," and then walk ten blocks to a Negro restaurant for a Coke. Now, irritated at being pictured as docile by the white establishment, the blacks from Shaw and St. Augustine planned and executed a series of massive sit-ins at Raleigh variety stores. Over forty would be arrested for trespassing before the mayor established an interracial committee to deal with desegregation.

On Lincoln's birthday, students in Nashville and Tallahassee demonstrated their readiness to rebel. A small CORE group at Florida A & M, responding to a call from their national office to follow the lead of Greensboro, staged a sit-in at Woolworth's. They were joined by fifteen white supporters from Florida State University. When the waitress told the blacks, "I'm sorry, I can't serve you," all the students propped books on the counter and began to read. They stayed until the counter closed. A week later they returned. Again, they sat silently, reading. This time, the police arrested eleven students and charged them with disturbing the peace by riotous conduct and unlawful assembly. The pace of sit-ins and arrests quickened, culminating in a protest march of nearly a thousand students. On March 18, the first group of eleven arrested students introduced a militant new tactic in the movement: the jail-in. Following their trial and conviction, they chose to serve sixty-day sentences in the Leon County jail rather than pay a fine.

Writing to a friend, Patricia Stephens described the "dank and cold" cells, the inedible food, and the hopeful determination of the jailed students. "We are all so very happy that we were (and are) able to do this to help our city, state and nation. This is something that has to be done over and over again, and we are willing to do it as often as necessary. We strongly believe that Martin Luther King was right when he said, 'We've got to fill the jails in order to win our equal rights.' " The A & M junior concluded her letter simply: "When I get out, I plan to carry on this struggle. I feel I shall be ready to go to jail again if necessary."

When the sit-in leaders in Greensboro at the beginning of February 1960 asked, "What can the students in Nashville do to support students in Greensboro?" a contingent of blacks from Fisk University and the American Baptist Theological Seminary, aided by some whites from Vanderbilt University, immediately decided on massive, nonviolent direct action in Nashville. James Lawson, studying theology at Vanderbilt, initially led the group. He had been conducting nonviolent workshops for a couple of years and drew up the rules. "Do show yourself friendly on the counter at all times. Do sit straight and always face the counter. Don't strike back, or curse back if attacked. Don't laugh out. Don't hold conversations. Don't block entrances." Lawson reminded each volunteer: "Remember the teachings of Jesus, Gandhi, Martin Luther King." On a snowy twelfth of February, forty students sat-in at Woolworth's in Nashville. They stayed for several hours, politely reading, studying, in their best Sunday clothes. Then they met with some five hundred other students in a local church to plan the next day's demonstration and to sing the spirituals and freedom songs that had started to characterize the student movement.

Each succeeding day, the number of students sitting-in grew. Tension mounted in Nashville. Violence began. White hecklers pushed lighted cigarettes against the backs of girls sitting at the counter. They beat and kicked "nigger lovers." They threw french fried potatoes and gum at the demonstrators. They spat on them and blew cigar smoke in their faces. Yet the police arrested only the protesters. Seventy-six students had been jailed by the fifth day. By early May, when the first downtown lunch counters announced an end to the color line, Nashville students had been arrested by the hundreds and had marched in protest by the thousands.

Day after day, sit-ins rocked the cities of the South. The arrest of thirty-three blacks sitting-in at the restaurant in Thalhimer's department store in Richmond on February 22 immediately provoked similar demonstrations in Petersburg, Hampton, Newport News, and Arlington. On February 23, high-school students sat-in at the Chattanooga Kress store. Students took to the streets in Knoxville, Memphis, and Oak Ridge. Over a hundred blacks from Friendship Junior College launched sit-ins and picketed against segregation in Rock Hill, South Carolina. Demonstrations in Orangeburg, Columbia, and Sumter, South Carolina, followed within the week. More than six hundred Allen University and Benedict College students marched to the dime stores of downtown Columbia and took turns sitting-in after being refused service.

In Orangeburg, the students from Claflin College and South Carolina State College painstakingly schooled themselves in the principles and practices of nonviolence. They read King's *Stride Toward Freedom* and the pamphlet "CORE Rules for Action." They constantly asked one another: "Could each one of us trust our God and our temper enough not to strike back even if kicked, slapped, or spit upon?" A CORE staffer instructed them:

> To protect the skull, fold the hands over the head. To prevent disfigurement of the face, bring the elbows together in front of the eyes. For girls, to prevent internal injury from kicks, lie on the side and bring the knees upward to the chin; for boys, kneel down and arch over, with skull and face protected.

Over a thousand students were trained. Their first wave of sit-ins closed the lunch counters of Orangeburg on February 25. They returned the next day, and the next. On March 1, nearly a

thousand blacks paraded through Orangeburg with signs reading "Down with Jim-Crow," "Segregation is Obsolete," and
"All Sit or All Stand." Two weeks later, police met another
mass march in support of the sit-ins with tear-gas bombs and
high-pressure water hoses. Over five hundred students, knocked
off their feet by streams of water, retching and temporarily
blinded, were arrested. They filled the city and county jails, so
the police herded more than three hundred into a chicken-coop
stockade that afforded no protection against the sub-freezing
weather. A photograph of those well-dressed, drenched students
shivering and herded behind a wire fence appeared all over
the country and throughout the world.

The sit-ins now spread southward. Thirty-five Alabama State
College students demonstrated for service at the Montgomery
County courthouse snack shop on February 25. When Governor
John Patterson ordered the president of the college to expel any
student involved in a sit-in, the campus staged a mass rally,
addressed by Martin Luther King. Nearly a thousand students
pledged to quit the college en masse if any expulsions followed
their protest. A week later, about a hundred Texas Southern
University students sat-in at the lunch counters of Houston.
Mass arrests followed a series of sit-ins in the east Texas city
of Marshall. Threatened with sit-ins, the managers of the variety
stores in San Antonio announced the desegregation of their
lunch counters on March 20. Sit-ins by high-school students
quickly produced a dramatic headline in the Galveston *Tribune*:
"City Lunch Counters Integrated."

More commonly, however, whites responded with violence
and savagery. In Houston, a white youth slashed a black with a
knife and three masked white men seized another black, flogged
him with a chain, carved the initials of the KKK on his chest,
and hung him by his knees from an oak tree. Unknown assail-
ants stabbed a student protester in Columbia and firebombed the
gymnasium of a Negro college in Frankfort, Kentucky. The
KKK pistol-whipped a young demonstrator in Jacksonville,

Florida. A crowd of whites in Biloxi, Mississippi, attacked blacks with clubs and chains, and wounded ten by gunfire. Jackson, Mississippi, police employed tear gas and police dogs against women and children. Acid was thrown in the face of a sit-in leader in Atlanta.

Not even such brutality could deter the students. There was no stopping them. Their parents often tried, and failed. School administrators tried, to no avail. When white officials and police tried, they succeeded only in solidifying the black community behind the students and in stimulating more protests. Young Southern blacks conquered their fears, courted arrest, braved fire hoses and police dogs, and planned larger sit-ins.

Their most ambitious campaign developed in Atlanta. On February 4, Julian Bond, an aspiring poet and student at Morehouse College, was relaxing at Yates and Milton's Drugstore, which functioned as an informal meeting place for Atlanta University Center students, when Lonnie King approached him with a copy of the Atlanta *Daily World*. The headline blared: "Greensboro Students Sit-In, Third Day." King, a veteran of military service and campus football hero, bluntly demanded of the influential Bond: "What do you think about it?" "Well, it's all right, pretty good stuff," Bond replied. "Don't you think it ought to happen here?" King pushed. "It probably will." King insisted: "Let's make it happen." And so they did.

They hoped to stage their first demonstration on Lincoln's birthday, sitting-in at Woolworth's, W. T. Grant's, and Kresge's simultaneously. Meetings were held with all the student leaders of Morris Brown, Clark, Morehouse, and Spelman colleges, the Interdenominational Theological Center, and the professional schools of Atlanta University. When the college administrators learned of the plan, however, they delayed the students by insisting on further consultation and more meetings. Out of these discussions came an agreement by the students to publish a clear, open statement of their aims before demonstrating. The

University presidents agreed to raise the funds to publicize their manifesto.

On March 9, a full-page advertisement appeared in the Atlanta *Constitution, Journal,* and *Daily World* entitled "An Appeal for Human Rights." It began with a pledge of "unqualified support" for the student sit-ins in other cities and then proclaimed:

> The students who instigate and participate in these sit-down protests are dissatisfied, not only with the existing conditions, but with the snail-like speed at which they are being ameliorated. Every normal human being wants to walk the earth with dignity and abhors any and all proscriptions placed upon him because of race or color. In essence, this is the meaning of the sit-down protests that are sweeping this nation today. . . . Today's youth will not sit by submissively, while being denied all of the rights, privileges, and joys of life. We want to state clearly and unequivocally that we cannot tolerate, in a nation professing democracy and among people professing Christianity, the discriminatory conditions under which the Negro is living today in Atlanta, Georgia—supposedly one of the most progressive cities in the South.

"We do not intend to wait placidly for those rights which are already legally and morally ours to be meted out to us one at a time," the appeal continued. It demanded an end to segregation in restaurants, movie theaters, concert halls, and other public facilities, the enfranchisement of blacks, and equitable law enforcement. It called for jobs for blacks and for equality in education, where only 4 percent of the state's expenditures for higher education went to the black colleges. They demanded equality in housing, where the blacks of Atlanta constituted over a third of the population and had to live in less than 16 percent of the city area. And they sought better health services; only 680 of the more than four thousand beds in the city hospitals could be used by blacks. "The time has come for the people of

Atlanta and Georgia to take a good look at what is really happening in this country, and to stop believing those who tell us that everything is fine and equal, and that the Negro is happy and satisfied." The students ended with a promise: "We must say in all candor that we plan to use every legal and non-violent means at our disposal to secure full citizenship rights as members of this great democracy of ours."

On March 15, some two hundred students staged a well-orchestrated protest at the lunch counters and restaurants in the City Hall, the State Capitol Building, the Fulton County Courthouse, two office buildings devoted exclusively to government agencies, and the city's bus and train stations. Bond led the group at City Hall, where a sign announced "Cafeteria, Public Is Welcome." "What do you want?" said the manager. "We want to eat." "Well, we can't serve you here." "Well," Bond replied, "the sign outside says the public is welcome and we're the public and we want to eat." The police arrested Bond and seventy-six of his fellow students. The next day they organized the Committee on an Appeal for Human Rights to negotiate with business and civic leaders.

Interminable meetings followed. But the Atlanta leadership had no intention of compromising. They counted on the upcoming summer vacation to end the sit-in craze; they expected to go back to business as usual in the fall. The students, however, used the summer months to plan large-scale sit-ins at the major department and variety stores and to organize a boycott of the downtown merchants. "Close out your charge account with segregation, open up your account with freedom," became their slogan. With military precision, the fall campaign began. In October 1960, Martin Luther King and thirty-six students were arrested when they sat down in the Magnolia Room of Rich's department store. Even more demonstrators appeared the next day, and police arrested fifty-seven protesters. They all vowed to stay in jail and not post bond. Then the mayor arranged a sixty-day truce. The sit-ins would cease; those arrested would be released; negotiations would resume. But the merchants refused to offer anything more concrete than vague assurances to try sincerely to end segregation sometime in the future. The students considered this response unacceptable and publicly announced the resumption of demonstrations:

> We intend to do it for as long as it takes. It has never been our intention to hurt our city, the merchants or anyone else. We do want, however, to remove the hurt from the hearts of Negroes who've been hurting for over one hundred years.

The students now had the support of the Atlanta black community. Many adults began to sit-in and picket. The boycott took its toll. Day after day, hundreds of protesters marched and clogged the downtown lunch counters. Equipped with two-way radios and cars to shuttle students quickly to any store where they might be needed, the Committee on an Appeal for Human Rights kept increasing the pressure on the merchants during the winter months. In February 1961, the arrests began again. Nearly a hundred students were behind bars by February 11. Finally, the business leadership budged. They pledged that their rest-room and eating facilities would be desegregated no later than October 15. The students dropped their demand for immediate integration. On September 27, 1961, desegregation came to Atlanta.

Long before that, however, scores of other cities in every Southern state, including Mississippi, confronted impatient young blacks. As the pace of victory quickened in desegregating lunch counters, the student movement focused on eradicating other vestiges of Jim Crow and experimented with new forms of nonviolent direct action. There were "kneel-ins" in churches, "sleep-ins" in motel lobbies, "swim-ins" in pools, "wade-ins" on restricted beaches, "read-ins" at public libraries, "play-ins" in parks, even "watch-ins" in movie theaters. Other targets of racial exclusion included amusement parks, employment agencies, laundromats, and museums. These demonstrations fundamentally transformed the use of public accommodations in the border and upper South states, where by the end of 1961 nearly two hundred cities had begun to desegregate. Try as they might, however, the students scored few victories in the Deep South. There, the segregationist wall of resistance held. The sit-ins, nevertheless, accelerated a train of consequences that would soon topple Jim Crow.

These subsequent developments and the meaning of the sit-ins can best be understood through the many who demonstrated collectively. Much has already been written about specific individuals involved, about particular groups, about single cities affected. There is a continuing debate on the causes and goals of the movement. In some instances, it is argued, a charismatic student or an especially galling local incident was the vital force. In others, sit-ins materialized spontaneously without definitive provocation, leadership, or incitement.

When asked to explain their motives, sit-in participants answered in about as many ways as their number. They stated that their inspiration come from parents engaged in the struggle for racial justice, or from teachers who dwelled on the long and noble tradition of Negro protest, or even from whites who urged the necessity to demonstrate against Jim Crow. Sometimes they stressed personal experiences. Quite a few had served in the armed forces or had lived in the North and found it difficult to adjust to Southern segregation. Some knew of the 1958 sit-ins staged by NAACP youth groups or the 1959 actions by CORE in Miami. Many more had heard about the Montgomery bus boycott and the doctrines of nonviolence preached by Martin Luther King, Jr. He had spoken in Greensboro in 1958, and Ezell Blair remembered King's sermon being "so strong that I could feel my heart palpitating. It brought tears to my eyes." The passive-resistance movement in Montgomery stirred innumerable students, pointed to a workable strategy, and shamed them. The bus boycotters "were at least trying to do something," remonstrated Joseph McNeill. "And we weren't."

"By coincidence," recalled Bernard Lee, the sit-in leader at Alabama State College, "I had just written a term paper on civil disobedience and non-violence—had read Gandhi for it." So had numerous others. King's popularization of Gandhi's concepts had become a staple of black discussion groups. Many students spoke vividly of their experience watching documentaries on the Indian nonviolent movement in their churches and schools. Prior to the sit-ins, some had already participated in nonviolent workshops; some had joined CORE; and some had already been in trouble with the law or with school authorities because of their opposition to racism. Yet another student emotionally recollected hearing Tom Mboya, a leader of the black liberation campaign in Kenya, speak at Fisk University and was stirred into realizing that he was a "part of a worldwide struggle of young black people to control their lives." Ghana's victorious revolution for independence in 1957 had initiated a wave of freedom movements against the African empires of Belgium, France, Great Britain, and Portugal. In 1960, a dozen African nations had gained independence. Afro-American students were not unaware; the successful struggles of black Africans both inspired and embarrassed them. "The pace of social change is too slow," exclaimed James Lawson in Nashville. "All of Africa will be free before we attain first-class citizenship." And black author James Baldwin jeered: "All of Africa will be free before we can get a lousy cup of coffee."

However much the student analyses of the cause of the sit-ins differed, impatience was a factor in virtually every explanation. Their generation, for the most part, had been in elementary school or beginning high school when the Supreme Court ordered an end to segregation in public education. The decision thrilled them. They believed they would finish their education in desegregated schools. John Lewis, a seminary student in Nashville who became one of the sit-in leaders in that city, recalled learning the news of *Brown* when he was fourteen. "I thought that the next year I would go to a real high school, and not the kind of training school that blacks were sent to. I thought I wouldn't have to be bused forty miles each day, past white schools, to maintain a system of segregation." But Lewis would never attend a desegregated school. Contrary to the Constitution, in defiance of numerous federal court orders, and despite a brilliant, costly, valiant campaign by the NAACP, six years after the Supreme Court outlawed segregation only 6 percent of the schools in the South had started to desegregate. Not even a beginning had been made in Alabama, Florida, Louisiana, Mississippi, and South Carolina. At this rate of compliance with the law, segregation would not be ended in their lives, perhaps not even in the lifetime of the children of the generation who sat-in.

The pace of progress in terminating disenfranchisement was equally painful. Again, despite intensive efforts by the NAACP and SCLC, despite decades of struggle for the suffrage, despite victories in the courts and in the Congress, fewer than one in four blacks of voting age in the South could register and vote in 1960. Many realized that not even their college diplomas would open the voting booth to them. Many understood that just the attempt to claim this most elementary right of citizenship entailed the risk of losing their jobs, their homes, possibly their lives.

Yet this generation of black students expected to mature in a different America. They grew up in an era of change. For the most part, they came from cities, not sharecropper shacks; their parents were professionals, industrial workers, civil servants, not dirt farmers. They were the middle class, certainly in aspiration if not in income. They were students in college, or expected to be there shortly. Their youth had been marked by sweeping changes in the economy, in demography, in national and international politics, and in American attitudes about race. All this had conspired to raise their aspirations, to fuel their hopes. But the promise of change far outran the reality. Massive resistance to racial equality throughout the South proved the rule. The minimal extent of enfranchisement and desegregation seemed ludicrously disproportionate to the monumental expenditures of energy, money, time, and courage. Southern blacks, no matter how wealthy or educated, still could not even have a cup of coffee with whites in public. In 1960 their patience ran out. They were no longer in a mood to wait silently, inactively.

Having a cup of coffee, sitting down, may not seem like much today, but in 1960 it epitomized the degradation of blacks induced by segregation. "Negro Americans throughout our country will be bruised in nearly every waking hour by differential treatment in, or exclusion from, public accommodations of every description," Roy Wilkins testified to Congress. "From the time they leave home in the morning, en route to school or to work, to shopping or visiting, until they return home at night, humiliation stalks them." Then the NAACP leader invited the lawmakers to imagine themselves black and planning an auto trip in the South.

> How far do you drive each day? Where, and under what conditions can you and your family eat? Where can they use a rest room? Can you stop driving after a reasonable day behind the wheel or must you drive until you reach a city where relatives or friends will accommodate you and yours for the night? Will your children be denied a soft drink or an ice-cream cone because they are not white?

John Williams, a black writer, echoed Wilkins in emphasizing the demeaning nature of Jim Crow. "Nothing is quite as humiliating," wrote Williams, "so murderously angering as to know that because you are black you may have to walk a half mile farther than whites just to urinate; that because you are black you have to receive your food through a window in the back of a restaurant or sit in a garbage-littered yard to eat."

Clearly, the students sought more than the opportunity to eat where and as others ate in public places. Their worthiness and self-esteem could not be attained within the framework of compulsory segregation. They sought, accordingly, the end of Jim Crow. The lunch counter, said one student, is only a symbol that we "aren't having it any more. . . . We're trying to eradicate the whole stigma of being inferior." Those demonstrating in Chapel Hill carried signs saying: "We do not picket just because we want to eat. We can eat at home or walking down the street. We do picket to protest the lack of dignity and respect shown us as human beings." The students sat-in to demand full equality in a way that could be neither misunderstood nor ignored.

That goal, and the brave, resourceful, unambiguous manner in which the students expressed it, awakened a generation of young activists. Ruby Doris Smith, a seventeen-year-old sophomore at Morehouse College, heard a rumor about the Greensboro sit-in and rushed home to watch it on the television news. "I began to think right away about it happening in Atlanta." So did John Lewis. "I had the feeling that we were involved in something like a crusade. . . . It was a sense of duty, you had an obligation to do it, to redeem the city—as Dr. King said so many times, to redeem the soul of America. . . . I will never forget it. . . . You felt that you were doing something that *had* to be done." "It made me so proud," recalled Bernard Lee in Montgomery, "I never had to think about whether to get involved." Neither did Charles McDew in Orangeburg, or Cleveland Sellers in Denmark, South Carolina. "I had a burning desire to get involved," Sellers wrote. Each evening he would rush to the student union to view the news broadcasts.

With the exception of the announcer's voice, the lounge would be so quiet you could hear a rat pissing on cotton. Hundreds of thoughts coursed through my head as I stood with my eyes transfixed on the television screen. My identification with the demonstrating students was so thorough that I would flinch every time one of the whites taunted them. On nights when I saw pictures of students being beaten and dragged through the streets by their hair, I would leave the lounge in a rage.

James Forman, a former Chicago schoolteacher doing graduate work in French, and Robert Moses, a Harvard graduate student and mathematics teacher in Harlem, had similar reactions. "They were kids my own age and I knew this had something to do with my life," remarked Moses. And thousands less well known, but just as angry, just as proud, just as impatient, would also act. As a Charlotte student put it: "The sit-ins were a means of expressing something that had been in our hearts for a long time."

Moreover, the intrepid resolution of their children inspired the black adult community to act. Many a dormant Negro betterment organization came to life to assist the students. They raised bail money for the jailed, provided legal counsel, defrayed organizational costs, and lent moral support. The astounding success of most of the economic boycotts launched to buttress the sit-ins testified to the involvement of adult blacks. Several cities reported black boycotts of targeted merchants that were nearly a hundred percent effective. An intangible yet profound shift in the psychology of the black community became manifest. The sit-ins dramatically illustrated the power of individuals to shape their own history, and a renewed will to struggle for equal rights appeared. "Something wonderful is happening in this town," commented Atlanta's Martin Luther King, Sr. "The low-down Negroes are getting tired. I mean the kind of folks who just come and go like the rain. White folks have never paid them any mind, but they're tired. They just aren't going to take it like they always have before." The behavior of the students taught their elders that the way it used to be did not have to be. As Jim Crow seemed less immutable, the paralyzing feeling of fatalism diminished.

The volume of public endorsements for the sit-ins also pointed to the new mood in black America. Privately, numbers of black clergymen, school administrators, and civic spokesmen opposed the student actions. They considered the tactics too brusque, or the strategy unwise, or the time not right. For reasons that ranged from narrowly selfish to sincerely altruistic, some older blacks tried to discourage the young. But rarely did they publicly announce their opposition; and those that did soon recanted. Everywhere, leaders hurried to catch up with their followers, lest they be stigmatized as Uncle Toms. The sit-ins pushed the established black leadership to a new plateau of militancy.

Some white students, and their parents, also responded positively to the spirit of nonviolent militance, redemptive love, and dignity expressed by the sit-in participants. "I have a moral obligation to support this movement," said one young white woman who joined the Greensboro sit-in. Just days after it began, the University of North Carolina *Daily Tar Heel* editorialized about the students demonstrating in Greensboro: "We hope they win. We hope they win BIG and we hope they win SOON." Student assemblies, faculty groups, interracial organizations, and church conventions spoke out to vindicate the demonstrators. "There are many white people in the South who recognize the injustice of the lunch counter system," pronounced the Greensboro *Daily News*. "It is based on circumstances which may have made sense 100 years ago; today it has a touch of medievalism. It smacks of Indian 'untouchables' or Hitlerian Germany's Master Race Theories." Florida's Governor LeRoy Collins told a statewide radio and television audience: "I don't mind saying that if a man has a department store and he invites the public generally to come in his department store and trade I think then it is unfair and morally wrong for him to single out one department though, and say he does not want or will not allow Negroes to patronize that one department." Frank P. Graham, former United States Senator and president of the University of North Carolina, added that the black protesters are "in their day and generation renewing springs of American democracy. . . . In sitting down they are standing up for the American dream."

Although such statements remained atypical in the South, many of those opposed to the student demonstrators grudgingly praised their courage and comportment. The contrast between the dignity of the blacks sitting-in and the ugliness of their opponents' tactics was repeatedly highlighted. In a widely reprinted editorial, the Richmond *News Leader* observed:

> Here were the colored students, in coats, white shirts, ties, and one of them was reading Goethe and one was taking notes from a biology text. And here, on the sidewalk outside, was a gang of white boys come to heckle, a ragtail rabble, slack-jawed, black-jacketed, grinning fit to kill, and some of them, God save the mark, were waving the proud and honored flag of the Southern States in the last war fought by gentlemen. *Eheu!* It gives one pause.

The sit-ins, moreover, opened the eyes of Southern whites as nothing had before to the depth of black discontent and determination. The risks taken by so many students, and the responses of black communities, made it painfully clear that their dissatisfaction with segregation could no longer be denied or attributed merely to a handful of Northern agitators. The black struggle could never again be dismissed as just the doing of the Supreme Court or the Kremlin. As surely as the sit-ins destroyed the myth of black contentment with the status quo, they demolished the image of a united white South committed to preserve Jim Crow at any cost.

The reaction of Northern whites also proved heartening to the black students. Within a fortnight, sympathy sit-ins and pickets appeared at the lunch counters of Grant, Kress, Liggett, Walgreen, and Woolworth stores in Boston, Chicago, and New York. Students from California to Connecticut demonstrated in support of the Southern sit-ins. Their slogan: "We Walk So

They May Sit." Campus groups raised scholarship money and bail funds to assist expelled or jailed blacks. The National Student Association, the National Student Christian Federation, and the Northern Student Movement, a new organization formed specifically to support the sit-in campaign, organized boycotts against the variety-store chains, helping to make lunch-counter discrimination a national issue. Eleanor Roosevelt termed the sit-ins "simply wonderful." Various labor, liberal, and religious organizations voiced their support. Even President Eisenhower responded, when queried at a press conference whether or not he approved of the sit-ins: "Now, let me make one thing clear. I am deeply sympathetic with the efforts of any group to enjoy the rights of equality that they are guaranteed by the Constitution."

Most of all, the sit-ins transformed the young blacks' image of themselves. Recalling the first of February in Greensboro, Franklin McCain asserted: "I probably felt better that day than I've ever felt in my life. I felt as though I had gained my manhood, so to speak, and not only gained it, but had developed quite a lot of respect for it." Such a psychological change occurred thousands of times. Each student had his own way of expressing "I became a man." And the net result of this wellspring of self-respect was a whetted appetite for further struggle. The students' new sense of their own determination and strength also intensified this impetus. An Atlanta student described a young woman from Spelman sitting-in next to her:

The manager walked up behind her, said something obscene, and grabbed her by the shoulders. "Get the hell out of here, nigger." Lana was not going. . . . She put her hands under the counter and held. He was rough and strong. She just held and I looked down at that moment at her hands . . . brown, strained . . . every muscle holding. All of a sudden he let go and left. I thought he knew he could not move that girl— ever.

In a thousand ways the students stated that they could not be moved, spurring themselves and others to protest yet more. "City officials pointed out that we had staged nineteen demonstrations during January," one of the Rock Hill "jail-inners" commented, "and suddenly we felt sort of ashamed of ourselves that we hadn't staged thirty-one."

Success further enhanced their commitment. They showed that blacks could challenge racism in their own communities; they demonstrated that the system was not impregnable; they proved that whites could, and would, accept integrated public accommodations. This strengthened their will to press harder against remaining discriminations. It was a heady moment in the black struggle. "I myself desegregated a lunch counter, not somebody else, not some big man, some powerful man, but little me," said a proud black student. "I walked the picket line and I sat in and the walls of segregation toppled. Now all people can eat there." Each small victory convinced thousands that "Nothing can stop us now."

The formation of the Student Nonviolent Coordinating Committee exemplified this new spirit. Soon after the sit-in fever became contagious, Ella Baker persuaded the SCLC to appropriate $800 and the president of her alma mater, Shaw University in Raleigh, to make its facilities available for an Easter-weekend conference of youth leaders. Then executive director of the SCLC, but soon to be replaced by Wyatt Tee Walker, Baker feared both the volatility of the young and the appetence of established civil-rights groups to harness the student commitment to their own organizations. She had spent most of her sixty years organizing for civil rights, and felt that the SCLC and NAACP had not kept pace with the new impatience and aggressiveness that the students had injected into the movement. She wanted young blacks to dare to go further, and so sought a structure and a direction for the student movement that would keep it both free from adult fetters and disciplined enough to remain active and nonviolent. Those answering her call for a meeting included some 150 students from 58 Southern communities, 19 delegates from Northern colleges, and about 50 representatives from the American Friends Service Committee, CORE, SCLC, and various student groups, such as the National Student Association and the Young Women's Christian Association.

The Youth Leadership Meeting convened on April 15, 1960. Baker's opening address, "More Than a Hamburger," dwelled on the need for the students to keep it a young people's movement and to change the whole social structure, not just integrate lunch counters. "The younger generation is challenging you and me," Baker added, eyeing the adults present, "they are asking us to forget our laziness and doubt and fear, and follow our dedication to the truth to the bitter end." Martin Luther King, Jr., echoed Baker's admonition in his speech to the students. The sit-in movement, he declared, "is also a revolt against the apathy and complacency of adults in the Negro community; against Negroes in the middle class who indulge in buying cars and homes instead of taking on the great cause that will really solve their problems; against those who have become so afraid they have yielded to the system." King made three specific recommendations: "some type of continuing organization" to coordinate the student struggle; a nationwide campaign of "selective buying" to punish segregating variety-store chains; and an army of "volunteers who will willingly go to jail rather than pay bail or fines." Above all, King accentuated his philosophy of nonviolence, preaching the values of reconciliation and the creation of the beloved community. "The tactics of nonviolence without the spirit of nonviolence," he expounded, "may become a new kind of violence."

"I don't dig all this," responded one student from Virginia, voicing the reaction to King's caveat felt by the majority of those at the Raleigh conference. Some of the divinity students present shared King's beliefs, but as subsequent events made clear, most blacks viewed nonviolence as a political weapon. That was the theme of James Lawson's address, which the students accepted enthusiastically. Lawson came to Atlanta a hero to young blacks because of his leadership in the Nashville movement and his expulsion from Vanderbilt University for his role in the sit-ins. He emphasized the tactical importance of direct action, underlined the impatience of black students, and rebuked the NAACP and SCLC for their lack of aggressive militancy.

In the discussions and workshops during the next two days, the young black leaders continually reaffirmed their goal of "full equality," their hope that black students had surpassed the ministry as the new driving, dynamic force in the civil-rights movement, and their insistence that litigation now take second place to civil disobedience. The most applause at the conference went to the workshop recommendation that demonstrators choose jail over bail and to the student who declared: "The greatest progress of the American Negro in the future will not be made in Congress or in the Supreme Court; it will come in the jails." The meeting ended with the establishment of a Temporary Coordinating Committee, chaired by Ed King, who had been bloodied leading the Frankfort, Kentucky, sit-ins.

The following month, fifteen student delegates met with Ella Baker, Ed King, James Lawson, and CORE's Len Holt in Atlanta. They voted not to affiliate with the SCLC or any other group but to be an independent enterprise named the Temporary Student Nonviolent Coordinating Committee. They elected Marion Barry of Nashville their new chairman and agreed to establish their headquarters in Atlanta. The students also adopted a Statement of Purpose, strongly redolent of Martin Luther King's rhetoric. Love was its central motif. "We affirm the philosophical or religious ideal of nonviolence as the foundation of our purpose," it began, "the presupposition of our faith, and the manner of our action." It ended: "By appealing to conscience and standing on the moral nature of human existence, nonviolence nurtures the atmosphere in which reconciliation and justice become actual possibilities."

In addition, the May conclave decided to offer testimony to the Democratic National Convention. In July, Barry appeared before the Platform Committee. He called for federal action to enfranchise blacks, enact a fair-employment law and speed school desegregation. Barry then defined the essence of the sit-in movement.

The ache of every man to touch his potential is the throb that beats out the truth of the American Declaration of Independence and the Constitution. America was founded because men were seeking room to become. . . . We are again seeking that room. . . . We want to walk into the sun and through the front door. For three hundred and fifty years, the American Negro has been sent to the back door. . . . We grew weary. . . . We seek a community in which man can realize the full meaning of the self which demands open relationship with others.

Finally, in October 1960, a plenary conference meeting in the Atlanta University Center dropped *Temporary* from its name and made the Student Nonviolent Coordinating Committee (SNCC) a permanent organization. Martin Luther King again spoke for the philosophy of nonviolence but the students made clear their primary desire to force overdue racial change. Charles McDew, SNCC's new chairman, articulated its temper. "The sit-ins have inspired us to build a new image of ourselves in our own minds. And, instead of sitting idly by, taking the leavings of a sick and decadent society, we have seized the initiative, and already the walls have begun to crumble." The student movement would not end, McDew promised, until "every vestige of racial segregation and discrimination are erased from the face of the earth."

Viewing themselves as no longer "temporary" demonstrators

but as leaders of a revolutionary direct-action movement, the students who met in Atlanta went forth to claim their inevitable victory. With Jane Stembridge, a young white from Virginia who left her studies at the Union Theological Seminary in New York to run the SNCC office, they believed: "What happened in Greensboro, the kick-off place, can happen and is happening all across the South. People can come to an understanding, barriers can be removed, a new South can be born, and America can become an actual democracy." They presumed the millennium only a few years of struggle away.

Burning with idealism and impatience, they would emblaze the fight for equality their parents had kindled. The students would no longer accept the presence of a single black child in a formerly all-white school as a major triumph. Tokenism was out. They wanted an end to Jim Crow, and they wanted it quickly. Convinced that civil disobedience provided the fastest and most effective route to desegregation, black youth insisted that the focus of the struggle be nonviolent direct action in the streets, not legal skirmishes in the courtroom. Moreover, the students assumed that their elders had wasted too much energy on fund-raising, public relations, and bureaucratic minutiae. They distrusted too much structure. Wishing to "stay loose," to remain spontaneous, to stress improvisation, the young blacks judged themselves by the maxim of Bob Moses: "Go where the spirit say go and do what the spirit say do."

The students did not consider the possibility of failure. They took pride in their lack of professionalism. They boasted that three-quarters of SNCC's first forty fieldworkers were under twenty-two years of age. They laughed away the hindrance of having a budget of only $14,000. They exuded faith in themselves and in the promise of America. None doubted that their spirit of nonviolent militance and redemptive love would ultimately make manifest the essential righteousness of the government and its white majority. The fervor which always accompanied their singing "We Shall Overcome" exhibited and augmented this conviction. "Deep in my heart"—all would rise —"I do believe,"—each clasping the hand of persons on either side—"That we shall overcome some day." Forming a human chain, swaying in unity, some hummed and others intoned: "We'll all go to jail. . . . We are not afraid. . . . We'll walk hand in hand." Their voices swelled: "Black and white together. . . . We *shall* overcome." The ritual expressed the creed and the certainty of SNCC in 1960. Few could imagine the anguish, frustration, and violence of the years ahead.

FOUR

The Long Journey

In 1961 and 1962 the movement for racial justice paid a fearful price in anguish and pain for minimal gains. Civil-rights workers learned that victory was not inevitable, that white resistance in the Deep South could hold firm. Consequently, new tactics and strategies evolved. The idea of changing hearts and minds gave way to confrontation politics that would induce federal intervention. SNCC led the way, augmented by the revitalized Congress of Racial Equality.

On March 13, 1961, James Farmer, CORE's new national director, issued a call for volunteers to conduct freedom rides through the South to test racial discrimination in interstate-travel terminals. Three months earlier, the Supreme Court in *Boynton v. Virginia* had extended its 1946 prohibition against segregation in vehicles engaged in interstate travel (*Morgan v. Virginia*) to include all terminal accommodations. Two CORE field secretaries, assisting students in the sit-in movement, discussed the court ruling and wondered how they could test the decision. At the February CORE national council meeting, they proposed a Freedom Ride. Farmer, who had just taken office that month, enthusiastically supported the idea and the council quickly approved the plan. "Our intention," the national director stated, "was to provoke the southern authorities into arresting us and thereby prod the Justice Department into enforcing the law of the land." CORE craved a crisis, Farmer later admitted. "We were counting on the bigots in the South to do our work for us."

Farmer had been chosen to invigorate CORE. A charismatic leader and dramatic orator, Farmer considered himself an "action man." Although he had studied for the ministry at Howard University, he refused ordination in 1941. "I did not see how I could honestly preach the gospel of Christ in a church that practiced discrimination." So he went to work for a variety of struggling pacifist and socialist groups, including the Fellowship of Reconciliation, where he served as race-relations secretary from 1941 to 1945. Believing that legal battles alone could not win the fight against Jim Crow, he helped to form CORE in 1942 and pioneered in the development of nonviolent direct action against racial injustice. After the war he became a union organizer, a youth secretary in the League for Industrial Democracy, and then program director of the NAACP. There he languished. None of his plans for bold, mass demonstrations came to fruition. The cautious NAACP leadership quietly filed away all his proposals for direct action. Having to watch from the sidelines as the student movement, practicing techniques he had devised, spread through the South particularly galled him. He longed to be in the thick of the action. Chafing at the bit, Farmer jumped when CORE offered him the lead post early in 1961. Though poor in finances, membership, and influence, CORE sought a dynamic leader who could make it a major power in the civil-rights movement. And Farmer considered

CORE's interracial, truly dedicated believers, committed to non-violent direct action, an ideal group to steer into the vanguard of the surging campaign against segregation and discrimination.

CORE consciously modeled its 1961 Freedom Ride on the 1947 Journey of Reconciliation. Organized by Bayard Rustin and George Houser, of CORE and the Fellowship of Reconciliation, the 1947 train and bus trip to fifteen cities in Kentucky, North Carolina, Tennessee, and Virginia sought to publicize the *Morgan* decision and to inspire blacks to practice the rights they had won in the courts. Eight blacks and eight whites met in Washington, D.C., for a weekend of sessions on the philosophy and tactics of nonviolence. They staged socio-dramas, acting out the roles of bus drivers, policemen, "hysterical segregationists," and protesters. Their journey began on April 9. It ended April 23. Most Americans never heard of it. With few arrests and little violence, the Journey of Reconciliation received scant or no attention in the press. No one even fancied the possibility of coverage by television, then in its infancy.

The 1961 ride, however, would have far-reaching consequences. Farmer's plan, like the earlier one in 1947, envisioned an interracial group to challenge Southern segregation and to demonstrate the extent to which the South disobeyed the law of the land. Like the Journey of Reconciliation, it would begin with training sessions on nonviolence in Washington, D.C. But there the similarities ended. The Freedom Ride would test Jim Crow in terminal restaurants, waiting rooms, and rest rooms, not merely the seating aboard buses. It would force the issue in the heart of the Deep South, not remain in the upper South. And, when arrested, the riders pledged to remain in jail rather than pay fines or bail out. Besides the publicity to be derived from this tactic, Farmer believed it would "make the maintenance of segregation so expensive for the state and the city that they would," Farmer hoped, "come to the conclusion that they could no longer afford it. Fill up the jails, as Gandhi did in

India, fill them to bursting if we had to." Farmer saw the Freedom Ride as a peripatetic continuation of the sit-ins, "putting
the movement on wheels, so to speak."

In April, CORE, "following the Gandhian technique," informed Washington of its intent to commit civil disobedience. It
wrote to President John F. Kennedy, to the Justice Department,
to the FBI, and to the bus companies involved. CORE received
not a single reply. On May 4, seven blacks and six whites, split
into two interracial groups, left Washington on a Greyhound
and a Trailways bus. Four were CORE staff members, including
Farmer and James Peck, a white pacifist who had been on the
Journey of Reconciliation. The blacks came primarily from the
ranks of the student sit-in movement; the whites from socialist
and peace organizations. Slowly they made their way southward,
from Richmond to Petersburg to Lynchburg, ignoring, without
incident, the signs reading "White" or "Colored" over lunch
counters and toilets. At some stops, local blacks told them that
the signs had just been removed.

Arriving in Charlotte on May 8, Charles Perkins strolled into
the Union bus-station barbershop, reserved for whites only, and
climbed into a shoeshine chair. When refused service, he remained seated. Minutes later he was arrested for his "shoe-in."
On the basis of the *Boynton* decision, Perkins won an acquittal
on May 10. The day before, however, violence erupted for the
first time. At the Greyhound station in Rock Hill, South Carolina, John Lewis started to enter a white waiting room. Already
a veteran of five arrests for his sit-in activities, the twenty-one-
year-old member of the Nashville Christian Leadership Conference had volunteered for the Freedom Ride because, "at this
time, human dignity is the most important thing in my life." He
had decided "to give up all if necessary for the Freedom Ride,"
Lewis wrote on his application, "that Justice and Freedom might
come to the Deep South." As Lewis approached, recalled
Farmer, "several young white hoodlums, leather jackets, duck-
tail haircuts, standing there smoking . . . blocked the door and

said, 'Nigger, you can't come in here.' He said, 'I have every right to enter this waiting room according to the Supreme Court of the United States in the Boynton case.' They said, 'Shit on that.' He tried to walk past, and they clubbed him, beat him, and knocked him down."

Several then began slugging Albert Bigelow, a former naval commander who turned pacifist out of revulsion over his World War II experiences. Not until one of the women with them had been pushed to the ground did the police intervene. They did not make any arrests, but allowed all the riders to enter the white waiting room unmolested. In Winnsboro, thirty-seven miles to the south, however, police arrested Peck and Henry Thomas, a black student, for attempting to eat at a white luncheonette. Without incident, the Freedom Riders then tested facilities in Sumter, Camden, Augusta, and Athens, before arriving in Atlanta on May 13 to regroup for the dangerous journey into Alabama and Mississippi.

Mother's Day, May 14, the Freedom Riders curved along U.S. 78 into the heart of the Black Belt. When the Greyhound bus arrived in Anniston, Alabama, an angry mob surrounded it. Armed with blackjacks, iron bars, clubs, and tire chains, they smashed windows and slashed tires. Only the arrival of the police made it possible for the bus to depart. The mob pursued in cars. Six miles out of town, the bus tires went flat. The mob again beat on the bus, denting its sides. An incendiary bomb sailed through a window. Suddenly the bus filled with thick smoke. The passengers tried to get out the door, but the mob held it shut from the outside. "Hey, the bus is gonna explode," somebody yelled, and the door opened. While the mob beat the exiting riders, the bus burst into flames, slowly turning into a charred metal skeleton. Local hospital personnel refused to treat the Freedom Riders cut by flying glass or overcome by smoke inhalation, and only an armed caravan of cars from Birmingham, led by the Reverend Fred Shuttlesworth, succeeded in extricating the wounded.

An hour later, the Trailways bus pulled into Anniston. Eight whites jumped aboard and demanded that the black students move to the formerly segregated rear section. They refused. The whites forced them back with punches and kicks. Peck and Walter Bergman, a sixty-one-year-old retired teacher, tried to persuade the whites to desist. The hoodlums set upon them, beating them to the floor. A blow on the head left Bergman close to death and permanently brain-damaged. The violence had only begun.

When the Trailways bus parked at its terminal in Birmingham, a mob of about forty whites lined the loading platform. The police had been warned to expect trouble. Commissioner T. Eugene "Bull" Connor's police headquarters was only two blocks from the terminal. Yet not a single law officer was in sight. According to an eyewitness report by CBS's Howard K. Smith, the white "toughs," who had been waiting all day, "grabbed the passengers into alleys and corridors, pounding them with pipes, with key rings and with fists. . . . Police did not appear until around ten minutes later, when the hoodlums had got into waiting cars and moved down the street." Peck, knocked unconscious, required fifty-three stitches. Still, the Freedom Riders wanted to continue. They decided to travel as a single contingent on the next lap, from Birmingham to Montgomery. But no bus would accept them. Asserting that he could not protect "this bunch of rabble-rousers," Alabama Governor John Patterson advised the CORE contingent to "get out of Alabama as quickly as possible." Stranded, frightened, the Freedom Riders reluctantly boarded a special flight to New Orleans arranged by the Justice Department. On May 17, the CORE-sponsored Freedom Ride disbanded. A new phase of the Freedom Ride began.

SNCC leaders in Atlanta and Nashville hurriedly conferred, agreeing that the Freedom Ride must continue to prove to the world that violence could not overcome nonviolence. Diane Nash quickly assembled some sit-in veterans to join John Lewis and Henry Thomas for a trip to Birmingham. On the outskirts of the city, police met the bus and escorted it to the terminal, where eight black and two white Freedom Riders were arrested and put in "protective custody." The students went on a hunger strike. Around midnight the next day, Police Commissioner Connor drove the students, against their wishes, some 150 miles to the Tennessee–Alabama line. There they managed to call Diane Nash for a car to take them right back to Birmingham, and to eat for the first time in nearly two days. The students returned directly to the Greyhound bus station. Again, no driver would make the trip to Montgomery with the Freedom Riders. The students just sat on the bus-station benches and waited, singing freedom songs. Eighteen hours later, now augmented by fresh volunteers from Atlanta and Nashville, twenty-one Freedom Riders boarded a Greyhound for Montgomery early on the morning of May 20.

The two-hour ride went without incident. "There were police cars all round the bus, and helicopters flying over head," recalled a young black woman from Atlanta. "But when we got inside the Montgomery city limits, it all disappeared. . . . There was not one policeman around." The "moment that we arrived in that station, it was the strangest feeling to me," John Lewis remembered. "It was really weird. It was an eerie feeling. There was a funny peace there, a quietness. . . . Complete silence. There were no cabs around that you could see. You couldn't see any other buses. Not anything. We stepped off the bus and . . . people just started pouring out of the station, out of buildings, from all over the place. White people. . . ." At that very moment, John Doar, second in command to Burke Marshall in the Civil Rights Division of the Justice Department, put through a call to the Attorney General from his post across the street from the terminal. "The passengers are coming off," Doar reported. "A bunch of men led by a guy with a bleeding face are beating them. There are no cops. It's terrible. It's terrible. There's not a cop in sight. People are yelling, 'Get 'em, get 'em.' It's awful."

"Get those niggers," a woman cheered the mob of nearly three hundred venting its fury on students and newsmen with sticks, metal pipes, and baseball bats. Several whites cornered John Lewis. They clubbed him to the ground. With a briefcase yanked from his hands, they smashed his head, leaving him with a brain concussion. While lying in a pool of blood, Lewis was handed a state-court injunction forbidding interracial travel in Alabama.

Meanwhile, another white group grabbed James Zwerg, an exchange student from the University of Wisconsin attending Fisk University. They pummeled and stomped him into the hot tar of the pavement. One of the mob put Zwerg's head between his knees to let others take turns at socking him and kicking in the front teeth of the Freedom Rider. "Kill the nigger-loving son of a bitch," several women chanted. "Zwerg never attempted to defend himself in any way," observed a black woman. "He never put his arms up or anything. Each time they knocked him down, he got back up."

The mob had now grown to over a thousand. Not a single policeman had yet arrived. They broke one boy's leg. They poured inflammable liquid on another and set his clothes afire. They slapped and chased the two white women Riders, who begged a motorist for help. "You deserve what you get," he replied. "I hope they beat you up good." "Come on, I'll help you," another driver offered, "I'm a federal man." As John Siegenthaler, the President's emissary to the Governor of Alabama, tried to get the women in his car, several whites slugged him from behind, knocking him unconscious. While people milled around, he lay on the sidewalk for nearly twenty-five minutes before the police finally drove him to a hospital. They left Jim Zwerg bleeding and in a state of shock, his spinal cord injured, for over two hours before getting him medical attention. It had taken the police more than an hour to halt the rioting. Montgomery's Police Commissioner stated: "We have no intention of standing guard for a bunch of troublemakers coming into our city."

The combination of mob violence and the callous indifference of Alabama officials combined to make the Freedom Ride page-one news throughout the world. Banner headlines and photographs of the burning and bloodshed played up the white South's brutality and crude defiance of the law. The Communist press harped on the theme that rampant racism "exposed" the "savage nature of American freedom and democracy." Editorials in Africa and Asia stressed that the federal government's compromising with racial discrimination would make it impossible for the United States "to sell to the outside world, especially the non-white world, that she stands for equality of all men." Non-Communist European papers generally deplored America's racial prejudice for encouraging and confirming anti-colonial and anti-Western feeling. And almost without exception, the American news media expressed its horror and disgust at the violence against the Freedom Riders. Even the Alabama Associated Press Association condemned "the breakdown of civilized rule" in that state. Most Southern newspapers followed the lead of the Atlanta *Constitution* in criticizing the irresponsibility of the Freedom Riders while insisting "that is not the point of what happened in Alabama."

Any man in this free country has the right to demonstrate and assemble and make a fool of himself if he pleases without getting hurt. If the police, representing the people, refuse to intervene when a man—any man—is being beaten to the pavement of an American city, then this is not a noble land at all. It is a jungle. But this is a noble land. And it is time for the decent people in it to muzzle the jackals.

The Kennedy Administration belatedly decided that the time had come when it must act. Private phone calls to Alabama authorities to secure safe passage for the Freedom Riders would no longer suffice. The President and Attorney General Robert Kennedy considered the international prestige of the Administration to be threatened. They could no longer tolerate either the deliberate failure of local authority to preserve civil peace or the open defiance of federal law. Yet they still sought to walk the tightrope between, as the Kennedys viewed them, the unreasonable militants on both sides. They shared the liberal faith in integration. They believed Jim Crow to be wrong. Racial prejudice and the inequalities it fostered bothered them. They hoped to better the life of Afro-Americans—but slowly, and at the proper time. They thought demands for freedom *now* to be just as irresponsible as calls for segregation forever. In 1961, the Kennedys saw the struggle against racism as a conundrum to be managed, not a cause to be championed.

"Tell them to call it off. Stop them!" had been the President's initial response to the Freedom Ride. The fervor of the young blacks clashed with his own calculating approach to political problems. He prided himself on being pragmatic, tough-minded. Idealists and romantics annoyed him. Quixotic crusades interfered with his careful plans and cautious timetables. Only in the battle against Communism did he think the United States should "pay any price, bear any burden, meet any hardship, support any friend, oppose any foe." Never in the struggle for black rights would he ask the American people for a commitment or sacrifice approaching that. On the civil-rights issue, the President's education reinforced his temperament. Like most in his generation, he had been taught that radical Reconstruction was a mistake, that the solution to the race problem required moderation, not coercion. He believed in using the absolute minimal amount of force in this sensitive matter. "I don't think we would ever come to the point of sending troops," Kennedy confided to an aide just a month before the Freedom Ride began.

Politics also strengthened that resolve. Kennedy's victory in the 1960 election, winning with less than 51 percent of the two-party vote, made him particularly solicitous of the white South. Nixon had received a majority of its vote and Kennedy did not want that to happen again in 1964. With the Catholic issue resolved, he looked forward to securing the bulk of Southern voters in his reelection bid. The Democratic margin in both House and Senate, moreover, had been cut in the 1960 elections, forcing the President to curry favor with the Southern Democrats. He needed their votes for his legislative program. Therefore, Kennedy refused to aid the liberals in their effort to eliminate the filibuster; he appointed notorious segregationists to lifetime federal judgeships in the South; he delayed issuing his promised Executive Order to end racial discrimination in federally assisted housing for nearly two years; and he remained aloof from the bills introduced to carry out the Democratic Party's 1960 campaign pledge on black rights. The President, said his press secretary, "does not think it is necessary at this time to enact civil rights legislation." Perhaps most important, Kennedy feared that the race issue would "divide the American people at a time when the international scene required maximum unity." Foreign affairs was his primary concern and he shunned potentially divisive domestic matters. Preparing to meet with Khrushchev early in June, the President considered the Freedom Riders an unnecessary burden. But the savagery of Alabama whites forced him to act.

On May 20, President Kennedy termed the situation "a source of the deepest concern." He called on Alabama officials to "meet their responsibilities," stated that the United States "intends to meet its," requested that Alabama citizens and visitors alike refrain "from any action which would in any way tend to provoke further outbreaks," and ordered the Attorney General "to take all necessary steps." Robert Kennedy then announced that the Justice Department would seek to enjoin the KKK and National States Rights Party from interfering with peaceful interstate travel, and that a contingent of 350–400 U.S. marshals under the command of Deputy Attorney General Byron White would be sent to Montgomery "to assist state and local authorities in the protection of persons and property and vehicles." Governor Patterson protested the moves as unconstitutional and unnecessary. The following evening made the need for federal marshals painfully obvious.

While the Kennedys acted, Martin Luther King rushed to Montgomery to urge on the stalled Freedom Ride. After conferring with representatives of CORE and SNCC, King announced a mass rally for May 21, sponsored by the Montgomery Improvement Association. A crowd of over twelve hundred crowded into Ralph Abernathy's First Baptist Church, more than twice its capacity. In a park across the street, a mob of whites gathered, bent on trouble. Without any local police to stop them, they began beating up local blacks standing in front of the church. Some whites charged into the church to fight. Others threw stones and bottles. Firebombs and stench bombs hurtled through the windows. The blacks in the church tried to sing to maintain their courage, but the smoke and the heat and the fright caused some to panic. Suddenly, recalled James Farmer, "the marshals materialized. . . . It seemed almost fictional . . . the marshals confronting the mob." Armed with nightsticks and tear-gas cannisters, their pistols hidden, the marshals formed a skirmish line to protect the church. They barely could. Then the governor declared "qualified martial rule," and ordered the National Guard and state troopers to reinforce the marshals. While they dispersed the mob, the troops ordered those inside the church to stay put and not attempt to leave until the next morning.

Undaunted, King, Farmer, and the Nashville student leaders announced the next day that the Freedom Ride would be resumed despite the continued threats of violence. CORE, SCLC, SNCC, and the Nashville Christian Leadership Council established a Freedom Ride Coordinating Committee and rejected Attorney General Kennedy's call for a temporary cessation of the Rides to provide a "cooling-off period." "We had been cooling off for a hundred years," Farmer announced. "If we got any cooler we'd be in a deep freeze." When Robert Kennedy said that racial turmoil would embarrass the President in his meeting with Khrushchev, Abernathy retorted: "Doesn't the Attorney General know that we've been embarrassed all our lives?" Even NAACP head Roy Wilkins urged black college students returning home at the end of the school year to "sit where you choose on a nonsegregated transportation basis" and to use terminal facilities "without discrimination." Additional volunteers for the Ride, meanwhile, arrived in Montgomery from Atlanta, New York, New Orleans, and Washington, D.C.

Escorted to the Trailways bus station by National Guardsmen on May 24, a bruised and bandaged corps of twenty-seven readied for the Freedom Ride to Jackson, Mississippi, and more danger. They all ate in the "white" dining room and then departed in two heavily guarded buses. Three airplanes and two helicopters flew reconnaissance overhead while motorized National Guard units scouted the road ahead and patrol cars escorted the shiny red-and-white buses. As they passed the sign "Welcome to the Magnolia State," Mississippi troopers and Guardsmen took over the task of safely conveying the Riders to Jackson. To keep up their morale, the two whites and twenty-six blacks aboard held workshops on nonviolence and sang with forced gaiety:

> *Hallelujah, I'm traveling*
> *Hallelujah, ain't it fine,*
> *Hallelujah, I'm traveling*
> *Down Freedom's main line.*

All the students wrote the names and addresses of their next of kin on notes which they shoved in their pockets or bosoms. "Everyone on the bus," said a Rider, "was prepared to die."

Determined that there be no violence, Robert Kennedy made a deal with Mississippi Senator James Eastland. In exchange for there being no mob violence in Jackson, the federal government would not interfere with the immediate arrests of the Freedom Riders. When the two buses reached the terminal in Jackson, police, state troopers, and National Guardsmen appeared everywhere and not a single group of white bullies could be seen. All twenty-seven Riders were quickly arrested when they tried to enter the "white" cafeteria and rest rooms, and they were found guilty, fined, and given two-month suspended sentences.

Farmer now announced that all would go to jail rather than pay the fine, and he urged other volunteers to keep violating Jackson's unconstitutional segregation ordinance until they filled the jails to overflowing. By the end of the summer, over a thousand persons of every age and faith, from every section of the country, had participated in Freedom Rides. Most were young, black, and Southern. Over three hundred had been jailed in Jackson, and nearly fifty others in Arkansas, Florida, Louisiana, and Texas. The movement spread to railroad and airport facilities. By creating a crisis, the Riders forced the federal government to act. The Attorney General petitioned the Interstate Commerce Commission to issue rules prohibiting racial discrimination in interstate facilities, a move supported by the Secretary of State as vital to our conduct of foreign affairs. On September 22, the ICC announced that interstate carriers and terminals must display signs stating that seating "is without regard to race, color, creed or national origin," effective November 1. The ICC also banned interstate carriers from using any terminal which practiced segregation. Although some towns in the Deep South initially evaded the order, CORE proclaimed at the end of 1962 that the battle of interstate travel had been finally won.

Beyond the removal of "White" and "Colored" signs in the terminals of the South, the Freedom Rides resulted in a complex combination of gains and losses for the civil-rights movement. They demonstrated that victory in the Deep South was possible; yet they intensified the fervor of white resistance. In 1960, Mississippi had been the only Southern state where there had been no sit-ins and Alabama had effectively used its state powers to wreck the student protests. Federal orders required both to begin integration in 1961. That outcome, and the method of its achievement, gave new strength to the KKK and similar groups and new life at the polls to the most hard-core segregationists. Rabble rousers like Alabama's George Wallace, profiting from the politics of confrontation, came to the fore. The Rides also underlined the benefits and dangers of federalism, the involvement of the Executive Branch, and the creation of crisis situations. When the Freedom Riders aroused a torrent of public sympathy, as they did after Birmingham and Montgomery, the federal government acted to protect them and to end the violation of federal law. But when, as in Jackson and other cities where the Riders met little or no violence, Southern officials engaged in peaceful defiance of the federal courts, the Kennedy Administration condoned the mass arrests of American citizens for attempting to implement a constitutional right clearly promulgated by the United States Supreme Court. Such behavior reinforced the urge of movement leaders to court white violence in the South to trigger the Administration into enforcing federal law. It also spurred segregationist officials to hamstring demonstrators in protracted legal battles and to prevent violence, and thus forestall federal action. The reluctance with which the Kennedys entered the fray, moreover, made them eager to influence, even manipulate, movement strategy. They did not want to have to fight again at a time and on a battlefield not of their choosing.

The Freedom Rides also rejuvenated the black-rights struggle while they tarnished its image. CORE quickly grew in membership, income, staff personnel, and stature, challenging King, the NAACP, and SNCC to press more vigorously for racial change. Competition among the civil-rights organizations intensified, forcing them to redouble their efforts to win yet greater gains. In turn, the heightened sense of immediacy among blacks brought more and more of them into the movement. To a far larger extent than any previous protest, the Freedom Rides also enlisted whites and non-Southerners in direct action. The Rides exposed to the nation the crudity of Southern racism. They revealed the ugly face of brutal mobs and the official connivance with violence. That appalled most whites. But their indignation did not last long. The absence of tumult was what they really cared about. Although a majority of whites approved of ending segregation in interstate travel, over two-thirds of those questioned in public-opinion polls disapproved of the Freedom Rides on the grounds that they "were causing too much trouble." In the South, particularly, the role of "outsiders" in the Rides revitalized the hoary myth of "uppity Northern niggers" and radical white agitators being responsible for the black demand for equal rights. Many viewed the Freedom Riders as unkempt, unreasonable nuisances, a contrast to their image of long-suffering Montgomery bus boycotters and idealistic sit-in students.

Finally, the impact of jail, the physical and psychological brutality encountered by the Riders, both enhanced and corroded the spirit of the black struggle. Even those who had been briefly imprisoned during the sit-ins were shocked by what they had to endure in Mississippi's Hinds County Jail and Parchman Penitentiary: the endless rounds of questioning and beatings, the pain of battery-operated cattle prods, the terror of wrist-breakers, and the sounds of friends groaning and crying; the back-breaking work in the fields from sunup to sundown, the execrable food, and the filthy cots in bug-infested cells; the capricious denial of cigarettes, reading materials, and showers; and the dreaded time in the sweatbox or solitary confinement for refusing to play Uncle Tom to the guards. Jail broke some. It strengthened others. Some became demoralized and dropped out. Others deepened their commitment and left jail to become full-time movement personnel. They went to work for SNCC, SCLC, and CORE changed men and women. Most had lost their faith in the ability to alter white attitudes and feelings. Most no longer believed that the South could be converted or even shamed into responsibility.

The themes of reconciliation and the beloved community preached by Martin Luther King, Jr., had little relevance to many who had suffered in the jails of Mississippi. They believed that power alone counted, that only power could induce change. The Freedom Rides had proved to them that Jim Crow's demise depended on the enforcement powers of the federal government. Accordingly, they searched for the lever that would move the Kennedy Administration into a firm alliance with the proponents of racial equality. Their protracted discussions while in jail often centered on just what tactics and strategy could make the federal government an unequivocal partner of the black struggle.

With the desegregation of interstate travel facilities accomplished, moreover, all the major protest leaders agreed that the time had come to set new priorities. They had to decide where the energies released by the sit-ins and Freedom Rides could now be utilized, where the new troops enlisted in the movement, especially the students choosing to become full-time civil-rights workers rather than return to school in the fall, could best be deployed. The Southern Regional Council (SRC) for several years had been urging a voter-registration campaign in the South. Some of the liberal foundations which funded the SRC had also been concerned about encouraging black voting. Shortly after the Freedom Rides began, the Justice Department informally communicated to the SRC its interest in helping the civil-rights movement attack black disenfranchisement. On the day after the bus burning at Anniston, Robert Kennedy made the same point to Roy Wilkins. Later in the month, the Attorney General lobbied Martin Luther King, Jr., on the matter.

On June 16, Robert Kennedy met with representatives of CORE, SCLC, SNCC, and the National Student Association. He and his aides argued that the vote held the key to change in the South and that registering blacks would be far more fruitful than further demonstrations. The Justice officials dangled the financial support of the Field and Taconic Foundations and the Stern Family Fund before the financially-pressed movement personnel. They also promised protection for the voter applicants and civil-rights workers against the anticipated reprisals by Southern whites. Timothy Jenkins of Howard University, a vice-president of the NSA, recalled the principal assistant to the President on racial affairs assuring those at the meeting "that if necessary in the course of protecting people's rights to vote, that the Kennedy Administration would fill every jail in the South." Martin Luther King left the meeting believing that they had been guaranteed "all steps necessary to protect those rights in danger."

During the June 1961 meeting of SNCC, Jenkins's proposal that the students shift their emphasis from demonstrations to voter registration precipitated bitter wrangling that traumatized the organization. Marion Barry and Diane Nash led the faction insisting that nonviolent direct action continue to be SNCC's primary strategy. They looked forward to larger and more sensational confrontations to desegregate public facilities, to gain equal employment opportunities for blacks, and to maintain the momentum generated by the sit-ins and Freedom Rides. They feared that an interminable registration effort, resulting neither in major new gains nor in dramatic news coverage, would diminish support for the movement and let the "white establishment off the hook." Furthermore, the fact that the plan emanated from the White House heightened the students' suspicions. Most saw it as a clever ploy by the Administration to increase Negro voting strength in preparation for Kennedy's 1964 reelection bid, and to "get the niggers off the streets." Robert Kennedy had already called on civil-rights leaders for a "cooling-off period," and this suggestion to divert the militancy of the movement smacked of another way to accomplish that. They no longer wanted to defer the black dream of freedom to the President's desire for safe, gradual change.

Another faction of SNCC admitted the benefits of the proposal to Kennedy, and insisted that the struggle for racial equality would profit the most from black enfranchisement. These students saw the vote as the lever to lasting change. They considered black political strength in the South a prerequisite for the mass of blacks to exercise the rights granted them and for the liberalization of Congress, a step vital to the passage of social and economic legislation necessary for black advancement. Why not take the money and federal protection offered, they argued, and develop the power of blacks to correct injustice themselves, to control their own destinies. To their mind, voter registration would be less cathartic than demonstrations in the short run, but ultimately more constructive. At the least, these SNCC staffers conjectured, a sizable increase in Southern black voters might cement the alliance of the federal government and the movement.

The debate within SNCC seethed throughout the summer of 1961, and came to a head at the August staff meeting. Neither faction would back down. Both angrily voiced proposals to disband SNCC and to resign. Indeed, some, like Lonnie King of Atlanta, did quit because of disgust at the Administration's manipulation of the movement. Then James Forman broke the impasse. Elected by the students to assume the post of SNCC's executive director in October, the thirty-three-year-old former Chicago schoolteacher had the respect of both sides. All viewed him as a thoughtful man of stature, of uncompromising militancy and total commitment to SNCC. Forman insisted that the effort to encourage people in the Black Belt to set aside their fears would inevitably interlock voter registration and direct action. To persuade blacks to register and face oppressive white power would indeed be direct action. He described registration work "as a tool by which consciousness might be aroused, politicized, and organized." Forman also predicted that SNCC's activities would bring white retaliation, and the resulting violence "would create more exposure and thereby more consciousness." To appease those inconsolably committed to boycotts and demonstrations, SNCC formally adopted Ella Baker's suggestion of two divisions within the organization: Direct Action Projects led by Diane Nash, and Voter Registration headed by Charles Jones.

CORE followed suit. The same debate had split its ranks. But at its September convention, CORE accepted Farmer's contention that direct action and voter registration were "not mutually exclusive" and approved a registration campaign in the Deep South. CORE and SNCC joined with the NAACP, SCLC, and the Urban League in a new Voter Education Project (VEP). Funded at $870,000 by the Stern Family Fund and the Taconic and Field Foundations, and scheduled to last two and a half years, the SRC-administered VEP formally began work in April 1962.

Bob Moses and SNCC, characteristically, initiated a voter registration project in rural Mississippi prior to any official resolution. Moses, who had gone to work for SNCC in Atlanta in July 1960, set out for Mississippi the following month to interest blacks in attending SNCC's fall meeting. In Cleveland, Mississippi, he became acquainted with Aimzie Moore, the courageous and resilient local NAACP leader, who convinced him of the potential of a campaign to register blacks. Together, they plotted a strategy. A year later, Moses came to live in McComb, a city of thirteen thousand in Pike County, where in 1960 fewer than two hundred blacks registered to vote out of an adult black population of more than eight thousand. In two adjoining counties, Walthall did not have a single one of its twenty-five hundred blacks of voting age registered, and Amite claimed one —but as Charles McDew commented: "We haven't been able to find him." Moses, with the help of local high-school students and the encouragement of some adults, began canvasing, going door-to-door to convince McComb blacks that SNCC would totally back their attempts to register. After a week, John Hardy of the Nashville student movement and Reggie Robinson of Baltimore arrived in McComb to assist Moses. And then other

SNCC students who had been jailed in Jackson began to leave Parchman Penitentiary and drift into McComb.

What happened in the next two months in these Delta counties set the pattern for voter-registration efforts in the rural South throughout 1962 and 1963. On August 7, a SNCC Voter Registration School opened in Pike County, the first in the history of Mississippi. Moses patiently explained the complexities of registering to vote in the Magnolia State; he struggled to inspire courage and build morale. A dozen or so blacks attempted to qualify to vote in the first few days. On August 10, one of the blacks who had tried to register was shot at by a white. Attendance at the Voter Registration School plummeted. Moses had to rebuild. Five days later he accompanied three blacks from Amite to register at the county seat, Liberty. None qualified.

On the drive back to McComb, a highway patrolman flagged the blacks over to the side of the road. Referring to Moses as the "nigger who's come to tell the niggers how to register," the patrolman arrested the SNCC organizer on a charge of impeding an officer in the discharge of his duties. Two weeks after that, Moses again drove several blacks to the registrar's office in Liberty. Billy Jack Caston, cousin of the sheriff and son-in-law of State Representative Eugene Hurst, met them at the door and smashed Moses across the head, opening a wound that required eight stitches to close. Undaunted, Moses filed assault-and-battery charges against Caston—the first time in Amite's history, and probably Mississippi's, that a black man legally contested the freedom of a white to beat him at will. During the farce of a trial, however, the sheriff informed Moses that he better leave the county before the "not guilty" verdict if he wanted to escape mass assault.

In McComb, meanwhile, Marion Barry had arrived on August 18, intent on initiating direct action. He began to hold workshops and formed the students too young to vote into the Pike County Non-Violent Movement. On August 26, two of the youths sat-in at the lunch counter of the local Woolworth's— another first in the history of the county. They were arrested and sentenced to thirty days in jail. Nearly two hundred McComb blacks then attended a protest meeting, and on August 30 a sixteen-year-old girl and five other high-school students sat-in at the lunch counter of the local bus station. For their "breach of peace" the students were expelled from school; the young men also were given eight-month jail sentences, and the young woman a term of one year in a state institution for delinquents.

The fear of Delta blacks began to turn to terror on September 5. As Moses and Travis Britt, a student from New York City, started toward the registrar's office in Liberty with four blacks, a clerk ordered them outside, where a belligerent group of whites awaited them. The white men accosted the "niggers from New York" for daring that they "could come down here and teach people how to register to vote." They then beat and kicked Britt into semi-consciousness, and threatened to kill the blacks if they did not immediately "get the hell out of town."

Two days later, John Hardy, who had set up the first voters' school in Walthall County, accompanied some black residents to register in Tylerstown. John Q. Wood, the registrar, would not let them apply. When Hardy heard this, he walked into Wood's office to introduce himself. He never had the opportunity. Wood instantly pulled a gun out of his desk and ordered Hardy to leave. As the Nashville student started to walk out, Wood smashed him on the back of the head. His head bleeding profusely, Hardy staggered out of the courthouse. He went to the county sheriff to report what had happened. The sheriff arrested Hardy for inciting to riot and breach of the peace, and he threatened to beat Hardy within an inch of his life if he dared complain. In due time, the Justice Department intervened on Hardy's behalf. But it would take until April 1963 before the county dropped the charges against the SNCC organizer. Long before that, the damage had been done.

The accumulating incidents, recalled Robert Moses, "just

about cleaned us out. The farmers in both those counties were no longer willing to go down. . . . There wasn't much we could do." To make matters worse, four men fishing in the Big Black River on September 13 discovered the remains of an unidentified black man whose body had been stuffed into a cloth sack and weighted down with rocks. Then, said Moses, "the boom lowered on September 25; Herbert Lee, a Negro farmer, was killed in Amite County." Lee, an NAACP member, had been actively assisting Moses. On that fateful morning, Lee's truck had been tailgated by Mississippi State Representative Eugene Hurst as he drove into Liberty to gin his cotton. When Lee stopped his truck, Hurst approached him with his gun drawn. They argued. Suddenly Lee was dead, a .38 bullet in his brain. "This was the story that three Negro witnesses told us on three separate nights as we went out, in Amite County," said Moses, "tracking them down, knocking on doors, waking them up in the middle of the night." On the afternoon of Lee's death, however, a coroner's jury ruled that Hurst killed in self-defense. The local symbol of white political power was never booked, charged, or tried, but one of the Negro witnesses, two years later, was killed by a shotgun blast. To complete the reign of terror, McComb police arrested over a hundred high-school students and a dozen SNCC activists on October 4, when they sought to march through town to protest the slaying of Lee and the expulsion of their classmates. At the sentencing of Moses and his colleagues, a judge warned the black townsfolk: "Those of you who are local residents are like sheep being led to the slaughter. If you continue to follow the advice of outside agitators you will be like sheep and be slaughtered."

Through it all, and with worse to come, SNCC refused to be run out of Mississippi. Despite the stark terror of living unprotected in a completely hostile environment, the young activists endured. They kept canvasing, holding literacy and citizenship clinics, and accompanying applicants to the courthouse, never knowing when they might be jailed, whipped, killed; they always suspected that the hatred they encountered would explode into savagery. The volunteers had to suffer excessive pain and anguish for their belief in, and hope for, American democracy. Threatening phone calls plagued them. Vicious beatings became commonplace. Night riders ransacked their homes and offices, riddled them with bullets, set them ablaze. Truckloads of whites holding loaded shotguns and pistols tailgated their cars. Patrolmen apprehended them for every imaginable offense. To survive, SNCC's cadre learned to live with unrelenting tension. "It was always there," wrote Cleveland Sellers, "always stretched like a tight steel wire between the pit of the stomach and the center of the brain."

The brave young men and women, black and white, subsisted in the face of abuse and death but could not remain unscathed. The anxiety that never slackened took its toll. "The whole uncertainty of the thing" left its scars, said one volunteer. "You would be taking someone down to register, and you would simply be trailed by two cars of whites. Maybe they would do nothing, but you would never know. Maybe they would get out and whip you. Maybe they wouldn't." SNCC's Sellers listed some of the consequences of such strain: ulcers, migraine headaches, constipation, nervous twitches. Another volunteer in the Delta campaign recalled the nightmare of always "wondering whether someone was going to sneak in and dynamite you or fire-bomb your home. Always checking your car before you got in it, because you were worrying about whether someone stuck a piece of dynamite under it. Always making sure your tires were in good condition, because you never know, you may have to race up the road at night." The grinding, omnipresent dread changed SNCC, further eroding its faith in nonviolence, in the decency of the federal government, in the American dream.

But SNCC barely changed Mississippi, or any of the rural Deep South. The Voter Education Project recorded 688,800 blacks qualifying to vote for the first time in the South between April 1, 1962 and November 1, 1964, a jump from 26.8 to 38 percent of the potential black registrants. Almost all the increase, however, came from the urban and upper South. In Mississippi, the proportion of black voters rose from 5.3 percent to just 6.7 percent. Indeed, the VEP, having spent more money in Mississippi with fewer results than in any other state, decided in 1963 to pour no further funds into the Delta campaign. Without the promised federal assistance, the movement had been stymied by dilatory registrars, economic intimidation, and a calculated reign of jailings and violence.

Intransigent registration officials mastered tactics of harassment and delay. To suit their purposes, they changed registration dates and procedures at will; they administered literacy and understanding tests arbitrarily; they forced blacks to wait interminably, to return time and time again. Not uncommonly, the office walls of registrars sported Confederate flags and signs proclaiming "Support Your Citizens' Council." Those blacks not yet discouraged by the foregoing had to face the derision of whites gathered near the courthouse and the hostile stares of sheriffs and deputies, ominously taking their pictures or noting their names. "Who do you work for?" was frequently the first question an angry registrar asked a black attempting to enroll, underlining the price to be paid for daring to exercise this right of citizenship. Blacks who worked for whites and tried to register lost their jobs. Landowners evicted tenants from their plantations. Black farmers found banks refusing to extend them credit, merchants refusing to sell them supplies, ginners refusing to process their cotton, and grain-elevator operators refusing to store their grain. Still other blacks who sought to vote were removed from the welfare rolls and denied the federal surplus commodities due them. Indeed, in Greenwood, Mississippi, the effort of a few to respond to SNCC's exhortations to register led county officials to discontinue the distribution of surplus food to over twenty thousand blacks.

To underscore the threat, local officers perverted the law to shackle black activists and voter applicants. They peremptorily

arrested civil-rights workers for breach of peace, traffic violations, trespassing, vagrancy, and whatever else they could con-
jure. The fact that few convictions were ultimately upheld did not
matter, wrote one lawyer, since the "primary effort is to use
arrests and threats of arrests, costly bail, to hamstring voter
registration." Such harassment forced CORE out of Monroe,
Louisiana, and doomed its most concerted voter-registration
campaign in Plaquemine in Iberville Parish. It had the same
effect when used against local residents. In nearby Clinton,
police arrested twelve blacks, who wrote a letter to the mayor
respectfully requesting the establishment of a biracial committee, on charges of intimidating a public official. Just outside
Greenwood, fifty-eight blacks who left a meeting in a church
into which smoke bombs had been tossed and marched to the
Itta Bena sheriff's house to ask for police protection for voter
registration were all arrested, tried, convicted, and sent to prison
on charges of disturbing the peace. Farther to the north, a
Clarksdale black who had the termerity to wear a CORE "Freedom Now" T-shirt was arrested for parading without a permit.
In Americus, Georgia, following the arrest of three hundred
blacks demonstrating for voter registration, three SNCC and one
CORE volunteer were charged with attempting to incite insurrection, a crime which carried the death penalty.

Violence by both law-enforcement officers and white terrorists capped the effort to stifle black enfranchisement. A SCLC
worker in Alabama testified to being arrested for canvasing for
voter registration. After the worker was kicked and beaten, the
local police chief "got out a brand new [electric cattle] prod
and applied it to me several times, but I took it. I began to get
weaker and dizzy, but I tried to take it. Then when he put it to
my genitals, I said to him, 'What about your God?' He stopped,
but he threatened to put the Klan on me. . . . For about two days
I was in a daze as a result of the prod treatment given me by the
police chief." In Winona, Mississippi, SNCC's Lawrence Guyot

went to check on the arrest of several civil-rights workers. The sheriff "said 'I got 'em. What you gon' do about it?' I said, 'All I want to do is find out what the charges are so we can raise the money to get them out. . . .' He said, 'You get the fuck out of here.' " Guyot walked to his car and the sheriff followed. " 'Nigger, what you causing all these problems?' and hit me in the mouth. . . . And then he just beat on me till he got me in the jail and just kept beating on me. One guy was a prizefighter, and he just stood me up to the wall and just beat on me, and then they used guns." Nine policemen worked him over, forced him to take all his clothes off and threatened to burn his genitals and pierce them with a sharp stick. After some four hours, "they called in a doctor and they said, 'Well, can he take any more?' And he said, 'Well, I'm not going to be responsible if you do.' " They charged Guyot with attempted murder.

With the connivance of those entrusted to uphold the law, white toughs wrecked a voter-registration campaign in a town midway between Greenwood and Jackson. They firebombed and dynamited several cars and homes, threatened the life of a black minister, set afire a new community center, and beat up the voting-rights volunteers working in the town. In Greenwood, while the police broke up peaceful marches to the courthouse and unleashed snarling dogs on black demonstrators, local whites blasted their shotguns at SNCC cars and offices and put them to the torch. This violence against the effort to enfranchise blacks, largely unnoticed by the nation and unhindered by the federal government, continued until the Mississippi Freedom Summer of 1964, when at least thirty homes were bombed, thirty-five churches burned, eighty persons were beaten, and there were more than thirty shooting incidents, and six known murders. A SNCC organizer in Georgia summed up the reasons for the failure of the registration effort in the rural Deep South: "How does one get it across to the people that we are not alone, when all around them white men are killing and getting away?

Not only getting away, but in many cases promoted. . . . How do you push a meeting when they tell you, 'I might be killed, my house may be burned, I may be fired from my job.' "

Only a significant federal presence in the rural Deep South might have saved the voter-registration program. It was promised. It was necessary. It never materialized. The Justice Department politely accepted all the phone calls it received from civil-rights volunteers in the field, respectfully replied to all movement correspondents, promptly conferred with black leaders when they requested it, but continued to maintain that the system of federalism tied its hands. "Careful explanations of the historic limitations on the federal government's police powers," admitted Robert Kennedy, "are not satisfactory to the parents of students who have vanished in Mississippi or to the widow of a Negro educator shot down without any reason by night riders in Georgia." Yet his Department of Justice insisted that it could not intervene unless local authorities proved wholly incapable of upholding law and order or defied a specific federal court order.

Only Mississippi's Governor Ross Barnett in 1962, in the limited realm of desegregated education, gave the Kennedy Administration the unimpeachable grounds that it required before it would act. Defying federal court orders directing the admission of James Meredith, the grandson of a slave and an air-force veteran of eight years, to the state university, Barnett announced a doctrine of interposition redolent of John C. Calhoun. President Kennedy met this challenge to his constitutional authority by sending several hundred federal marshals to the campus of Ole Miss to guarantee Meredith's admission. When they were met by a rioting mob, the President dispatched army troops and federalized the state National Guard. Two died and 375 were injured in the melee. Much of the nation, save diehard segregationists, applauded Kennedy's stand and accepted it as dramatic evidence of the Administration's commitment to racial justice.

Black leaders, knowing the hundreds of unlawful acts by white supremacists that the Kennedy Administration did nothing about, viewed the matter differently. They saw Kennedy as a temporizer and manipulator, devoid of any true sense of moral urgency concerning the race issue. He would act when it suited his needs, not the movement's. He would act the hero in the victory at Ole Miss but remain on the sidelines during the really fundamental attempt at racial change in Albany, Georgia.

In that Black Belt city of southwest Georgia, segregationist officials proved impervious to nonviolent direct action when the federal government chose not to enforce the constitutional rights of blacks. Beginning in November 1961, and lasting for more than a year, thousands of Albany blacks marched, boycotted, and sat-in to win enfranchisement and the full integration of public facilities. Over a thousand spent time in jail. Countless others sacrificed and suffered. Yet at the end of 1962 only the merest handfuls of blacks could vote in Baker, Lee, Mitchell, or Terrell counties, and an Albany black still could not get a cup of coffee at a downtown lunch counter. The local schools, bus terminal, and municipal library and swimming pool remained as segregated as ever.

The first city-wide campaign of massive civil disobedience totally failed to achieve its objectives because the Kennedy Administration never acted against white Albany's clear violations of federal law. The Kennedy brothers, wanting calm so that the moderate Democrat Carl Sanders might triumph over his extremist opponents in the 1962 gubernatorial contest, chose not to intervene as long as Albany's segregationists could keep the peace. And that Chief of Police Laurie Pritchett did masterfully. He met Martin Luther King's nonviolence with his own, and outmaneuvered the SCLC and SNCC staff workers participating in the Albany movement. He filled the jails with black demonstrators, but kept their mistreatment to a minimum and prevented white mobs from running amuck as they had in Anniston, Birmingham, and Montgomery. Consequently, the Kennedy Administration never sent federal marshals to Albany, never enforced the Interstate Commerce Commission ruling against segregation in bus terminals, and never applied pressure to the city fathers to rectify black grievances. In the absence of tumult, few whites throughout the nation demanded that the federal government do more.

The collapse of the Albany movement proved to segregationists that police action "to keep the peace" could be their most effective instrument of oppression. Albany gave the leadership of white resistance a renewed confidence that, if they minimized outrageous public disorder, they could use local force in defiance of the law. Conversely, the strategists of the black struggle understood the lesson of Albany, the voter-registration campaign, and the Freedom Rides to be the clear need for dramatic crises of greater and greater magnitude and disorder. Black freedom would be achieved neither through persuasion of Southern whites nor through orderly protest. Sweeping, coercive civil-rights legislation was indispensable. That would come only when massive violence had aroused a national consensus to cry out for federal intervention.

FIVE

We Shall Overcome

Martin Luther King's determination to provoke a confrontation in Birmingham in 1963 resulted in a massive wave of nonviolent action—"the Negro Revolution." His action decisively changed both the nature of the struggle for racial justice and white attitudes toward civil rights. After more than twenty thousand blacks were jailed in hundreds of demonstrations, King's action eventuated the passage of the most comprehensive anti-discrimination legislation in American history.

The decision to launch a campaign to end segregation in Birmingham had been reached in a three-day strategy session conducted by the SCLC at its retreat near Savannah at the end of 1962. The motives were both personal and political, practical as well as philosophical. The Albany debacle weighed heavily on King and his aides. Malcolm X had said "the civil rights struggle in America reached its lowest point" in Albany, and many in the movement agreed. Albany brought into the open doubts about King's leadership and disillusionment with the established techniques of protest. The head of the SCLC wanted desperately to prove that nonviolence could still work, that "you can struggle without hating, you can fight without violence." King also believed it imperative to demonstrate his own courage and effectiveness. His reputation, and SCLC's influence, necessitated a daring, dramatic effort, especially since 1963 would be the year of the one hundredth anniversary of the Emancipation Proclamation.

King realized the need for some majestic achievement to rekindle the morale and momentum of the freedom struggle. Social movements require victories for sustenance, and civil-rights gains had not kept pace with the rising expectations of blacks. Despair mounted in 1962, and King feared that if the movement faltered, blacks would turn to leaders like Malcolm X, who mocked nonviolence and had nothing but scorn for "integration"—a word, Malcolm said, "invented by a northern liberal." The SCLC leadership craved and needed a major triumph.

The time had come, moreover, to force Kennedy's hand. The President's policy of trying to show concern for blacks while at the same time avoiding action to inflame the white South, said King, had brought the movement nothing but delay and tokenism. By 1963, thirty-four African nations had freed themselves from colonial bondage, but more than two thousand school districts remained segregated in the South. Only 8 percent of the black children in the South attended class with whites. At this rate of progress, civil-rights leaders moaned, it would be the year 2054 before school desegregation became a reality, and it would be the year 2094 before blacks secured equality in job training and employment. Kennedy would have to be pushed, and pushed hard. "We've got to have a crisis to bargain with," Wyatt Tee Walker explained at the SCLC retreat. "To take a moderate approach hoping to get white help, doesn't help. They nail you to the cross, and it saps the enthusiasm of the followers. You've got to have a crisis."

Birmingham appeared to answer King's diverse needs. The Reverend Fred Lee Shuttlesworth, the head of the Alabama Christian Movement for Human Rights, a SCLC affiliate, had just invited King to conduct nonviolent demonstrations in Birmingham, the most segregated big city in America. No other undertaking would be more audacious. Absolute segregation was the rule—in schools, restaurants, rest rooms, drinking fountains, and department-store fitting rooms. Municipal officials closed down the city parks rather than comply with a federal court order to desegregate them. Birmingham abandoned its professional baseball team rather than allow it to play integrated clubs in the International League. Although over 40 percent of the population was black, fewer than ten thousand of the 80,000 registered voters were black. Despite the city's industrial prosperity, moreover, blacks remained restricted to menial and domestic jobs. Describing race relations in Birmingham, Harrison Salisbury wrote in *The New York Times*:

> Whites and blacks still walk the same streets. But the streets, the water supply and the sewer system are about the only public facilities they share. Ball parks and taxicabs are segregated. So are libraries. A book featuring black rabbits and white rabbits was banned. A drive is on to forbid "Negro music" on "white" radio stations. Every channel of communication, every medium of mutual interest, every reasoned approach, every inch of middle ground has been fragmented by the emotional dynamite of racism, reinforced by the whip, the razor, the gun, the bomb, the torch, the club, the knife, the mob, the police and many branches of the state's apparatus.

To crack Birmingham's solid wall of segregation would be a mighty achievement.

Birmingham was more than unyielding on segregation. It had

the reputation of a dangerous city. Blacks dubbed it "Bombingham" for the eighteen racial bombings and more than fifty cross-burning incidents that occurred between 1957 and 1963. Leading the vanguard of the brutal, last-ditch defenders of segregation was Eugene T. ("Bull") Connor. The jowly, thickset police commissioner prided himself on being as vigilant as he was cruel in "keeping the niggers in their place." The SCLC could count on Connor to respond viciously to any effort to alter the city's racial order, and that just might create the crisis that would force the President to act. King decided to aid Shuttlesworth, but to avoid having their nonviolent campaign used as a political football, they postponed the demonstrations until after the April 2 mayoralty runoff election. In the meantime, King and his associates prepared a top-secret plan which they called "Project C"—for *Confrontation.*

King and his task force arrived in Birmingham the day after the election. They promptly issued a manifesto spelling out the grievances of blacks in that city. It called for an immediate end to racist employment practices and Jim Crow public accommodations, and for the rapid formation of a biracial committee to plan for further desegregation. "The absence of justice and progress in Birmingham demands that we make a moral witness to give our community a chance to survive," the manifesto concluded; it reasoned that since Birmingham officials had resisted every attempt at mediation and compromise, the only recourse left to blacks was open protest. "We're tired of waiting," Shuttlesworth angrily reiterated to a packed church meeting that evening. "We've been waiting for 340 years for our rights. We want action. We want it now." As the congregation responded with feverish renditions of "Woke up This Mornin' with My Mind Stayed on Freedom" and "Ain't Gonna Let Nobody Turn Me 'Round," King rose to vow that he would lead an economic boycott and demonstrations against the downtown merchants until "Pharaoh lets God's people go."

The first stage of Project C began the next morning. Small groups of protesters staged sit-ins at the segregated downtown lunch counters. The anticipated arrests followed. King continued this tactic for several days, patiently piquing the concern of the Kennedy Administration and the interest of the national news media while arousing the black community. He carefully avoided provoking the racist fury of white Birmingham until these objectives were reasonably accomplished. To accelerate the process, King ordered Project C's second stage to start on April 6.

Some fifty blacks led by Shuttlesworth marched on City Hall that Saturday morning. Connor arrested them all. The next day, Palm Sunday, Connor similarly intercepted and jailed a column of blacks marching on City Hall headed by Martin Luther King's brother, the Reverend A. D. King. Day after day the public marches and arrests continued, all in the full glare of newspaper photographers and television cameras. King had counted on these incidents and the economic boycott accompanying them to activate larger numbers of Birmingham blacks, to focus national attention on the issue of civil rights, and to discomfort the city's economic elite. He had calculated right. On April 10, city officials secured an injunction barring racial demonstrations. They thought it would stop the SCLC campaign in its tracks, robbing King of his desired publicity and dampening the fervor of the black community. But King announced that he saw it as his duty to violate this immoral injunction and that he would do so on Good Friday, April 12. Accompanied by Abernathy and Al Hibbler, the popular blind blues singer, King led some fifty hymn-singing volunteers on yet another trek toward City Hall. Chanting "Freedom has come to Birmingham!" nearly a thousand blacks lined their route. An infuriated "Bull" Connor, now assisted by a squad of snarling, snapping police dogs, ordered their arrest. The national spotlight illuminated Birmingham's racial crisis as never before.

King used his time in jail to compose an eloquent essay justifying the strategy of the black freedom struggle. Ostensibly written to the eight Birmingham clergymen who had condemned the SCLC campaign as "unwise and untimely," King addressed his reply to the many whites and blacks who apparently shared his goals but questioned his tactics, especially those who urged the movement to be patient, moderate, and law-abiding. Begun in the margins of newspapers and continued on bits of scrap paper smuggled to him by a prison trusty, King worked for four days on his nineteen-page "Letter from the Birmingham Jail." Soon after, several national periodicals published it in its entirety and reprints were distributed across the nation. The news media frequently quoted it and, for the most part, cited it favorably. The letter proved to be a potent weapon in the propaganda battle to legitimate the direct-action movement. It quieted numerous critics of civil disobedience; it won significant new support for "Freedom Now."

King's letter began with a refutation of the charge of "outside agitator," arguing that as a Christian and an American he had the duty to combat injustice wherever it existed. Then King explained how the white leadership of Birmingham left blacks no alternative but to demonstrate at this time. He detailed the broken promises and refusal to negotiate by the white elite, juxtaposing them against his portrayal of the dismal, brutal plight of black Birmingham. The advocates of civil rights, therefore, had to turn to nonviolent direct action to dramatize the issue. Something had to be done to break the crust of apathy and indifference that enabled white America to ignore such injustice; something had to be done to create a crisis so the city could no longer evade a solution. To those who asked blacks "to wait," King retorted that "wait" generally meant "never." He had never "yet engaged in a direct action movement that was 'well timed,'" King observed, "according to the timetable of those who have not suffered unduly from the disease of segregation."

I guess it is easy for those who have never felt the stinging darts of segregation to say wait. But when you have seen vicious mobs lynch your mothers and fathers at will and drown your sisters and brothers at whim; when you have seen hate-filled policemen curse, kick, brutalize, and even kill your black brothers and sisters with impunity; when you see that vast majority of your twenty million Negro brothers smothering in an air-tight cage of poverty in the midst of an affluent society; when you suddenly find your tongue twisted and your speech stammering as you seek to explain to your six-year-old daughter why she can't go to the public amusement park that has just been advertised on television, and see tears welling up in her little eyes when she is told that Funtown is closed to colored children, and see the depressing clouds of inferiority begin to form in her little mental sky, and see her begin to distort her little personality by unconsciously developing a bitterness toward white people; when you have to concoct an answer for a five-year-old son asking in agonizing pathos: "Daddy, why do white people treat colored people so mean?"; when you take a cross-country drive and find it necessary to sleep night after night in the uncomfortable corners of your automobile because no motel will accept you; when you are humiliated day in and day out by nagging signs reading "white" men and "colored"; when your first name becomes "nigger" and your middle name becomes "boy" (however old you are) and your last name becomes "John," and when your wife and mother are never given the respected title "Mrs."; when you are harried by day and haunted by night by the fact that you are a Negro, living constantly at tiptoe stance never quite knowing what to expect next, and plagued with inner fears and outer resentments; when you are forever fighting a degenerating sense of "nobodiness"—then you will understand why we find it difficult to wait.

King next turned to a philosophical vindication of civil disobedience. Because segregation laws injured the soul and degraded the human personality, he defined them as unjust. Then

King cited Augustine, Thomas Aquinas, Paul Tillich, and Martin Buber in support of his contention that one has a moral responsibility to disobey unjust laws. He reminded his fellow ministers that the laws of Hitler had been technically "legal," and further emphasized the undemocratic nature of the segregation ordinances by demonstrating that blacks had been excluded from the political process which enacted these state and local laws. To those still unpersuaded of the justness of civil disobedience, King posed the alternative. "If this philosophy had not emerged I am convinced that if our white brothers dismiss us as 'rabble rousers' and 'outside agitators'—those of us who are working through the channels of nonviolent direct action—and refuse to support our nonviolent efforts, millions of Negroes, out of frustration and despair, will seek solace and security in black nationalist ideologies, a development that will lead inevitably to a frightening racial nightmare." King concluded with an expression of his disappointment with moderates who care more about law and order than about justice. He looked forward to the day when the nation would recognize its real heroes.

They will be the James Merediths, courageously and with a majestic sense of purpose, facing jeering and hostile mobs and the agonizing loneliness that characterizes the life of the pioneer. They will be old, oppressed, battered Negro women, symbolized in a seventy-two-year-old woman of Montgomery, Alabama, who rose up with a sense of dignity and with her people decided not to ride the segregated buses, and responded to one who inquired about her tiredness with ungrammatical profundity: 'My feets is tired, but my soul is rested.' They will be the young high school and college students, the young ministers of the gospel and a host of their elders, courageously and nonviolently sitting in at lunch counters and willingly going to jail for conscience's sake. One day the South will know that when these disinherited children of God sat down at lunch counters they were in reality standing up for the best in the American dream and the most sacred values in our Judeo-Christian heritage, and thus carrying our whole nation back to great wells of democracy which were dug deep by the founding fathers in the formulation of the Constitution and the Declaration of Independence.

That day had certainly not yet arrived in Birmingham. As the disinherited children of God continued to try to march to City Hall, "Bull" Connor's police acted with less and less restraint. The movement responded to police violence with larger and larger demonstrations. And Birmingham blacks reacted by tightening the economic boycott which pinched the merchants more and more. As the racial tension mounted, events outside of Birmingham heightened the sense of impending crisis.

On April 21, William L. Moore, a white Baltimore mail carrier and CORE member, set off from Chattanooga on his "freedom walk." Wearing a sandwich-board sign proclaiming "Equal Rights for All—Mississippi or Bust," Moore intended to hike to Jackson and personally deliver a letter to Mississippi Governor Ross Barnett protesting Southern segregation. On the afternoon of April 23, he walked through Gadsden, Alabama. That evening he was found murdered on a lonely road ten miles outside the city. Moore had been shot in the neck and head.

The killing of Moore embittered many in the movement. As officials throughout the nation bemoaned the outrageous crime, Diane Nash Bevel led a group of eight Birmingham blacks to Gadsden to complete Moore's pilgrimage. All were jailed. Then an interracial group of CORE and SNCC staffers left Chattanooga on May 1 to take up the freedom walk. Nearly a hundred cars filled with bottle- and rock-throwing whites followed them across the Alabama state line, shouting "Kill them!" "Throw them niggers in the river!" Alabama highway patrolmen immediately arrested the freedom walkers, repeatedly shocking them with electrical cattle prods. The CORE–SNCC contingent refused to accept bail and spent a month in prison. Two weeks later, a third attempt to resume Moore's freedom walk, organized by CORE, resulted in the arrest of another six blacks and five whites. Their incarceration, unlike the earlier arrests, barely made news. By this time King had been released from jail and had launched the third stage of his confrontation with Birmingham's establishment.

D Day, May 2, an astonished national audience, generated by the sit-ins, protest marches, police brutality, and the slaying of William Moore, watched over a thousand black children, some only six years old, march out of the Sixteenth Street Baptist Church to demonstrate and be arrested. Before the cameras, the young blacks sang freedom songs, chanted freedom slogans to the hundreds of cheering adult spectators, and knelt to pray as the police corraled them. They offered no resistance to Connor's stupefied forces, clapping, dancing, laughing, and skipping to the patrol wagons waiting to take them to jail. "Black and glad," determined yet not somber, the children stunned the nation.

Criticism of King for his "children's crusade" came from every quarter. Moderates anguished about the safety of the children. Conservatives denounced the tactic as cynical and exploitative. Radicals demeaned it as unmanly. "Real men," objected Malcolm X, "don't put their children on the firing line." King retorted that, by demonstrating, the children gained a "sense of their own stake in freedom and justice," as well as a heightened pride in their race and belief in their capacity to influence their future. He asked his white critics pointedly: Where had they been with their protective words when down through the years, Negro infants were born into ghettos, taking their first breath of life in a social atmosphere where the fresh air of freedom was crowded out by the stench of discrimination?

Words of reason no longer mattered, however. Action had taken precedence. The rules of the game had changed. Another thousand black children of Birmingham packed the Sixteenth Street Baptist Church that evening to shout their approval of

King and his promise "Today was D Day. Tomorrow will be Double-D Day."

The *New York Times* account of the May 3 demonstrations began: "There was an ugly overtone to the events today that was not present yesterday." No one would accuse the reporter of overstatement. As an enraged "Bull" Connor watched a thousand more students gather in the church to receive their demonstration assignments, he abandoned all restraint. He ordered his forces to bar the exits from the church, trapping inside about half the young protesters, and then had his men charge into those who escaped and had gathered in Kelly Ingram Park in front of the Sixteenth Street Baptist Church. The police, swinging nightsticks brutally and indiscriminately, beat demonstrators and onlookers. They sicced their dogs on the young, wounding several. When some adults in the park, horrified at the mistreatment of the children, hurled bricks and bottles at the policemen, Connor commanded the firemen with their high-pressure hoses: "Let 'em have it." With a sound like gunfire, streams of blistering water roared from the nozzles, blasting blacks against buildings and sweeping kids down slippery streets. The hundreds of pounds of pressure ripped the bark off trees; it also tore the clothes off young people's backs and cut through their skin. Those jailed that Friday brought the number of children arrested in two days to nearly thirteen hundred.

King had his confrontation, and more. On Saturday, an additional two hundred students were arrested, and several thousand adult blacks skirmished with the police, pelting them with rocks and stones. Again, scenes of clubbing, police dogs, and fire hoses appeared on the front pages of newspapers and on television sets throughout the country. The appalling pictures of snarling dogs lunging viciously at youthful marchers, of bands of policemen ganging up to beat children and women, of high-pressure hoses knocking the very young and the very old off their feet or into the air, brought a surge of anger and determination across black America and aroused the conscience, or guilt, of millions of whites. King suddenly had the support of much of the nation. Kennedy now had to act.

The pictures of violence in Birmingham made him "sick," the President admitted to a delegation from the Americans for Democratic Action that Saturday. Yet he doubted aloud that he had a constitutional mandate to act. He termed impossible the liberals' suggestion that he intervene immediately and forcefully in Birmingham, but acknowledged: "I am not asking for patience. I can well understand why the Negroes of Birmingham are tired of being asked to be patient." Privately, the President knew that the time had come to act. He had to resolve the conflict with the least possible political damage to himself. He shared the sense of national outrage at Southern white atrocities yet shrank from the prospect of using federal force to impose a new racial order. Kennedy simply wanted the quickest possible restoration of civil peace. Secretly he ordered Justice Department mediators to Birmingham to persuade the contending groups to negotiate a settlement. Concurrently, key Administration officials began an intensive campaign to pressure Birmingham's most influential businessmen, especially those connected with U.S. Steel, to accept a compromise agreement.

Until this moment in the crisis, the Senior Citizens' Committee, covertly organized by the Birmingham Chamber of Commerce to deal with desegregation problems, would not even talk with King and his associates. They were the so-called white moderates of the South—the gentlemen who said "nigra" rather than "nigger"—supposedly too busy making money to hate, yet for a month they had avoided even a hint of willingness to end the disorder and violence. Now, suddenly, they were ready to talk. They had felt the heat from Washington. They feared the city was on the verge of a major bloodletting. And they had reckoned the toll of the black boycott: sales in April had dropped more than a third in the downtown stores. So Birmingham's economic elite started to negotiate in earnest on May 4, even agreeing to hold all-night sessions. They talked and listened but would not accede. The SCLC would not back down. Deadlock. King ordered the demonstrations to continue.

The most massive black protest to date began early Monday, May 6, and police violence intensified accordingly. A flyer distributed near Negro schools urged all students: "Fight for freedom first, then go to school. Join the thousands in jail who are making their witness for freedom. Come to the Sixteenth Street Baptist Church now . . . and we'll soon be free. It's up to you to free our teachers, our parents, yourself and our country." Once again, thousands of young blacks heeded the call. In some schools, attendance dropped nearly 90 percent. Preaching to a jammed church and to the thousands more in Ingram Park listening to loudspeakers, King reminded the students of their stake in this "righteous struggle for freedom and human dignity." He reiterated the necessity for nonviolence: "The world is watching you." Violence is impractical as well as immoral; the power of nonviolence is a greater weapon.

Dick Gregory, the well-known black comedian, led the first group of demonstrators out of the church. Police hurried them into the waiting paddy wagons as the students chanted: "Don't mind walking, 'cause I want my freedom now." Then another group left the church, shouting: "Freedom! Freedom! Freedom!" They, too, were quickly herded off to jail. Out came another group of young blacks, and then another, and another. For an hour, wave after wave of twenty to fifty black students, chanting and shouting for freedom, defiantly offered themselves up for arrest. The huge crowd in the park roared their approval for each contingent leaving the church. Many sang a new ditty: "It isn't nice to go to jail/There are nicer ways to do it/But the nice ways always fail."

The audacity of the students, the contempt of the blacks, stirred Connor's fear and loathing. After more than a thousand demonstrators had been seized, he turned his police on the crowd in the park. Shoving and kicking, the men in blue now vented their fury. As the television cameras rolled and the photographers focused their lenses, snapping police dogs once again leaped at the throats of taunting children, fire hoses bowled over rock-throwing blacks, and Connor's minions indiscriminately clubbed onlookers.

A shocked nation demanded federal action to end the conflict. Kennedy's mediators redoubled their efforts. They pressed King to yield on his demands for immediate desegregation and an end to discrimination in employment. They warned him of the folly of prolonging the crisis in the expectation of intervention by federal troops. Separately, the Justice Department officials urged the city's business establishment to make real concessions, not merely promises of future action. They threatened the white elite with the probable consequences of federal action and the economic effects of a bloodbath in Birmingham. Neither negotiating team would budge. The talks resumed, and so did the confrontation.

Tuesday, May 7, the conflict peaked. A larger number of students than ever before, and far less submissive, appeared on the streets. Rather than march from the church and orderly court arrest, some two thousand young blacks suddenly converged on the downtown area at noon. Most staged sit-ins. Others picketed the major stores. Some held pray-ins on the sidewalks. Several thousand adult spectators then spontaneously joined a raucous black parade through the business section. Over and over they sang "I ain't scared of your jail 'cause I want my freedom! . . . want my freedom!" "We're marching for freedom!" others chanted. "The police can't stop us now. Even 'Bull' Connor can't stop us now."

Connor certainly tried. Adding an armored police tank to his arsenal of hoses, dogs, clubs, and cattle prods, he ordered his men to drive the protesters back into the black ghetto. Brutally, they did so, eventually penning nearly four thousand in Ingram Park. Connor commanded that the high-pressure hoses be turned on the trapped blacks. The water shot from the nozzles whacked the bark off trees. It tore bricks loose from the walls.

The crowd screamed, some for mercy, some in anger. Rocks flew. Bottles and bricks were hurled at the police. SCLC aides circulating in the crowd pleaded for nonviolence. Few could even hear them over the crashing of the huge hoses; and not many who could hear wanted to listen. Soon after Shuttlesworth entered the park to try to calm his followers, a blast of water slammed the minister against the side of a building. On hearing that an injured Shuttlesworth had just been placed in an ambulance, Connor laughed. "I waited a week to see Shuttlesworth get hit with a hose. I'm sorry I missed it. I wish they'd carried him away in a hearse." Not until the crowd had been thoroughly pacified and dispersed did the dogs cease biting, the clubs stop crashing bones, and the hoses end knocking blacks down and washing them along the sidewalks. A reporter who watched in despair mumbled "God bless America."

That noon, as the blacks demonstrated tumultuously downtown, a secret emergency meeting of the Senior Citizens' Committee resolved to end the disorder that had caused Birmingham to become an international byword for unrestrained police brutality. With the din of freedom chants in their ears, the business leaders directed their negotiators to come to terms with the SCLC. That evening a three-hour bargaining session brought the two sides close to agreement. Differences remained, but the premonition of unchecked violence affected both negotiating teams. Following three more days of talk, they reached agreement.

"I am very happy to be able to announce," King stated, "that we have come today to the climax of a long struggle for justice, freedom and human dignity in the city of Birmingham." The SCLC had won its demands for the "desegregation of lunch counters, rest rooms, fitting rooms and drinking fountains"; for the "upgrading and hiring of Negroes on a nondiscriminatory basis throughout the industrial community of Birmingham"; and for the formation of a biracial committee. It accepted, however, a timetable of planned stages, relenting on its insistence that these changes take effect immediately. The SCLC, moreover, acceded to the release of arrested demonstrators on bond, giving up its demand for the outright dismissal of all charges against them. Still and all, King could well claim with pride "the most magnificent victory for justice we've ever seen in the Deep South."

King concluded his May 10 press conference with a plea for brotherhood and reconciliation, but too many in Birmingham, black and white, wanted neither. That Saturday, Connor and other leading local and state officials broadcast their denunciations of the biracial accord. In language dripping with venom, they assaulted the Senior Citizens' Committee and the Kennedy brothers as well as King and the SCLC. At nightfall, over a thousand robed Ku Klux Klansmen met to hear further diatribes against the agreement. Shortly after the rally ended, two dynamite bombs rocked the home of A. D. King, strewing glass and timber in every direction. No one was injured, but the front porch had been replaced with a large crater and the house was a shambles. Sullen neighbors milled about, vowing vengeance. The Police and Fire Department officials inspecting the rubble were jostled and threatened. As the crowd grew, so did calls for retribution. Some angry blacks slashed the tires of police cars and fire trucks. A. D. King pleaded for peace, and only his herculean effort contained the assemblage's rage.

Minutes later, another bomb exploded, blasting a gaping hole in the Gaston Motel, the SCLC's headquarters in Birmingham. Thirsting for vengeance, the black underclass of Alabama's steel town streamed out of the bars and pool halls in the ghetto. They pelted the arriving police and firemen with stones and bottles. They stabbed one officer and assaulted several others. When some of King's aides urged them to stop throwing rocks and go home, the mob shouted back: "They started it! They started it!" "Ladies and gentlemen," Wyatt Tee Walker pleaded into a megaphone, "will you cooperate by going to your homes.

Please. Please go home." "Tell it to 'Bull' Connor," came the reply. "This is what nonviolence gets you."

As police reinforcements swarmed into the area, additional rioters joined the rampaging mob. Many were parents of arrested children who had just heard tales of brutality and mistreatment in the prison. Martin Luther King, Jr., to the contrary, they would not love their enemy. Others had been so ground down by racist oppression that they wanted only to kill "whitey." They had never accepted King's talk of nonviolence, and this night they felt emboldened to display their hatred. Pandemonium reigned for several hours. Sporadic battles between the mob and the police flared. A white cabdriver, lost in the ghetto, was attacked by blacks, his car overturned and set on fire. Two grocery stores owned by whites were put to the torch. Soon an entire block was ablaze. "Let the whole fucking city burn," Walker heard a young black scream. "I don't give a good goddamn—this'll show those white motherfuckers!" Some blacks, however, struggled throughout the night to prevent bloodshed. Their exertions managed to keep the surge of violence from becoming a flood. Still, over fifty had been injured and the Birmingham *News* estimated property damage at more than $40,000.

King hurried back from Atlanta the next day to calm black Birmingham and to see that the accord held. He and other SCLC officials made the rounds of black bars and pool halls, schools, and churches, preaching the necessity of avoiding any provocation that might jeopardize the agreement. King pleaded that blacks stay on the nonviolent road to freedom. "Don't stop," he urged. "Don't get weary. There is a great camp meeting coming." How long? He was asked; not long, he promised. "We *shall* overcome." The familiar refrain reassured and comforted. The furor subsided. City officials and business leaders began to implement the desegregation pact on schedule. Order returned to Birmingham.

Further racial disorder, however, swept across much of the rest of the nation as a result of the impact of Birmingham on black America. The audacity of taking on "Bull" Connor's "Johannesburg" and vanquishing it, the unprecedented children's crusade and savage white response, the determination of all strata of black Birmingham to fight racial oppression by whatever means they chose, all combined to affect more Afro-Americans, more deeply, than any previous civil-rights protest. The black struggle had reached a new plateau.

Birmingham fully awakened blacks to a sense of their new power; it ignited a mighty confidence in the potency of mass social dislocation to overcome white intransigence. Blacks took to heart King's description of the accord as a great victory, and heard repeatedly that the lesson of Birmingham was that if such a bastion of segregation could be defeated then any other city or area could be brought to heel by an aroused and determined black community. Birmingham also spurred self-pride, a spirit of black unity, a willingness to join the struggle. James Farmer termed this optimistic assertiveness "a spiritual emancipation" and journalists trumpeted the emergence of a "New Negro," dwelling endlessly on his loss of fear, his readiness to go to jail, and his urgent quest for Freedom Now!

In part, the bravery of Birmingham's black children inspired this commitment. The image of the young, first seen on television and then seared in memory, volunteering to face down Connor's bullies and dogs and hoses, goaded thousands more to demonstrate. The same images also shamed blacks into the struggle. If children could court jail so that all blacks could be free, how could their elders do less. Simultaneously, the pictures of violence against women and kids engendered new depths of anger and widespread bitterness. The catalysts of hatred and retaliation in part dissolved black apathy and helped spark a brushfire of "little Birminghams" across the country in mid-1963.

More significantly than the increased number of demonstrators, the nature of black protest changed after Birmingham. Blacks en masse forsook gradualism for immediacy. The era of tokenism had ended. Limited gains—a handful of students in an integrated school or the desegregation of a specific public accommodation—would no longer suffice. The insistence on *Freedom Now* meant, unmistakably, sweeping basic changes without either delay or dilution. "The package deal is the new demand," wrote Bayard Rustin. Instead of accepting further protracted, piecemeal alterations in the racial system, blacks clamored now for "fundamental, social, political and economic change." The price of racial peace, they insisted, must be decent jobs and housing for blacks as well as the franchise, an end to police brutality as well as immediate desegregation of all schools and public accommodations. To underscore their determination, moreover, blacks demonstrated for these concerns in an exceedingly bellicose and relentless manner.

Birmingham also induced the previously torpid, very poorest blacks to participate in the racial struggle. Their entry into the movement both reflected and accelerated the radicalization of civil-rights strategies and goals. The unemployed and working poor had little interest in the symbolic and status gains that the college students, professionals, and religious Southern middle-class blacks, who had constituted the bulk of the movement prior to Birmingham, had centered their energies on. They had even less sympathy for, or knowledge of, the spirit of *Satyagraha.* King's talk of love left them cold. His request that they nobly accept suffering and jailing made them snicker. As the black struggle became more massive and encompassing, impatience multiplied, disobedience became barely civil, and nonviolence often a mere stratagem.

In addition, both deliberately and inadvertently, all the major civil-rights organizations further radicalized the movement. All responded to the changes wrought by Birmingham with an increasing militancy. "There go my people," King often quoted Gandhi at this time. "I must catch them, for I am their leader."

And as King hurried to capitalize on the new spirit and participants in the struggle, so did James Forman and John Lewis of SNCC, James Farmer of CORE, Roy Wilkins of the NAACP, and even Whitney Young, the executive director of the National Urban League since 1961. Far more outspoken than his predecessors, Young in 1963 constantly harped on the themes that civil rights are not negotiable, that the time for compromise or delay had passed, and that the nation owed blacks a "domestic Marshall Plan." "The only fair and realistic way of closing the gap and correcting historic abuses," Young insisted, "calls for a transitional period of intensified special effort of corrective measures in education, in training and employment, in housing and in health and welfare." Although never a direct-action organization, the Urban League in 1963 publicly defended that strategy and urged blacks to demonstrate and protest.

So did the NAACP. And it backed it up with action. Wilkins, who had chided black demonstrators in Jackson in 1961, returned to that city two years later to be arrested for picketing a Woolworth store that refused to desegregate. At the NAACP annual convention in July, Wilkins demanded that the association "accelerate, accelerate, accelerate" the civil rights attack. For the first time, moreover, the national office provided all-out support for its local branches engaging in direct action, especially in the Carolinas, Mississippi, and Philadelphia, where Cecil Moore, the branch president, led blockades of the job sites of lily-white construction unions and boasted: "My basic strength is those 300,000 lower-class guys who are ready to mob, rob, steal and kill."

CORE, however, took the lead in the North in 1963. From New York to San Francisco, it organized rent strikes and school boycotts, demonstrated against job bias and for compensatory employment, and focused public attention on police brutality in the ghetto. And as CORE involved more urban blacks in the struggle, its stridency escalated. Militancy for the sake of militancy took hold, spurring ever more radical demands and tactics. At the same time, similarly responding to pressure from local blacks, CORE put forth a greater effort than ever before in the South. Often in conjunction with the SCLC and SNCC, it mounted major voter-registration campaigns in Louisiana and Mississippi and participated in massive demonstrations against segregation in Alabama, Florida, Maryland, North and South Carolina, and Virginia. All these struggles exhibited the uncompromising impatience and sweeping demands of the thousands of new active-movement adherents, which CORE field secretaries did their best to articulate and channel. The followers were leading, the leaders following.

Competition *among* the civil-rights organizations added to the militancy injected into the movement by those most recently mobilized. All the groups in the fight against racism sought the manpower and money necessary to battle successfully. Each tried to gain influence in Washington and standing in a local community, as well as the approval of the masses and the active support of true-believers. And each group, believing its solution best, sought power to affect the outcome of events. Competition among organizations in the civil-rights movement had always existed. Prior to 1963, however, it had been muted. Despite tactical differences, their goals had remained close, and their combined weakness relative to the opposition had placed a premium on cooperation or, at a minimum, absence of open opposition.

Birmingham changed the rules of the competition, and the stakes. There was a lot more to compete for, and more reason to win. The pool of prospective dues-paying members, of bodies to be utilized in demonstrations, and of committed activists willing to work full-time in the movement increased spectacularly after Birmingham. So did the potential of white backing. The door swung open to the possibilities of immense financial contributions, alliances with powerful business and political leaders, and public endorsements and assistance from the nation's major white religious, civic, and labor groups. At the

same time, the probability of victory, of making real changes
in the racial order, also zoomed following Birmingham, intensifying each civil-rights organization's desire to shape the future
according to its light. Variances between the groups, in style
and substance, once easily glossed over, now began to appear
insurmountable. CORE, SNCC, SCLC, and the NAACP each
hungered for the lion's share of the resources they believed
would enable them to set the terms of future agreements and
legislation. Each tried to outdo the others, to be more successful
in its campaigns, to be more devoted to the struggle. The
NAACP and CORE demonstrated that in their competing
efforts in a score of cities in the North and in the Carolinas;
the same was true of the rivalry of SNCC and SCLC in Dan-
ville, Virginia, and in Gadsden and Selma, Alabama; and the
contest for primacy in the civil-rights struggle in Mississippi
among the NAACP, SNCC, and CORE generated still further
momentum and militancy within the movement.

Impatience, tactics, and demands escalated, moreover, because the civil-rights leadership recognized that the new mood
in black America would not be long sustained. They feared that
delay could dissipate the intense involvement generated by
Birmingham. Worrying that anything smacking of "business as
usual" might precipitate individual blacks' hasty withdrawal into
the private struggle for a better life, the leaders pressed for
"all, now!" The civil-rights organizations concertedly demanded
as much as they could as quickly as possible. In tandem, the
NAACP, CORE, SNCC, and SCLC schooled their followers
in the politics of disorder, planning ever more provocative
demonstrations.

Blacks responded with a siege of direct action. A far greater
number of blacks participated in many more demonstrations
against a broader array of discrimination than ever before, and
with unprecedented verve. Describing the change, King indicated that prior to 1963 "the quiet sobbing of an oppressed
people had been unheard by millions of white Americans."

Then, starting with Birmingham, "the lament became a shout and then a roar and for months no American, white or Negro, was insulated or unaware." Nearly eight hundred boycotts, marches, and sit-ins in some two hundred cities and towns across the South occurred in the three months after the Birmingham accord. Over eighty thousand disenfranchised blacks cast ballots in a Mississippi freedom election to protest their being denied the vote. And hundreds of thousands of Northern blacks paraded to demonstrate their solidarity with their Southern brothers and sisters. In addition to staging their own school walk-outs against de facto segregation, they picketed against discrimination in employment, and conducted rent strikes against racism in housing. Indeed, vivid daily accounts of blacks demonstrating and being brutally attacked by police and white mobs became the number-one feature of the news media in mid-1963.

This onslaught of disruptive militancy forced the white South to retreat. Many Southern white leaders suddenly began bargaining for peace, as a result of fear or a sense of fairness. Further, they were concerned for business profits and they also calculated that some reform might best forestall a revolution in race relations. No longer able to count on the indifference of the North or the intransigence of their white constituents, white officials acceded to the desegration of public accommodations in some fifty Southern and border cities in the five months from May to the end of September. Scores of localities established biracial commission and hired their first black policemen. And demagogues who had vowed "Never" registered Afro-Americans to vote and enrolled blacks in previously all-white schools. More racial change came in these few months than had occurred in three-quarters of a century. But it did not come everywhere in the South; and even in those areas that did start to alter their racial system, numerous whites remained unreconciled to any black advance.

From southwest Georgia across the Black Belt to the delta land of Louisiana, white supremacists mobilized for a last-ditch stand. They viewed themselves as the defenders of an isolated outpost—abandoned by the rest of white America, outnumbered by blacks, and under attack by an alliance of the federal government and civil-rights agitators. Embattled and endangered, they grew desperate, anxious to go down fighting and wound the hated black movement in whatever ways they could. First they tried all manner of harassment and intimidation, especially economic coercion. When that failed to stop the civil-rights troops, they called on sheriffs and deputies, who arrested over fifteen thousand demonstrators in the Deep South during the spring and summer of 1963. In one citadel of white racism after another, police brutally clubbed protesters, teargassed them, scarred their bodies with electric cattle prods, and turned biting dogs and high-powered hoses on the volunteers in the movement. Still, the demonstrations continued.

Fearful, frustrated, angry whites turned to terrorism and murder. Fiery crosses placed on the lawns of civil-rights spokesmen and carloads of whites night-riding ominously through the black part of town served as preludes to the burning and bombing of homes and businesses owned by integrationists, or the destruction of schools due to be desegregated. In Mississippi, still the most closed society in the feudal South, where most cars owned by whites bore license-plate legends such as MOST LIED ABOUT STATE IN THE UNION, FEDERALLY OCCUPIED MISSISSIPPI, KENNEDY'S HUNGARY, whites put to the torch several NAACP leaders' homes and stores in Gulfport, demolished the cars of civil-rights workers in Biloxi, wounded five SNCC staffers by shotgun blasts in Canton, and shot and killed a young movement organizer in Tchula. In Greenwood, 1963 brought the destruction of the SNCC office, the gasoline bombing of at least a half dozen black businesses and homes, the shooting of as many voter-registration workers, and the machine-gunning of SNCC's Jimmy Travis. Not to be outdone, whites in Jackson burned a restaurant that agreed to hire blacks, ravaged the homes and churches of several integrationists, and frequently fired rifles at cars driven by civil-rights workers. Returning from a mass meeting to his home in the capital shortly after midnight on June 11, Medgar Evers, the NAACP field secretary in Mississippi, was murdered by a sniper lying in ambush. Evers had just vowed to fight to end "all forms of segregation in Jackson."

Three months later, after two dozen black youths in defiance of Governor George Wallace had desegregated several previously all-white schools in Birmingham, a bomb constructed from fifteen sticks of dynamite shattered the Sunday-morning peace of the Sixteenth Street Baptist Church, the staging center of the spring protests. Dozens of children attending a Bible class and worshipping God were injured by the explosion. Four black girls, two of them fourteen, one eleven, and one ten, who had been changing into choir robes in the basement, lay dead and buried under the debris. Later in the day, a sixteen-year-old black youth was shot in the back and killed by a policeman with a shotgun, and a black thirteen-year-old riding his bicycle was shot to death by some white boys.

Revolted by this orgy of racist violence, mainly perpetrated by members of the Klan and the White Citizens' Council, public opinion in the North swung decisively behind the demand of the movement for an effective civil-rights law. From the May demonstrations in Birmingham through the September bombing in that city, white support for the black struggle steadily mounted and grew potent. Birmingham aroused the dormant conscience and sense of justice of millions of white Americans, and subsequent protests ended the complacency of still millions more. Dozens of student associations, labor unions, and religious organizations provided financial and political backing. Hundreds of liberal groups went on record in resolutions of support for the movement, and in certain white circles, being jailed in a civil-rights demonstration became as much a badge of honor as it was in the black community. Polls and surveys in the summer of

1963 disclosed overwhelming majorities in favor of laws to guarantee blacks voting rights, job opportunities, good housing, and desegregated schools and public accommodations. For a season, at least, Birmingham had altered the minds and hearts of millions of white Americans.

Northern whites, like their Southern counterparts, responded from fright as much as from conscience. Birmingham revealed how easily black discontent could flare into rioting, and melees throughout the summer, especially in Cambridge, Maryland, in Jackson after the assassination of Evers, and in Birmingham again, highlighted the disposition of blacks to meet racist violence with retaliatory rampages. In the main, blacks in 1963 vented their accumulated hostility against whites with rhetoric, but the words were so brutally frank, so uncompromising, so filled with fury, that they constituted an act as foreboding to whites as an assault. What whites heard and read, mostly for the first time, chilled them, and forced many to acknowledge the reasonableness of the civil-rights movement's tactics and goals.

The news media accentuated such fears, popularizing many of the most apocalyptic prophets of doom and destruction. The press played up Robert F. Williams's 1962 tract, *Negroes with Guns*, which preached the necessity of armed force by blacks to gain their freedom. It stressed the growing impatience with nonviolence among the more aggressive CORE and SNCC field secretaries, and their dire warnings of race riots to come unless the demands of blacks, North and South, were fully met. It sensationalized the terrorist fantasies of quasi-Maoist black revolutionaries.

Mostly, the media focused on the black threat vividly articulated by James Baldwin and Malcolm X. Baldwin's *The Fire Next Time* forced into the consciousness of whites a new sense of the rancor of blacks and the destruction awaiting America if it did not quickly and completely change its racial ways. He described the Afro-American's past of rope, fire, torture, castration, infanticide, rape; death and humiliation; fear by day and night, fear as deep as the marrow of the bone; doubt that he was worthy of life, since everyone around him denied it; sorrow for his women, for his kinfolk, for his children, who needed his protection, and whom he could not protect; rage, hatred and murder, hatred for white men so deep that it often turned against him and his own and made all love, all trust, all joy impossible.

He evoked the bleakness blacks presently faced. "For the horrors of the American Negro's life," he wrote, "there has been almost no language." Neither religion nor reason has persuaded whites to treat blacks decently, so, not surprisingly, the appeal of the Black Muslims keeps growing. "There is *no* reason that black men should be expected to be more patient, more forbearing, more farseeing than whites; indeed, quite the contrary." Whites must expect retaliation, unless they change and accept the unconditional freedom of blacks. The price of white security, Baldwin summed up, "is the liberation of the blacks—the total liberation, in the cities, in the towns, before the law, and in the mind." Anything less, he warned in the words of a Negro spiritual: *"God gave Noah the rainbow sign/ No more water, the fire next time!"*

The popularity of the Black Muslims' incitement of violent enmity, described by Baldwin, had first been impressed on white America by CBS's inflammatory documentary in 1959, *The Hate That Hate Produced.* The Nation of Islam was depicted as an army of black fanatics planning for the inevitable race war. Little or nothing most whites read and heard informed them of Muslim success in rehabilitating blacks that others considered beyond reclamation, or of the Muslim gospel that blacks had to conquer their own shame and poverty by adhering to such traditional American virtues as hard work, honesty, self-discipline, mutual help, and self-respect. Rather, the media spotlighted Malcolm X's most extremist visions of separatism and violence; and Malcolm quickly learned that the more shocking his comments, the more white attention the Black Muslims received. He played to the media, conjuring fantasies of jet fleets, piloted by blacks, someday bombing all-white neighborhoods, and publicly thanking *his* God for answering black prayers on the occasion of a plane crash in France which killed 120 white Atlantans. Malcolm X appeared on television more than any other black spokesman in 1963, and few whites remained unaware of his expressions of contempt for all things white, his appeal to blacks to fight racism "by any means necessary," and his insistence that the "day of nonviolent resistance is over."

What often frightened whites instilled a fighting pride in blacks. An apostle of defiance, Malcolm particularly gave voice to the anger and pain of young blacks in the ghetto. His hostility and resentment toward whites epitomized their feelings, and they cheered when Malcolm preached "an eye for an eye" or when he brought "whitey down front." Such utterances expressed the rarely publicized longings of the dissident black masses. Malcolm's insistence on black unity and the right of self-defense, and especially his affirmation of blackness and his contention that blacks must lead and control their *own* freedom struggle, struck still deeper chords among the many in Afro-America who demanded faster and more fundamental changes in racial conditions and called for more forceful means to achieve these ends. To them, of all black leaders, only Malcolm seemed to understand the depth of the racial conflict; and only Malcolm appeared to view the black struggle for equality as a power struggle, not a moral one. To virtually all blacks, moreover, Malcolm X stood as an implacable symbol of resistance and a champion of liberation.

Malcolm X remained a reproach to all white hypocrites and compromising blacks. His extremism, together with the threats of violence and revolution epitomized by Robert F. Williams and *The Fire Next Time*, provided a sharp cutting edge to the black struggle. They kept the pressure on civil-rights leaders to be bolder, more militant. Simultaneously, their radicalism made the movement's leadership and objectives appear responsible and moderate. And they scared some white leaders into accepting the civil-rights demands as the only effective way to avert potential disaster. The more Malcolm loomed as the alternative that whites would have to confront if CORE, SNCC, and SCLC failed, the more white officials acceded to the stipulations posed by the established leadership of the campaign for racial equality.

The threat of black insurrection, and even of more Birminghams and the intensification of black economic boycotts, especially touched the national corporate community. Businessmen saw no profit in turbulence, and many concluded in mid-1963 that meeting the reasonable aims of the civil-rights movement was the best way to lay to rest the specter of increasing racial violence and disorder. They suddenly became, King wrote, "prepared to tolerate change in order to avoid costly chaos." Corporate leaders began to put pressure on local governments, where they had substantial plants and offices, to negotiate their differences with movement organizers; they also started to endorse and to lobby for the proposed civil-rights bill. On June 19, 1963, nearly a hundred chairmen of corporations and foundations answered the call of the president of the Taconic Foundation to aid the civil-rights movement financially. Meeting at the Hotel Carlyle in Manhattan, they pledged over a million dollars to the five major civil-rights groups. These leaders of finance and industry perhaps assumed that by assisting the established black organizations to secure their goals they could preclude the emergence of radicalism that would fill the vacuum if the movement failed. Whatever their intentions, these funds, and the sizable contributions from other whites and blacks, enabled the black struggle to expand, to reach more potential supporters, and to plan larger, more ambitious campaigns. The national staffs of SCLC and SNCC nearly trebled; scores of new field secretaries were added; the number of CORE chapters jumped from sixty to over a hundred; and NAACP membership increased by a third, to more than half a million.

As King observed: "The sound of the explosion in Birmingham reached all the way to Washington." The profound consequences of that campaign on both blacks and whites forced the President's hand, altering his perception of what needed to be done and what could be done. In response to Birmingham and the rush of spring and summer events that followed, Kennedy traveled in fits and starts toward a commitment to civil rights, and an identification with the movement, that he had previously resisted. Although he never fully reached that destination, he moved nearer to it than any previous American President.

Kennedy began to act decisively on civil rights in the summer of 1963. He did so in part because of his personal sense of morality and in part because of his calculations as party leader and Chief Executive on how to respond to new pressures. He needed to satisfy the millions of Americans, white and black, liberal and moderate, protesting federal inaction and wanting an end to disorder. The President also had to dampen the explosive potential of widespread racial violence and to maintain the confidence of the mass of blacks in government. Additionally, Kennedy considered it necessary to assist Farmer and King and Wilkins in securing their objectives lest the movement be taken over by extremists.

Kennedy's first chance to demonstrate his new intentions came shortly after the Birmingham accord had been reached. On May 21, a federal district judge ordered the University of Alabama to admit two black students to its summer session. Governor George Wallace immediately threatened to defy the court order and to bar the entrance of any black who attempted to desegregate the university. "I draw the line in the dust and toss the gauntlet before the feet of tyranny, and I say, Segregation now! Segregation tomorrow! Segregation forever!" Wallace had announced in his inaugural address, and he now promised his white constituents, "I will not let you down." The nation braced for a repeat of the confrontation at Ole Miss. But Kennedy was determined to keep Tuscaloosa from becoming another Oxford. Unlike his behavior in the events leading to the crisis at the University of Mississippi in 1962, Kennedy in 1963 acted promptly and forcefully, leaving Wallace no doubt as to the President's resolve. The governor capitulated.

Several hours after the first black students at the University of Alabama had registered, just a couple of hours before the assassination of Medgar Evers, Kennedy spoke to the nation on the race issue in a televised address that most of his advisors had counseled him against. He had decided to assert his leadership on what he called "a moral issue . . . as old as the Scriptures and . . . as clear as the American Constitution." It ought to be possible, Kennedy intoned,

> for American students of any color to attend any public institution without having to be backed up by troops. It ought to be possible for American consumers of any color to receive equal service in places of public accommodation, such as hotels and restaurants and theaters and retail stores, without being forced to resort to demonstrations in the street, and it ought to be possible for American citizens of any color to register and to vote in a free election without interference or fear of reprisal. . . . In short, every American ought to have the right to be treated as he would wish to be treated, as one would wish his children to be treated. But this is not the case.

The President reviewed with intense emotion the plight of the American Negro, and asked:

> If an American, because his skin is dark, cannot eat lunch in a restaurant open to the public; if he cannot send his children to the best public school available; if he cannot vote for the public officials who represent him; if, in short, he cannot enjoy the full and free life which all of us want, then who among us would be content to have the color of his skin changed and stand in his place?

Who among us would then be content with the counsels of patience and delay? One hundred years of delay have passed since President Lincoln freed the slaves, yet their heirs, their grandsons, are not fully free. They are not yet freed from the bonds of injustice; they are not yet freed from social and economic oppression. And this nation, for all its hopes and all its boasts, will not be fully free until all its citizens are free.

Then Kennedy warned that "events in Birmingham and elsewhere have so increased the cries for equality that no city or state or legislative body can prudently choose to ignore them. The fires of frustration and discord are burning in every city," and the moral crisis "cannot be met by repressive police action" or "quieted by token moves or talk. It is a time to act in the Congress, in your state and local legislative body, and, above all, in all our daily lives."

A week later, saying that "the time has come for this nation to fulfill its promise," to "make a commitment it has not fully made in this century to the proposition that race has no place in American life or law," Kennedy asked Congress to enact the most comprehensive civil-rights law in history. A far cry from the eviscerated bill he had proposed in February, his June measure included provisions for desegregating public accommodations; granting authority to the Attorney General to initiate school-desegregation suits; establishing a Community Relations Service to prevent racial conflicts; improving the economic status of blacks; and empowering the government to withhold funds from federally supported programs and facilities in which discrimination occurred. Mississippi's Senator James Eastland termed the bill a "complete blueprint for a totalitarian state," but congressional liberals moved quickly to strengthen it further, adding provisions for a permanent Fair Employment Practices Commission and for federal registrars to enroll black voters.

On August 28, over two hundred thousand Americans, black

and white, and from almost every state in the union, converged on the Capitol, chanting: "Pass that bill! Pass that bill! Pass that bill!" Joyously, harmoniously, they marched to signify their belief in equal rights. Gathered in unity before the Lincoln Memorial, the vast, exalted throng cheered the nation's religious and civil-rights leaders' concerted declarations of support for black freedom. They accepted with delight the approval offered by the scores of government officials and dignitaries crowded on the platform behind the speaker's stand. Afterward, the President stated publicly that he had been "impressed with the deep fervor and the quiet dignity" of the marchers, and he lauded the demonstration as one of which "this nation can properly be proud." In the next day's *New York Times*, Russell Baker commented: "The sweetness and patience of the crowd may have set some sort of national highwater mark in mass decency." Few newspapers depicted it any differently. It appeared to be the apogee of the civil-rights movement. But it had not been so conceived, the unanimity was deceptive, and many of those who participated in and praised the march had opposed it when first announced by A. Philip Randolph.

The legendary head of the Brotherhood of Sleeping Car Porters, Randolph had long nurtured a hope for a march on Washington. He had previously broached the idea in 1941 to get President Roosevelt to open defense jobs to blacks and in 1948 to pressure President Truman to desegregate the armed services. In December 1962, he and Bayard Rustin began to plan a march for economic justice for blacks, centered on demands for fair-employment legislation and the passage of an increased minimum wage. Desultorily, CORE, SNCC, and SCLC approved Randolph's February call "for a broad and fundamental program of economic justice" and for a mass pilgrimage to Washington to dramatize the black-unemployment crisis. The NAACP and NUL bowed out. The idea drifted until Birmingham. Then it picked up steam as Rustin oriented it toward civil rights, rather than economic legislation, and Randolph agreed to bill the demonstration as "the March on Washington for Jobs and Freedom."

The President met with the civil-rights leadership on June 22 to dissuade them from encouraging blacks to march on Washington. "We want success in Congress, not just a big show at the Capitol," he stressed. "Some of these people are looking for an excuse to be against us; and I don't want to give any of them a chance to say 'Yes, I'm for the bill, but I am damned if I will vote for it at the point of a gun.'" There had been much loose talk of demonstrations and encampments on the White House lawn and mass sit-ins in the legislative galleries. Kennedy warned that their only effect would be "to create an atmosphere of intimidation—and this may give some members of Congress an out." Vice-President Lyndon B. Johnson added that to get the necessary uncommitted votes "we have to be careful not to do anything which would give those who are privately opposed a public excuse to appear as martyrs." Wilkins and the more moderate black leaders concurred. They, too, worried that a mass demonstration might erupt into violence and discredit the movement. Others were concerned that this attempt to pressure Congress might backfire and stimulate congressional resistance.

Randolph, King, and Farmer stood fast. "The Negroes are already in the streets," Randolph firmly informed the President. "It is very likely impossible to get them off. If they are bound to be in the streets in any case, is it not better that they be led by organizations dedicated to civil rights and disciplined by struggle rather than to leave them to other leaders who care neither about civil rights nor about non-violence?" Sustaining the argument, King stated that it was not a choice of a demonstration or legislation. The march "could serve as a means through which people with legitimate discontents could channel their grievances under disciplined non-violent leadership. It could also serve as a means of dramatizing the issue and mobilizing support in parts of the country which don't know the problems at first hand." "We understand your political problem in getting the legislation through," Farmer added, "and we want to help in that as best we can." Then the head of CORE reinforced the contentions of King and Randolph. "We could be in a difficult if not untenable position if we called the street demonstrations off and then were defeated in the legislative battle. The result would be that frustration would grow into violence and would demand new leadership." The President seemed almost persuaded, but he held off approving the march until he felt secure in its content and logistics. "I have my problems with the Congress," he ended the meeting, "you have yours with your own groups. We will undoubtedly disagree from time to time on tactics. But the important thing is to keep in touch."

The march organizers turned their energies, after the conference, to alleviating the qualms of the President and the moderates in the civil-rights camp who still did not back the proposed demonstration in Washington. They shelved all plans for civil disobedience in favor of staging a mass rally. Instead of laying siege to Capitol Hill, they would parade peacefully from the Washington Monument to the Lincoln Memorial. The economic demands favored by Randolph were further downgraded. By July, Rustin had the active cooperation of the NAACP, NUL, and nearly two hundred religious, labor, and civic organizations. Endorsements poured in. At his July 17 press conference, Kennedy characterized the coming demonstration as being "in the great tradition" of peaceful assembly "for a redress of grievances." "I'll look forward to being here," he added pointedly. His aides worked closely with the march leaders on arrangements. A month later, the President even worried that the march might not be massive enough, that the promised one hundred thousand people might not materialize.

The turnout exceeded all expectations. Nearly a quarter of a million attended the March on Washington to petition for black rights, including at least seventy-five thousand whites. They took heart in their numbers, and in the hundreds of celebrities who joined them. The day became a celebration. The assemblage clasped hands as Joan Baez intoned "We shall overcome," sang along with Peter, Paul and Mary when they asked "How many times must a man look up before he can see the sky?" and hushed to hear Bob Dylan sing a ballad about the death of Medgar Evers. They clapped and cried their accompaniment to "If they ask you who you are, tell them you're a child of God" by Odetta, and Mahalia Jackson's renditions of "I been 'buked and I been scorned." Good-naturedly, they endured the heat and humidity and the seemingly endless introduction of notables and repetition of clichés by speaker after speaker. As the afternoon wore on, some grew listless, and chose to nap, to play with the many children brought by parents, and to wade in the Reflecting Pool between the Washington Monument and the Lincoln Memorial. It did not matter. They had made their point by their presence and demeanor. Then Randolph introduced Martin Luther King, Jr., who had been, as Wilkins put it, "assigned the rousements."

"Five score years ago," King began to the sound of a thunderous ovation, "a great American in whose symbolic shadow we stand, signed the Emancipation Proclamation." The crowd grew quiet as King surveyed the century that had passed since that day, declaiming over and over "One hundred years later . . ." and finding that not much had changed. "So we have come here today to dramatize an appalling condition." He termed the promises of the Declaration of Independence "a sacred obligation" which had proved to be, for blacks, a bad check—"a check which has come back marked 'insufficient funds.'" But, King shouted to the standing tens of thousands who roared their agreement, "we refuse to believe that the bank of justice is bankrupt. We refuse to believe that there are insufficient funds in the great vaults of opportunity of this nation."

Melodiously, King's rich baritone praised the "veterans of

creative suffering" and urged them to continue the struggle. "*Now* is the time to make real the promises of Democracy. *Now* is the time to rise from the dark and desolate valley of segregation to the sunlit path of racial justice. *Now* is the time to open the doors of opportunity to all of God's children. *Now* is the time to lift our nation from the quicksands of racial injustice to the solid rock of brotherhood." He reminded the nation that there "will be neither rest nor tranquility in America until the Negro is granted his citizenship rights," and in rising tones answered those who asked, "When will you be satisfied?"

We can never be satisfied as long as our bodies, heavy with the fatigue of travel, cannot gain lodging in the motels of the highways and the hotels of the cities. We cannot be satisfied as long as the Negro's basic mobility is from a smaller ghetto to a larger one. We can never be satisfied as long as our children are stripped of their selfhood and robbed of their dignity by signs stating: "For Whites Only." We cannot be satisfied as long as the Negro in Mississippi cannot vote and the Negro in New York believes he has nothing for which to vote. No, no, we are not satisfied and we will not be satisfied until justice rolls down like the waters and righteousness like a mighty stream.

He appealed to the multitude: "Go back to Mississippi, go back to Alabama, go back to South Carolina, go back to Georgia, go back to Louisiana, go back to the slums and ghettos of our modern cities, knowing that somehow this situation can and will be changed."

King had a dream, a vision of racial justice and social harmony. Rhythmically, the words describing it rolled over the crowd, becoming more utopian and yet believable as the audience's antiphonal response rose tumultuously.

I have a dream that one day on the red hills of Georgia the sons of former slaves and the sons of former slaveowners will be able to sit down together at the table of brotherhood.

I have a dream that one day even the State of Mississippi, a state sweltering with the heat of injustice, sweltering with the heat of oppression, will be transformed into an oasis of freedom and justice. I have a dream that my four little children will one day live in a nation where they will not be judged by the color of their skin but by the content of their character. I have a dream today.

I have a dream that one day down in Alabama with its vicious racists, with its Governor having his lips dripping with the words of interposition and nullification—one day right there in Alabama, little black boys and black girls will be able to join hands with little white boys and white girls as sisters and brothers.

I have a dream today.

Spines tingled and eyes teared as King ended:

When we let freedom ring, when we let it ring from every village and every hamlet, from every state and every city, we will be able to speed up that day when all God's children, black men and white men, Jews and Gentiles, Protestants and Catholics, will be able to join hands and sing in the words of that old Negro spiritual, "Free at last! Free at last! Thank God almighty, we are free at last!"

In less than fifteen minutes, King had transformed an amiable effort at lobbying Congress into a scintillating historic event. "The thundering events of the summer required an appropriate climax," King later wrote, and he had provided it. His dream, judged by its impact both on those in Washington and on those watching on television, had buoyed the spirit of blacks and touched the hearts of whites. Not all, to be sure. It changed neither votes in Congress nor the minds of those most opposed or indifferent to racial equality. But, for most, King's eloquence and vision offset the ugly images of black violence that the demonstrations had started to evoke, replacing them with an inspiring picture of the movement at its benevolent best. To the extent that any single public utterance could, this speech made the black revolt acceptable to white America. King's dream capped the wave of direct action starting in Birmingham which in 1964 resulted in the passage of the civil-rights act.

Some blacks, however, felt betrayed by King and those responsible for the March on Washington. As most in the crowd cried and cheered when King perorated, one young black shouted furiously: "Fuck that dream, Martin. Now goddamit, NOW!" Others mocked "De Lawd." Malcolm X called the demonstration the "Farce on Washington." "Who ever heard of angry revolutionists swinging their bare feet together with their oppressor in lily-pad park pools, with gospels and guitars and 'I Have a Dream' speeches?" Malcolm asked. James Farmer spent the day in a Louisiana jail, refusing bail. Annoyed at the moderating influence of Kennedy and King, he stayed in his cell to make the point that he did not consider the March on Washington sufficiently militant. SNCC staffers were livid that John Lewis, their chairman, had been forced to soften his words in deference to the demand of some of the white speakers. Lewis had prepared a speech describing the civil-rights bill as too little, too late, denouncing both Republicans and Democrats as frauds, threatening the South with a Sherman-like "scorched earth" march through the heart of Dixie, and demanding of Kennedy: "I want to know—which side is the federal government on?" Those words were laundered from the talk by Lewis, but the angry reactions to the March on Washington and King's leadership, largely hidden from view that serene August afternoon, forecast the divisions and differences that would one day wreck the movement.

Nevertheless, throughout 1963, the black struggle remained outwardly united. An end to segregation appeared at hand, although Congress dawdled. In November the sudden crack of a rifle in Dallas precipitated the overdue legislation. The assassination of the President immediately stirred sympathy for the attainment of the goals Kennedy sought and an abhorrence of violent fringe politics, like those associated with the Klan and other extreme white supremacists. Many considered passage of the civil-rights bill the most fitting memorial to their slain leader.

The House of Representatives acted quickly after the 1964 session began. It considered the measure for eleven days and passed it overwhelmingly. The Senate took nearly three months to debate before voting 73 to 27 for the bill. On July 2, President Lyndon Johnson signed the act which prohibited discrimination in most places of public accommodation, authorized the government to withhold federal funds to public programs practicing discrimination, banned discrimination by employers and unions, created an Equal Employment Opportunity Commission, established a Community Relations Service, and provided technical and financial aid to communities desegregating their schools. The movement barely had time to celebrate. It was in the midst of the Mississippi Freedom Summer and a mighty effort to secure the franchise for blacks, the final item on the established civil-rights agenda.

SIX

How Many Roads

The struggle for black equality reached its crest and rapidly began to recede in the two years following the March on Washington. It swept aside the last vestiges of legal discrimination and segregation and ended black disenfranchisement. But, in the process, all the fissures in the movement became major cleavages. In part a victim of its own success, the movement created aspirations it could not fulfill and developed a new sense of racial pride that verged on being anti-white. Many in the struggle for racial justice became disenchanted with American society, disinclined to compromise, and disdainful of white support, as white racist violence did not abate. "The paths of Negro–white unity that had been converging," Martin Luther King, Jr., would later write, "crossed at Selma and like a giant X began to diverge." The split, however, started in Mississippi, not Alabama. And SNCC, not SCLC, charted the course.

CORE and SNCC staffers returning to the South after the

March on Washington plunged into the work of voter registration, deemphasizing direct action against segregation. Most felt that the massive protests in the spring and summer had forced the nation to confront the anachronism of Jim Crow, and they confidently expected passage of a federal civil-rights act outlawing segregation in public accommodations. The time had come for the next item on the Southern black agenda: enfranchisement. Funds from the Voter Education Project and other sources, possibly even from the Democratic National Committee, they believed, would support such an effort. Moreover, by mid-1963, the more radical Southern field secretaries in CORE and SNCC viewed desegregation as a middle-class affair. They belittled the issue as one remote from, and unresponsive to, the needs of the rural black masses.

These movement workers, following the lead of SNCC's Bob Moses, believed that the ballot box held the key to empowering the dispossessed. They sought to organize the political strength of the black masses as a weapon against both racism and poverty. Time and again they cited the statistics proving the stark nexus between disenfranchisement and indigence. In Mississippi, where only one out of twenty adult blacks could register to vote, the median black-family income was a paltry $1,444, barely one-third that of Mississippi whites. Blacks in Dallas County, Alabama, where one percent were registered to vote, had a median income of $28 a week; in neighboring Lowndes and Wilcox counties, where Afro-Americans constituted nearly 80 percent of the population and eked out a median income of $20 a week, not a single black had been registered to vote. To assist the poorest black sharecroppers and tenants, still largely untouched by the civil-rights movement, CORE concentrated its voter registration effort in Florida, Louisiana, and South Carolina; SNCC operated in Alabama and, especially, Mississippi.

"The Closed Society," Professor James Silver pictured Mississippi to the Southern Historical Society in 1963; the state's problems dramatically appealed to the temperament and philosophy of Bob Moses. The poorest, most backward and illiterate state in the nation, as well as the stoutest bastion of discrimination and segregation, Mississippi remained impervious to the black struggle for equality. "Every datum of economics and every fact and twist of history," stated the Southern Regional Council, "have conspired to keep its white people deeply and ofttimes harshly resistant to change and its Negro people ill-equipped for it." To Moses, the clear and compelling necessity for reform, both economic and racial, was matched by the potential for black political power, for Mississippi's 916,000 blacks totaled 42 percent of the state population and a majority in more than a third of its counties. A massive effort to register blacks to vote, moreover, would surely trigger a violent white reaction, and that, Moses reasoned, might force the national government to act to protect the lives of civil-rights workers and to enforce the voting rights of blacks.

The very enormity of the challenge appealed to Moses. No other battle on the civil-rights front posed greater risks than voter registration in Mississippi. No other campaign required such commitment and courage. An exemplification of bravery and sacrifice meant more to the existentialist Moses than the achievement of concrete political gains.

Following the withdrawal of the VEP from Mississippi in the fall of 1963, Moses redoubled his efforts to make voter registration in the Magnolia State the focus of the movement. He revitalized the Council of Federated Organizations, a statewide composite of racial-advancement groups which had been established in 1961 to secure the release of jailed Freedom Riders, and became its program director; he chose David Dennis of CORE as his assistant, and persuaded Aaron Henry, the respected Clarksville druggist and head of the state NAACP, to serve as its president. COFO and SNCC became indistinguishable; the NAACP and SCLC participated only nominally and CORE confined its energies to one of the state's five congressional districts. The preponderance of funds and workers for

COFO came from SNCC. Shortly before the regular November elections in 1963, Moses improvised a Freedom Election to prove that blacks wanted to vote. On the same day that Mississippi whites went to the polls, nearly eighty thousand disenfranchised blacks cast freedom ballots for Henry for governor and for the Reverend Edwin King, the white chaplain of Tougaloo College, for lieutenant governor.

Moses considered the Freedom Vote Campaign of 1963 a stunning success. It disproved the white assertion that Mississippi blacks did not vote because of apathy. It also provided the psychological reinforcement that Moses thought necessary for organizing blacks politically. Black morale had been boosted as a result of actually participating in a political process, even one not legally recognized. He looked forward to additional black political involvement that would inspire black self-confidence. Furthermore, Moses grasped the potential of using white volunteers in a massive voter-registration campaign. About a hundred white college students, largely from Stanford and Yale, had taken two weeks off from school to assist in the Freedom Election. This had brought both national attention to the campaign and increased FBI protection for registration workers. Moses's thoughts raced ahead to a full-scale summer project to register Mississippi blacks, aided by thousands of white students.

A week after the Freedom Election, COFO met in Greenville to consider the question: "Where do we go from here?" In Moses's absence, Dennis presented the idea for a Freedom Summer in 1964. The forty SNCC and five CORE representatives present immediately began considering the role of whites in the movement. Charles Cobb of SNCC stated that the invitation to whites to join in massive numbers indicated an admission of weakness by blacks, a concession that blacks could not deal with the situation. Many seconded his contention, grumbling about how the whites participating in the Freedom Election had rushed into leadership positions, elbowing aside blacks less skilled in typing, writing press releases, handling budgets, coordinating different schedules and just about everything else necessary in a large-scale organization. Others complained that the white volunteers unwittingly perpetuated the stereotype of black inferiority and reinforced the notion of white paternalism. Still others asserted that Southern blacks had to develop their own leaders, and condemned the white students for rushing unprepared into the state, hogging the publicity, and then quickly going home, leaving Mississippi blacks to face reprisals alone. Almost all agreed that blacks ought to control the struggle for their own freedom. Decisively, they voted down the proposal.

Moses returned the next day. "Look, I'm not gonna be a part of anything all-black," he told the meeting. "We're gonna have the Summer Project. We need it. We need it for these reasons," and he enumerated the psychological and tangible goals a Freedom Summer could achieve. Moses then stressed the federal protection whites would bring; he emphasized the national attention that would follow a thousand white college students attempting to register Mississippi blacks. Everyone understood that the country would respond because young white men and women were involved, rather than just black organizers. Moreover, everyone knew the risks involved in bringing Northern whites into Mississippi, the potential for violence, even murder. And silently they calculated how the death of a white student would benefit the movement. "That's cold," Dennis recalled, "but that was also in another sense speaking the language of this country. What we were trying to do was get a message over to the country, so we spoke their language. . . . We didn't plan any of the violence. But we just wanted the country to respond to what was going on."

Gradually, the SNCC staffers reached a consensus reaffirming their traditional view of the irrelevancy of skin pigmentation. They agreed with Mrs. Fannie Lou Hamer's perspective—"If we're trying to break down segregation, we can't segregate ourselves"—and with Moses' notion that it is not a matter of

"Negro fighting white, it's a question of rational people against irrational people." Not everyone was reconciled. Some remained adamant that the struggle should be led and waged by blacks. "I always thought," Moses quietly rejoined, "that the one thing we can do for the country that no one else can do is to be above the race issue." The COFO assemblage resoundingly approved the plan for a Mississippi Freedom Summer.

While the COFO staff planned the logistics of the summer project, Mississippi whites prepared for what the Jackson *Daily News* characterized as an "invasion." The state legislature and most municipalities enacted scores of ordinances to harass and hamper the movement. The State Highway Patrol was expanded from 275 to 475 men. The city of Jackson doubled the size of its police force. For the first time in the modern era, a Mississippi KKK was organized, as were several other similar groups with names like "Americans for the Preservation of the White Race." As summer approached, white violence rose throughout Mississippi. Bombs exploded outside the headquarters of COFO, CORE, and SNCC. Fire destroyed at least a half a dozen black churches connected with the project. Unprovoked killings of blacks and unpunished crimes against blacks multiplied. And not a single summer volunteer had entered the state.

On June 15, the first three hundred of the more than eight hundred volunteers for the Mississippi Summer Project assembled at the Western College for Women in Oxford, Ohio. After they had learned some new freedom songs, Bob Moses began quietly: "When Mrs. Hamer sang, 'If you miss me from the freedom fight, You can't find me nowhere, Come on over to the graveyard, I'll be buried over there . . .' that's true." He dwelled on the dangers they faced and the lack of federal protection they could expect. "The guerilla war in Mississippi is not much different from that in Vietnam," Moses stated. "But when we tried to see President Johnson, his secretary said that Vietnam was popping up all over his calendar and he hadn't time to talk to us." He paused. "Our goals are limited. If we can go and come back alive, then that is something." Almost whispering, Moses concluded: "Mississippi has been called 'The Closed Society.' It is closed, locked. We think the key is in the vote. Any change, any possibility for dissidence and opposition, depends first on a political breakthrough." There followed six days of intensive instruction on the intricacies of voter registration. The volunteers learned how to organize community centers, instilling political awareness while teaching the 3 Rs, and how to protect themselves nonviolently if they were beaten. Then in cars and buses they headed for Mississippi, singing:

> *They say that freedom is a constant struggle.*
> *They say that freedom is a constant struggle.*
> *They say that freedom is a constant struggle,*
> *Oh, Lord, we've struggled so long,*
> *We must be free, we must be free.*

The next day, several hundred more volunteers arrived in Oxford. But as Moses began his opening address a SNCC staffer interrupted him, whispering. Moses turned to the hundreds of whites: "Yesterday morning, three of our people left Meridian, Mississippi, to investigate a church-burning in Neshoba County. They haven't come back, and we haven't had any word from them." As best they could, COFO workers carried on the week-long classes to prepare the college students for the Mississippi Summer Project. But everybody's mind was on the three missing freedom fighters. Suddenly everyone learned that the car the three had been driving in had been found badly burned just outside Philadelphia, Mississippi. Fear enveloped the group. Moses said: "The kids are dead." Officially, the three were missing, but no one disputed Moses. Only a handful went home. Expecting the worst, the rest left for Mississippi.

By then, President Johnson had ordered a massive search for

the three civil-rights workers and an exhaustive FBI investigation of their disappearance. Secretly, the President also commanded the Bureau to protect the Mississippi Freedom Summer volunteers. It did James Chaney, Andrew Goodman, and Michael Schwerner no good. Six weeks after the search began, FBI agents uncovered their bodies in a newly constructed earthen dam five miles southwest of Philadelphia. Goodman and Schwerner had each been killed by a single bullet. Chaney, the sole black, had been brutally beaten with a chain, shot once in the head and twice in the body. In December the FBI, having infiltrated the Mississippi Klan in the previous few months to obtain the evidence, arrested twenty-one men, including the sheriff and deputy sheriff of Neshoba County. Then the nation learned the details of the murders plotted by the KKK.

Michael Schwerner and his wife, Rita, deeply affected by the Birmingham demonstrations, had joined CORE in June 1963 and left New York City in January 1964 to run COFO's community center in Meridian. There the young white couple worked closely with a local high-school dropout and black CORE fieldworker, twenty-one-year-old James Chaney. For five months Rita taught reading, sewing, and citizenship to Meridian blacks, while Chaney and her social-worker husband canvased the surrounding rural areas to prepare for a voter-registration campaign. In mid-June the three went to Oxford, Ohio, to serve as instructors in the training school for volunteers. When Michael was informed that a black church in Neshoba County, planned for use as a Freedom School, had been burned to the ground and that several of their supporters had been beaten, he decided to return to Mississippi to investigate and bolster the morale of Neshoba's blacks. Chaney insisted on accompanying him, and they asked twenty-one-year-old Andrew Goodman, assigned to work in Neshoba County, if he cared to join them. Goodman, a Summer Project volunteer and a junior at Queens College in New York, readily agreed. All three thought the long drive from Oxford to Meridian would give them ample opportunity to discuss the details of the summer activities.

Early Saturday, June 20, they said goodbye to Rita and headed south. They paused in Meridian on Sunday morning just long enough for Chaney to inspect carefully the CORE station wagon and for Schwerner to remind a volunteer working in the COFO office: "There's an immutable rule here—no one is to remain in Neshoba after 4 p.m. If for any reason we aren't back by 4 p.m., you should alert Jackson and begin checking every city jail, county jail, sheriff's office, police station, and hospital between Meridian and Neshoba. O.K.?"

The three civil-rights workers made the fifty-mile drive to the Mt. Zion Methodist Church, passed through the county seat, Philadelphia, did what they could to check the destroyed building and to reassure the local blacks that the Summer Project would continue, and then started their return trip to Meridian. The Philadelphia Klan was ready for them. Just outside town, Deputy Sheriff Cecil Price apprehended Chaney, Goodman, and Schwerner on a fictitious charge of speeding and jailed them in Philadelphia. The KKK waited until dark. Then the deputy took the three young men to a deserted road where three cars filled with Klansmen awaited them. According to William Bradford Huie, an investigative reporter who learned the details of the murders from a paid informant, later confirmed by testimony at the federal court trials of the killers, the Klan jeered at the three as they were pulled out of their car. "Several of the murderers chanted in unison, as though they had practiced it:

"Ashes to ashes, Dust to dust, if you'd stayed where you belonged, You wouldn't be here with us."

Another said: "So you wanted to come to Mississippi? Well, now we're gonna let you stay here. We're not even gonna run you out. We're gonna let you stay here with us."

When Schwerner was pulled from the car and stood up to be shot, I was told that the man with the pistol asked him:

"You still think a nigger's as good as I am?" No time was allowed for a reply. He was shot straight through the heart and fell to the ground.

The Klansmen killed Goodman the same way, and then beat Chaney, because he struggled to escape, before shooting him three times. Their bodies were buried by a bulldozer and their car burned. The next day, as concern for the missing men began to grow, Sheriff Lawrence Rainey told reporters he saw no cause for alarm: "If they're missing, they just hid somewhere, trying to get a lot of publicity."

The COFO staff and volunteers never believed Rainey and they labored throughout the summer under a pall of fear and suspicion that widened every cleavage between whites and blacks in the movement, and at the same time radicalized both groups. No one would dispute the truth of Rita Schwerner's statement: "We all know that this search with hundreds of sailors is because Andrew Goodman and my husband are white. If only Chaney was involved, nothing would've been done." It intensified the guilt and estrangement of most white volunteers. It traumatized COFO blacks, killing the idealism that had still been predominant in SNCC at the start of 1964, and making overt all the tendencies previously latent: lack of faith in nonviolence as a tactic, much less as a way of life or moral principle; distrust of all government institutions; and antagonism toward white liberals.

Although President Johnson made much of the vastly increased FBI presence in Mississippi, its failure to apprehend the killers during the summer or even to offer much protection to the Mississippi Summer Project workers deeply angered both blacks and whites. While the President talked of extending the federal authority in the state, white terrorists bombed another thirty homes, burned thirty-five more churches, assaulted at least eighty COFO partisans, and shot at some thirty civil-rights workers. On the flimsiest of pretexts, local law-enforcement officers made some one thousand arrests to hinder the movement. All the while, COFO officials kept asking: "How come the government tries to protect the South Vietnamese from the Vietcong and tells us that it will not accept the moral responsibility of protecting the black people in Mississippi?"

Johnson would not respond. But his special emissary to Mississippi, Allen Dulles, former director of the CIA, met with the COFO leadership and told them: "Look, I'm going to meet with the governor in an hour and we want this mess cleaned up." Aaron Henry said, "What do you mean?" and Dulles replied: "Well, these civil-rights demonstrations are causing this kind of friction, and we're just not gonna have it, even if we have to bring troops in here." Worse, the President's head of the FBI traveled to Jackson to decry what he called an "overemphasis" on civil rights. J. Edgar Hoover declared that his Bureau "most certainly" would *not* give special protection to the summer volunteers. Such words, and the FBI's patent lack of success in solving the murders or ending white terrorism, caused the white students to return to their colleges with little faith in liberalism or the governmental system. SNCC's skepticism about American justice and the political process became institutionalized.

By the middle of the summer, most SNCC workers in Mississippi carried a gun. All the despair, frustration, and rage that had been slowly building because they had been victimized too often, too brutally, with too little to show for it, burst when the FBI uncovered the bodies of Chaney, Schwerner, and Goodman. SNCC and CORE would be sacrificial lambs no longer. "I'm sick and tired of going to the funerals of black men who have been murdered by white men," David Dennis cried out for all of them as he delivered a eulogy at Chaney's funeral. "I'm not going to stand here and ask anyone not to be angry, not to be bitter tonight. We've defended our country. To do what? To live like slaves?" His voice rose: "I've got vengeance in my heart tonight." Sobbing and shouting, Dennis continued: "Don't just look at me and go back and tell folks you've been to a nice service. Your work is just beginning. And I'm going to tell you deep down in my heart what I feel right now. If you go back home and sit down and take what these white men in Mississippi are doing to us . . . if you take it and don't do something about it . . . then God damn your souls!" Tears streaming from his face, he stopped suddenly. Never again would Dennis speak of nonviolence. Nor would most COFO staffers. At the end of the year, SNCC would be officially defending the right of its field secretaries to wield weapons and CORE in Louisiana would openly accept the armed protection of the black vigilante Deacons for Defense and Justice.

The shock of the murders accentuated the bitterness corroding relations between blacks and whites in the movement. The concerns that had come up at the Greenville meeting regarding white volunteers flared into the open as many of the battle-weary volunteers cracked under the strain. Bitterly resenting the fact that the whites could, and would, go back to pleasant suburban homes, and prestigious colleges, and affluent careers, while blacks left alone would have to struggle on, many in COFO ridiculed the white students as "fly-by-night freedom fighters" and relished assigning them the most menial tasks. Angered that the nation paid attention only when whites were killed, or jailed, or beaten, blacks blamed the volunteers for unleashing the terror in Mississippi.

Bewildered and hurt, few white students could stand back from their feelings and understand the black rage. They judged harshly, or not at all. Many of the whites particularly recoiled from the heavy use of alcohol and marijuana by movement personnel seeking refuge from the strain of struggling amidst pervasive hatred. These whites could not fathom the depth of fear experienced by the SNCC staffers nor comprehend the black cultural forms of escape. They were particularly bothered by the rumors that SNCC males forced white women volunteers to have sex with them to prove they were not prejudiced. Black women in the movement, concurrently, grew furious with the female students after hearing the same tales.

Despite the development of these hostilities, the Mississippi Summer Project persisted. It succeeded in establishing and operating nearly fifty Freedom Schools throughout the state and about the same number of community centers. The volunteers taught blacks to articulate their needs and discontents, and aided in the creation of bases for further political power. They encouraged the emergence of new local leaders and helped Mississippi blacks understand their society and the mechanisms of change. Their very presence inspired blacks in the state, boosting morale. And the deaths of Chaney, Schwerner, and Goodman led to a feeling that if young people could risk so much to struggle for them, then the least they could do was fight for themselves. Additionally, the Summer Project riveted the attention of the nation on Mississippi racism as nothing before had. The almost one thousand white volunteers who had given up their summers to assist the movement, many of them sons and daughters of prominent politicians, lawyers, and community leaders, insured the Mississippi Freedom Summer constant and favorable front-page coverage. Assisted by the flagrant brutality of white racists, the project fostered a national consensus declaring the racial situation in Mississippi intolerable and in need of immediate change. For all its exertions, however, COFO managed to add only twelve hundred blacks to the registration rolls.

Unable to register blacks, and kept by the regular Mississippi Democratic Party from participating in the precinct, county, and state conventions, COFO set up a new party open to all. It enrolled nearly sixty thousand disenfranchised blacks in the Mississippi Freedom Democratic Party. Following the rules prescribed by the Democratic National Committee, the MFDP elected forty-four delegates and twenty-two alternates to attend the national convention in Atlantic City. Pointedly, the

MFDP pledged itself to support the Democratic Party's nominees and platform, which the lily-white regulars refused to do. The insurgents planned to contest the seats traditionally held by white Mississippians, on the grounds that the MFDP representatives belonged to the only freely chosen party in the state, blacks being systematically denied access to the delegate-selection process of the Mississippi Democratic Party, and that the regulars had disloyally endorsed Republican and Dixiecrat candidates in the past and would not presently commit themselves to back the principles and nominees of the national party.

Initially, COFO conceived its challenge to the white Mississippi delegation as a means of dramatizing the illegal exclusion of blacks from the political process. But it stirred an unexpectedly widespread sympathetic response. Joseph Rauh, the noted liberal attorney and close associate of Hubert Humphrey and Walter Reuther, prepared the MFDP's case against the seating of the Mississippi regulars, and resolutions of support for the Freedom Democrats poured in from Northern state delegations. Many of the Democratic Party's liberal luminaries promised aid. The dramatic events of the Mississippi Freedom Summer had clearly produced a groundswell for championing the MFDP's cause. By the time the Democratic National Convention opened on August 24, the MFDP believed it would triumph.

"I have only an hour," began Joseph Rauh to the nationally televised hearings of the Credentials Committee, "to tell you a story of moral agony that could take years." He emphasized how the constitutional rights of Mississippi blacks had been trampled on. He stressed the violence and intimidation employed to keep blacks from registering. "Are you going to throw out of here the people who want to work for Lyndon Johnson, who are willing to be beaten and shot and thrown in jail to work for Lyndon Johnson?" Rauh asked. "Are we for the oppressor or the oppressed?" Then Rauh called a stream of witnesses to Mississippi barbarity: Rita Schwerner, James Farmer, Roy Wilkins, Aaron Henry. The Reverend Edwin King recounted the consequences of his voter-registration activities: "I have been imprisoned, I have been beaten, I have been close to death. The Freedom party is an open party. They"—pointing to the spokesmen for the regulars—"are a closed party of a closed society." Martin Luther King, Jr., dwelled on the anguish and suffering of Mississippi blacks wanting to vote, and pleaded: "If you value your party, if you value your nation, if you value the democratic process, you must recognize the Freedom party delegation."

More than anyone else, the heroic, unlettered Fannie Lou Hamer made the seating of the MFDP *the* issue of the convention. Her account of the "woesome times" that followed her effort to register to vote in the home county of Senator James Eastland stunned the listening delegates and the nation. In simple rhythmic words evoking all the pain of the blues, Hamer described how her attempt to exercise the most elementary right of citizenship caused her to be thrown off the plantation she had labored on for eighteen years, to be shot at, and to be beaten until her skin turned blue and she could no longer walk. "Is this America, the land of the free and the home of the brave," Mrs. Hamer ended the retelling of her travail, "where we are threatened daily because we want to live as decent human beings?"

Hamer's words haunted the delegates, but Lyndon Baines Johnson's authority compelled them. The President wanted nothing to interefere with "his" convention in Atlantic City or *his* plans for a stunning triumph in November. There would be no divisive floor fight over the MFDP. Johnson insisted on a compromise solution acceptable to a majority of Southern delegates. In just six months he had given blacks and liberals a civil-rights act, an urban mass-transit and a food-stamp program, new education and health legislation, and an Office of Economic Opportunity to wage war on poverty. Now the President de-

manded that the blacks and liberals show their gratitude. Moreover, Johnson mused: Where else could they go? Certainly not
to the GOP, which had nominated Barry Goldwater in a blatant
turn to the far right. Johnson believed he had the blacks and
"conscience liberals" securely in his corner. It made sense now
to solidify his support among Southern white and working-class
Democrats.

The President particularly wanted to head off a bolt of the
South to the Republican Party, and that meant averting a Dixie
walkout from the convention over the MFDP issue. "If you
seat those black buggers," his friend John Connally, Governor
of Texas, told him, "the whole South will walk out." Five Southern delegations had already promised to leave Atlantic City if
the convention seated the Freedom Democrats. Johnson knew
he would not stand a chance in the South in November if he
was pictured as throwing the region's white politicians out of
the party. He also knew, looking beyond November, that he
needed the cooperation of the powerful Southern committee
chairmen in Congress to enact the social and economic reform
bills of his Great Society. Johnson, moreover, feared not just a
Southern defection. George Wallace had proved the potency of
the "white backlash" in the spring, garnering 34 percent of the
Democratic primary vote in Wisconsin, 30 percent in Indiana,
and 43 percent in Maryland. The President did not want to lose
working-class Democrats to Goldwater, and that necessitated
that he not appear to capitulate to black militancy.

Johnson got his way. He called in Hubert Humphrey, dangled
the Vice-Presidential nomination before him, and made the
leading advocate of civil rights in the Senate his salesman for a
compromise solution to the MFDP challenge. Northern liberals,
very much wanting Humphrey as the number-two man on the
ticket, did not dare buck the President. They fell quickly in line.
And they applied intense pressure on the established civil-rights
leadership to accept the compromise Johnson proffered.
Humphrey and his emissaries, moreover, pushed the black

spokesmen hard to disassociate themselves from the SNCC staffers who threatened disruptive direct action if the convention failed to seat the Freedom Democrats. Above all, L.B.J. did not want a bruising floor battle over credentials to shatter the image of Democratic consensus being broadcast nationwide.

For three days, Farmer, King, Rustin, and Wilkins wrestled with the conflict of politics and principles. They bargained with Rauh, Reuther, and Humphrey's floor leader, Walter Mondale; they beseeched the MFDP delegates; and they wrangled among themselves. But Johnson ordained the outcome, and the civil-rights leadership relented. The black strategists believed they had no other choice, since they now wanted to move from protest to politics—to make, said Rustin, "real gains and not only bear witness to injustice." What they desired for black advancement had to come from the federal government, and they risked losing all they had struggled for if they now rejected an alliance with a powerful President and a majority coalition. Nor could they easily spurn all the liberal, labor, and religious groups, which provided the bulk of funds for the movement, who now demanded a compromise. Virtually every ally insisted that the blacks accept Johnson's offer: "It's not what any of us wanted, but it's the best we could get." To do anything else would be futile and result not in the seating of the MFDP but in the isolation of the movement and the strengthening of its opposition. Forsaking morality for political expediency, Farmer and King reluctantly agreed with Rustin and Wilkins to lobby for a resolution providing for the seating of two of the Freedom Party leaders as delegates at large with full right to vote, the seating of no Mississippi regular delegate unless he pledged allegiance to the ticket, and the refusal at all future conventions to seat delegations from states which disenfranchised blacks.

The civil-rights leaders had gained far more than Johnson's initial proposal to admit the MFDP to the convention as "honored guests," but not enough to satisfy SNCC. Although Edwin King and Aaron Henry seemed ready to accept the agreement as a symbolic victory legitimating the MFDP's basic claims, and as the start of the real inclusion of blacks in the nominating process, the young black veterans of COFO derisively labeled the compromise a "back-of-the-bus" agreement. Fiercely idealistic, they argued that the MFDP must never place politics over principles and that to compromise now meant conciliating the forces responsible for the murder of their colleagues. Angry at the betrayal of their supposed friends and allies, SNCC lashed out that "this token offer of recognition was too much like the usual bone thrown to Negroes who showed signs of revolt." Mrs. Hamer agreed, describing the proposal as "a token of rights on the back row that we get in Mississippi. We didn't come all this way for that mess again." Most of the Freedom Democrats seconded her, adding that they had not come to Atlantic City "begging for crumbs." The MFDP's bond with SNCC stunned the established civil-rights and liberal leadership. James Farmer began to hedge, reflecting the deeper ambivalence of most of those in the movement. He spoke for and against the compromise, calling rejection of it "morally right but politically wrong."

The MFDP voted down the compromise decisively. "We must stop playing the game," it declared, "of accepting token recognition for real change and of allowing the opposition to choose a few leaders to represent the people at large." The Freedom Democrats bitterly resented the brazen paternalism of the Credentials Committee choosing who the MFDP at-large delegates would be. "That is the way things have been done in Mississippi for a long time," the MFDP added. Even more, the "sell-out" by their "false friends" disillusioned the COFO veterans. The liberal politicians who had promised total support to SNCC betrayed them to protect their own jobs and programs. It proved to SNCC and CORE's Southern organizers that white liberals could not be counted on, that they would compromise black needs whenever it suited them, and that real change would come only when blacks possessed the independent power to "remain a threat to the power structure."

The President's manipulative attempt to force the MFDP to endorse the compromise, moreover, completed SNCC's alienation from the mainstream of the movement and its estrangement from the federal government and the Democratic Party. It viewed Johnson as racist as Goldwater, and it mistrusted Martin Luther King, Jr., as much as it did the President. The treatment of the Freedom Democrats snapped the frayed ties that bound SNCC to liberal values, to integration and nonviolence, and to seeking solutions through the political process. The time had come for SNCC to formulate new goals and methods. To its battered and bloodied field troops, the American dilemma had become irreconcilable and the American dream a nightmare. "Things could never be the same," SNCC's Cleveland Sellers wrote later. "Never again were we lulled into believing that our task was exposing injustices so that the 'good' people of America could eliminate them. We left Atlantic City with the knowledge that the movement had turned into something else. After Atlantic City, our struggle was not for civil rights, but for liberation."

SNCC returned to the South demoralized as well as disillusioned. SNCC's leadership of the MFDP's rejection of the compromise and sit-in at the convention gained little more than embarrassment for the movement. Most Americans followed the President in seeing SNCC as inexplicably extremist, as both unamenable to reasonable compromise and ungrateful for real concessions. Malcolm X praised the Southern black radicals, adding: "We *need* a Mau Mau. If they don't want to deal with the Mississippi Freedom Democratic Party, then we'll give them something else to deal with." But the preponderance of black leadership tried to explain and excuse SNCC's behavior as a consequence of battle fatigue. Exhausted from overwork and tension, filled with pain and disappointment, SNCC expressed its rage rather than political acumen. Rustin noted: "They had nothing but death and destruction and fear all around them and to come up to Atlantic City and take any other position I think was psychologically impossible." But still wrong, Rustin insisted: the time had come for the movement to think politically.

The election results in November buoyed the spirit of all those who shared Rustin's faith in a coalition of labor, liberals, and blacks. The six million blacks who voted in 1964, two million more than in 1960, went 94 percent for L.B.J., who won an astounding 61 percent of the popular vote and carried every state but Goldwater's Arizona and the five Deep South states of Alabama, Georgia, Louisiana, Mississippi, and South Carolina, where fewer than 45 percent of the eligible blacks could vote. Where southern blacks did freely participate in the election, their ballots gave Johnson the margin of victory. Without the black vote, the Democrats would have lost Arkansas, Florida, Tennessee, and Virginia. Blacks hoped the message was clear: voter registration in the Deep South would benefit the Democrats. And the Democrats could now do something about it, for the 1964 election shattered the Republican–Dixiecrat coalition in Congress. The Democrats controlled the Senate 68 to 32 and the House 295 to 140. Racial justice no longer seemed utopian.

"Hurry, boys, hurry," the President implored his aides to draft the Great Society bills he wanted enacted. "Get that legislation up to the Hill and out. Eighteen months from now, Ol' Landslide Lyndon will be Lame-Duck Lyndon." But voting rights was not on Johnson's agenda. He feared the adverse effect of the "white backlash" on his socio-economic plans and he remained piqued at the civil-rights movement for the MFDP antics at the convention. The President particularly distrusted Martin Luther King, Jr. Jealous of his stature as *Time*'s 1964 Man of the Year and as winner of the Nobel Peace Prize, Johnson did nothing to stop an FBI vendetta against King. He remained silent when Hoover denounced King on November 18, 1964, as "the most notorious liar in the country," and when the FBI head implied a week later that SCLC was "spearheaded by Communists and moral degenerates." Nor did Johnson move to halt the Bureau's trying to blackmail King into inaction on the civil-rights front. Indeed, L.B.J. supposedly relished playing the tapes supplied by the FBI which recorded King's amorous adventures in bugged hotel rooms. Hoover hoped to use them to "completely discredit the effectiveness of Martin Luther King, Jr., as a Negro leader." Johnson certainly did not want to do anything that would enhance King's reputation. The Justice Department, moreover, advised the President that voting-rights legislation was unnecessary, and his closest aides counseled him not to submit any civil-rights bills in 1965.

Once again, King and the SCLC staff plotted a strategy to force the federal government to act on behalf of blacks. In late 1964, they set as their goal a strong voting-rights law. They had changed and learned much on the long road from Montgomery to Albany to Birmingham to St. Augustine. Unlike the CORE and SNCC cadres who no longer even paid lip-service to non-violence, the years of anguish and chagrin transformed SCLC's commitment to nonviolence from *satyagraha,* peaceful persuasion to change the hearts and minds of their oppressors, to *duragraha,* tactical nonviolence as an effective means to coerce a demanded end. Birmingham had convinced them that white savagery against unresisting civil-rights protesters could provoke the national response necessary to move the Administration and Congress. King outlined the desired scenario for Project Alabama: (1) "nonviolent demonstrators go into the streets to exercise their constitutional rights"; (2) "racists resist by unleashing violence against them"; (3) "Americans of conscience in the name of decency demand federal intervention and legislation"; and (4) "the Administration, under mass pressure, initiates measures of immediate intervention and remedial legislation." Success required Southern racists to act their brutal worst to arouse national indignation, so King and his aides carefully chose Selma as the focal point of their campaign to have the federal government end all barriers to black voting.

Birthplace of the Alabama Citizens' Council, Selma epitomized the difficulty of black voting throughout the Deep South. As King wrote in *The New York Times*: "Selma has succeeded in limiting Negro registration to the snail's pace of about 145 persons a year. At this rate, it would take 103 years to register the 15,000 eligible Negro voters of Dallas County." Selma, moreover, was already infamous within the movement for the vicious and violent treatment of civil-rights workers by its county sheriff, James G. Clark. His behavior toward SNCC's voter-registration efforts in Selma since early 1963 convinced King that his adversary would be another "Bull" Connor, that Clark's actions would provide the notoriety and martyrdom necessary for the national attention and support that would result in voting-rights legislation. SCLC staffers arriving in Selma were neither surprised nor disappointed when they encountered Sheriff Jim Clark wearing a huge button on his shirt containing one word: "Never!"

"We will dramatize the situation to arouse the federal government by marching by the thousands to the places of registration," King announced in Selma on January 2, 1965, just weeks after accepting the Nobel Peace Prize in Oslo. "We are not asking," he warned, "we are demanding the ballot." As in Birmingham, SCLC started slowly. In daily marches to the Dallas County Courthouse, King led dozens, then scores, and finally hundreds of blacks to attempt to get their names on the voter lists. By the end of the month, over two thousand blacks had been arrested. The media had made Selma a focus of national concern. But Sheriff Clark had controlled his temper, denying SCLC the confrontation it wanted and forestalling a sense of national outrage.

To try to provoke Clark, King led a giant demonstration on February 1, getting himself arrested along with 770 other protesters, many of them schoolchildren. The following day, Clark imprisoned some 520 blacks for parading without a permit, and on February 3 he arrested another 300 students. Throughout the month, marches and demonstrations persisted. As the number of the arrested grew, Clark became more high-handed and brutal; yet he contained himself enough to frustrate SCLC's calculated strategy of confrontation. SCLC failed to arouse the national indignation it needed to pressure the federal government, despite the severe beating of Reverend James Bevel, King's main strategist in Selma, and the killing of Jimmie Lee Jackson, a young black, in a voter demonstration in nearby Marion.

Checkmated, King on March 6 called upon blacks to march from Selma to Montgomery to present a petition of grievances to the governor. "I can't promise you that it won't get you beaten," King intoned at Selma's Brown Chapel. "I can't promise you that it won't get your house bombed. I can't promise you won't get scarred up a bit. But we must stand up for what is right." Governor Wallace responded: "Such a march cannot and will not be tolerated," and he issued an order proscribing the demonstration. Surprisingly, King and Abernathy left for Atlanta and cancelled the march, claiming that they had to minister to their congregations. In all probability, King neither thought it wise to be jailed at this critical juncture in the campaign nor desired to antagonize Lyndon Johnson, who made it clear that he did not want King to lead the march. The next day, however, Hosea Williams, director of the SCLC field staff, gave in to pressure from SNCC militants and aggressive Selma blacks and led five hundred chanting protesters out of Brown Chapel and toward U.S. Highway 80, the route to Montgomery.

As the television cameras whirred, and scores of newsmen looked on, the long column of freedom-singing blacks approached the Edmund Pettus Bridge, the gateway out of Selma. About a hundred of Sheriff Clark's deputized possemen lined both sides of the bridge, and another hundred state troopers, commanded by Major John Cloud, barred the opposite end.

Twice Hosea Williams sought to speak to Cloud. "There is no word to be had," the major responded. "You have two minutes to turn around and go back to your church." Williams began to confer with his aides and Cloud suddenly ordered: "Troopers forward!" As the state forces surged toward the blacks, Clark's vigilantes attacked from the sides. Totally unprepared, the marchers panicked and ran, fleeing the tear gas, the charging horsemen, the flailing nightsticks and chains and electric cattle prods. The troopers and deputies rioted, savagely attacking women and children, old and young, protesters and bystanders.

The nation saw it all and responded as never before in the history of the black struggle. The pictures on television and in newspapers of irrational white violence and of black helplessness and fright stimulated an uproar of indignation. The White House was besieged by labor unions and state legislatures with demands for federal intervention. Some four hundred rabbis, pastors, and nuns rushed to Selma, and at least ten times that number of clergymen converged on Washington to press Congress for voting-rights legislation and to denounce the President for his "unbelievable lack of action" in the crisis. Fourteen students insisting that the President send troops to Selma staged a seven-hour sit-in at the White House, while another three hundred students sat-in in the snow to support their call. Tens of thousands, white and black, showed their solidarity with the disenfranchised Alabamians by joining Selma sympathy marches in cities across the country.

Overwhelmed by the response, King promised in Atlanta to lead a second march on Tuesday, March 9, and to seek a federal injunction to prevent Governor Wallace and Alabama police authorities from interfering with the march. Monday morning, Judge Frank M. Johnson, Jr., heard the SCLC and Justice Department attorneys' request for an order to guarantee the safety of the marches and to void the governor's ban. Pending further hearings, however, Judge Johnson enjoined the SCLC from undertaking the march. King had never before defied a federal court order, but returning to Selma that evening, he told a rally: "We've gone too far to turn back now. We must let them know that nothing can stop us—not even death itself."

Again, King found himself trapped by conflicting needs and constituencies. For two months he had been nurturing the militancy of Selma's blacks and now, embittered by the Sunday violence, they insisted on marching across the bridge, and continuing on to Montgomery. The youth, many of whom had been jailed in the previous demonstrations, proclaimed that they would march regardless of what the adult leaders decided. SNCC organizers, who had remained aloof from the March 7 trek, now clamored for a rematch. "We were angry," wrote Cleveland Sellers. "And we wanted to show Governor Wallace, the Alabama State Highway Patrol, Sheriff Clark, Selma's whites, the federal government and poor Southern blacks in other Selmas that we didn't intend to take any more shit. We would ram the march down the throat of anyone who tried to stop us." In addition, such civil-rights leaders as James Farmer, Jim Forman, and Fred Shuttlesworth had hurried to Selma to resume the march. To postpone the confrontation until the injunction was lifted, King understood, meant risking the split of the Selma movement. He would surely be accused of being a toady of L.B.J. and a coward, and by default, leadership of the movement would fall into the hands of the irresponsible demagogues waiting for him to fail.

Yet, in no uncertain terms, President Johnson demanded that the illegal march not take place. Administration officials and congressional leaders pressed King to avoid a repetition of "Bloody Sunday." The SCLC leader knew he could not forfeit their support. His goal was voting-rights legislation and enforcement, and it would not come to pass without the cooperation of the White House. When Leroy Collins, head of the federal government's new Community Relations Service, arrived in Selma Tuesday morning with a face-saving plan to avert a clash, King accepted the arrangement. In return for an agreement by

Alabama authorities not to molest the marchers, King would lead his followers across the Pettus Bridge, stop when halted by the troopers, pray briefly, and then order the marchers to turn back. None of the marchers or other civil-rights leaders knew of King's compromise when he entered the Brown Chapel shortly after noon to lead the assemblage to Montgomery. "We have the right to walk the highways," King began,

> and we have the right to walk to Montgomery if our feet will get us there. I have no alternative but to lead a march from this spot to carry our grievances to the seat of government. I have made my choice. I have got to march. I do not know what lies ahead of us. There may be beatings, jailings, tear gas. But I would rather die on the highways of Alabama than make a butchery of my conscience. . . . I ask you to join me today as we move on.

Nearly a thousand blacks and half as many white sympathizers from the North proudly filed out of the church after King. Singing stanza after stanza of "Ain't Gonna Let Nobody Turn Me 'Round," the column crossed the bridge and stopped fifty feet from Major Cloud's line of state troops. "This march will not continue," Cloud commanded. "It is not conducive to the safety of this group or the motoring public." The major granted King's request to pray; then, departing from the agreed-upon scenario, to embarrass King further, Cloud ordered his men to break ranks and move to the sides of the highway. The road to Montgomery lay open. King hesitated, then turned to his astonished followers and instructed them to return to the Brown Chapel. At the church King tried to gloss over his decision, pretending that the demonstrators had made their point, rather than explaining why he had acted as he did. Few could accept the hollow rhetoric, and King stirred no excitement when he promised that there would yet be a march on Montgomery "in numbers that no one can count." That Tuesday evening the Selma movement came close to expiring.

One more time, however, white racist violence revived the struggle for equality. While militant blacks voiced their disillusionment with King, a gang of white hoodlums attacked three white Unitarian ministers who had come to Selma to participate in the march. Beaten unconscious with a club, the Reverend James J. Reeb of Boston died two days later of multiple fractures of the skull. His death kindled anew demands for federal action and expressions of support for the movement. Hundreds of clergymen, union officials, schoolteachers, and college students began their pilgrimage to Selma. Tens of thousands of letters and telegrams poured into Washington petitioning for voting-rights legislation, a plea echoed by most of the nation's press.

On Monday evening, March 15, President Johnson delivered a televised address to a joint session of the Congress to request the passage of a voting-rights bill. He compared the struggle at Selma to that at Lexington and Concord, and stated that the problem of racial equality "lay bare the secret heart of America itself. Rarely are we met with a challenge . . . to the values and purposes and the meaning of our beloved nation. The issue of equal rights for American Negroes is such an issue. And should we defeat every enemy, and should we double our wealth and conquer the stars, and still be unequal to this issue, then we will have failed as a people and a nation." Johnson told the legislators that the "real hero of this struggle is the American Negro. His actions and protests, his courage to risk safety, and even to risk his life, have awakened the conscience of this nation. His demonstrations have been designed to call attention to injustice, designed to provoke change, designed to stir reform. He has called upon us to make good the promise of America. And who among us can say that we would have made the same progress were it not for his persistent bravery and his faith in American democracy?"

Because local officials had deviously denied suffrage to blacks, Johnson went on, he would submit a bill to "establish a simple uniform standard which cannot be used, however ingenious the effort, to flout the Constitution." Many of "the issues of civil rights are complex and difficult," stated the President. "But about this there can be no argument. Every American citizen must have an equal right to vote. There is no reason which can excuse the denial of that right. There is no duty which weighs more heavily on us than the duty to ensure that right." To those who want "to maintain purely local control over elections, the answer is simple: Open your polling places to all your people."

"Even if we pass this bill, the battle will not be over," President Johnson sternly began his peroration. "What happened in Selma is part of a far larger movement which reaches into every section and state of America. It is the effort of American Negroes to secure for themselves the full blessings of American life." Eloquently he pleaded: "This cause must be our cause too. It is not just Negroes, but all of us, who must overcome the crippling legacy of bigotry and injustice. And," the President concluded emphatically, "we *shall* overcome." Johnson had expressed all that the movement hoped for, and even the most militant praised the address. SNCC's John Lewis termed it "historic, eloquent, and more than inspiring." Just a decade earlier, another President of the United States would not even state his agreement with the Supreme Court's school-desegregation ruling.

President Johnson also acted. He prevailed upon Judge Johnson to issue quickly a ruling to permit the march and he called in Governor Wallace and laid down the law: the marchers would be protected and he would brook no interference with their demonstration.

Six days after Johnson's address to Congress, King spoke to the more than three thousand black and white marchers gathered in front of Brown Chapel: "You will be the people that will light a new chapter in the history books of our nation. Those of us who are Negroes don't have much. . . . Because of the system, we don't have much education. . . . But thank God we have our bodies, our feet and our souls. Walk together, children," King preached, "don't you get weary, and it will lead us to the Promised Land. And Alabama will be a new Alabama, and America will be a new America." The joyous throng surged forward, singing and laughing, barely noticing the white hecklers lining the route with crude placards reading "Bye, Bye, Blackbird," "Nigger Lover," and "Martin Luther Coon." Protected by the federalized Alabama National Guard, the marchers tramped uneventfully through fifty miles of Alabama countryside. Four days later, on the outskirts of Montgomery, nearly thirty thousand more blacks and whites joined them for the final three miles to the grounds of the Alabama capitol. The list of prominent educators, entertainers, politicians, and black spokesmen topped the galaxy that appeared at the March on Washington.

As at that other historic gathering in support of equal rights, the huge interracial crowd in Montgomery waited patiently for King, while one civil-rights leader after another spoke. Then the nation on its television sets, and Governor Wallace through the slats of his venetian blinds, watched King stride to the podium and heard the assemblage's amens begin to rise. "We have walked on meandering highways and rested our bodies on rocky byways," he began rhythmically.

They told us we wouldn't get here. And there were those who said that we would get here only over their dead bodies, but all the world together knows that we are here and that we are standing before the forces of power in the state of Alabama, saying, "We ain't goin' let nobody turn us around."

"We are on the move now," he shouted to the throng at the capitol, "and no wave of racism can stop us." He called for more marches, everywhere—on segregated schools, on poverty, and on "ballot boxes until race baiters disappear from the political arena. Let us march on ballot boxes," King reiterated, "until we send to our city councils, state legislatures, and the United States Congress men who will not fear to do justice, love mercy and walk humbly with their God."

"My people, my people, listen! The battle is in our hands," King went on. "I know some of you are asking today, 'How long will it take?' I come to say to you this afternoon," he concluded with a syncopated chant, "however difficult the moment, however frustrating the hour, it will not be long because truth pressed to earth will rise again. How long? Not long, because no lie can live forever. How long? Not long, because you will reap what you sow. How long? Not long, because the arm of the moral universe is long but it bends toward justice." Then to the ecstatic thousands he boomed his crescendo from the Battle Hymn of the Republic: "How long? Not long. Because mine eyes have seen the glory of the coming of the Lord. . . . His truth is marching on! Glory hallelujah! Glory hallelujah! Glory hallelujah!"

Demented white violence had made this glorious moment possible, and it struck again that evening, ending all doubt that Congress would speedily enact an uncompromising voting-rights bill. Mrs. Viola Liuzzo, the white wife of a Detroit labor-union official and mother of five children, had come to Alabama, she told her husband, because "it was everybody's business—she had to go." Following King's speech, she volunteered to transport marchers back to Selma in her car. Returning to Montgomery later in the night to pick up a second group of marchers, she was shot to death by four Klansmen. Sixteen hours later, an angry Lyndon Johnson appeared on television to deplore "the horrible crime" and to announce the arrest of the Ku Klux Klan members. He called upon Congress to investigate these "enemies of justice who for decades have used the rope and the gun and the tar and feathers to terrorize their neighbors." He pledged to submit legislation to bring this "hooded society of bigots" under "effective control of law." Praising Viola Liuzzo for having gone to Selma to "serve the struggle for justice," Johnson again demanded the quick passage of his suffrage legislation.

That August, the President signed the act which authorized federal examiners to register qualified voters and suspended devices like literacy tests. Together with the 1957 and 1960 voting statutes, and with the Twenty-third Amendment outlawing the poll tax in federal elections (ratified in 1964) and the 1966 Supreme Court decision invalidating the poll tax in all elections, the 1965 Voting Rights Act transformed the face of Southern politics. The lock on the ballot box for blacks had been broken. Following the arrival of a federal examiner in Selma, the percentage of voting-age blacks registered rose in just two months from less than 10 to more than 60 percent. The 24 percent of Alabama blacks registered in 1964 became 57 percent in 1968. In Mississippi, the percentage of black registrants leaped from 7 in 1964 to 59 percent in 1968. In those four years, the number of Southern black voters increased from 1 million to 3.1 million.

The movement for racial justice could indeed be proud. But the struggle to gain this elementary right of citizenship left indelible scars and open sores that festered until they poisoned the movement. King's children would walk together no more.

SEVEN

The Dream Deferred

Black and white, few paid much attention to the rumblings of discontent within the movement and within the black ghettos as the nation celebrated Independence Day in 1965. Most accepted the civil-rights gains of the first half of the decade as necessary and just; many saw them as a prelude to further progress. Addressing the graduating class of Howard University in June, President Lyndon Johnson promised bold, new efforts in housing, employment, welfare, and education to assist the blacks' struggle to move beyond the goal of equality of opportunity to racial equality as a reality. Early in August, in a grandiose ceremony televised from the Capitol rotunda, the President signed the voting-rights bill into law and vowed swift and vigorous enforcement. Even as he spoke, federal voting registrars hurried into action in nine Southern counties. The Leadership Conference on Civil Rights had never seemed to be more popular, or more aided by religious, student, women's, and labor organizations interested in improving race relations, or more potent in influencing the three branches of the federal government. At this relatively peaceful and prosperous moment, public support for King's dream appeared unprecedented.

On August 11, however, just five days after Johnson signed the voting-rights act, the most destructive race riot in more than two decades began in Watts, Los Angeles's largest black ghetto. That explosion of bitterness over unmet demands for black dignity and a stop to racial oppression sparked a succession of "long hot summers" and proclaimed an end to the era of nonviolence. It hastened King's loss of power and the ascendancy of Malcolm's angry heirs within the movement. Strategies of social change gave way to cries of rage. "Black Power" drowned out "Black and White Together." "Burn, Baby, Burn" succeeded "Freedom Now." By the end of 1968, police reported some fifty thousand arrests and over eight thousand casualties in the nearly three hundred race riots and disturbances since 1965. An estimated half million blacks had participated in the burning and looting. An equal number of Americans served in Vietnam in 1968. The war in Asia had among its many unintended consequences the dismembering of the civil-rights alliance and the destruction of the consensus for racial reform. As the United States disgorged its firepower into Vietnam and the ghettos burst into flames, the hopes of the blacks went up in smoke and King's dream turned to ash.

A confrontation between white police and young blacks ignited the tinder in Watts, as it would in most of the subsequent racial disorders of the 1960s. Shortly before 8 p.m. on a sultry Wednesday evening, an ordinary arrest for drunken driving brought a typical crowd of onlookers. Such incidents were everyday occurrences in the ghetto. On this particular night, however, the arrested youth's mother scuffled with the patrolmen, and blacks observing the tussle responded with menacing jeers, causing the arresting policemen to brandish rifles and to radio for reinforcements. The black spectators refused to be cowed by a show of superior force; they pelted the newly arrived law officers with rocks and bottles. By 10 p.m. the angry crowd had become a rampaging mob, overturning the cars of passing white motorists and smashing shop windows. Looting began at midnight, and for several hours a few thousand blacks openly vented the anger they had so long repressed and concealed. Calm returned at dawn. The police confidently announced that the riot was over.

But the mob reassembled the next evening. Many carried arms. In the shabby, littered streets of the ghetto, the hostility toward all whites suddenly grew palpable. Black violence raged. This time it did not cease with the light of day. Indeed, the more than five thousand rioters roaming Watts on Friday morning, crying "Long live Malcolm X," protested against indignity and against the brutality of the Los Angeles Police Department with ever more boldness and destruction. Most looted and trashed. Some firebombed white-owned businesses and attacked whites wandering in the ghetto. A few returned police fire, sniped at them from rooftops, and ambushed firemen responding to the increasing number of alarms. Law-enforcement officials called for help, and National Guard troops rushed to Watts on Friday afternoon to restore order. They could not. The number of rioters multiplied. The damage soared. By late Saturday, over fourteen thousand Guardsmen augmented the fifteen hundred law officers struggling to contain the insurrection of an estimated fifty thousand blacks. Traditional restraints on black anger had evanesced and for three more days and nights the burning, looting, and sniping continued. When the six-day melee ended, thirty-four had been killed, some nine hundred injured, nearly four thousand arrested, and about $30 million of property had been devastated.

While a shocked nation viewed the Watts conflagration on its TV sets, the outrage of Chicago blacks erupted after a fire truck accidentally struck and killed a black woman on August 12. For two days and nights, the West Side of Chicago resembled the Watts battlefield. Thousands of blacks rushed to the ghetto streets to battle police and National Guardsmen, and to loot and burn the stores owned by whites. Then the arrest of eighteen blacks outside a nightclub in Springfield, Massachusetts on August 14, ignited another outbreak of collective violence. Once again, blacks looted and burned and returned the fire of the police and National Guard.

In retrospect, the racial tumult of 1965 was merely a prelude to the acts of destruction and desperation to come. The summer of 1966 brought more than a score of race riots and an even larger number of serious racial disturbances. Across the nation, ghetto blacks went on a rampage, violently declaring their fury over unmet demands for dignity, for meaningful work, for housing without rats and police protection without brutality or contempt, for a decent measure of control over their own destiny. Hardly a day seemed to pass without the evening news showing film of surging black mobs breaking windows, smashing cars, ransacking stores, putting the torch to white businesses, and hurling bricks and bottles at embattled police and firemen. To quell the turbulence in 1966, National Guard troops patrolled the streets of Chicago, Cleveland, Dayton, Milwaukee, and San Francisco, where arsonists, looters, and vandals damaged property worth $5 million. At least seven blacks died in the racial disorders, more than four hundred were injured, and another three thousand arrested.

The most intense and destructive wave of racial violence the nation had ever witnessed came in 1967. The National Advisory Commission on Civil Disorders, appointed by President Johnson to investigate the turmoil, recorded nearly 150 racial outbreaks that summer and described twoscore of the riots as "major or serious." Violence convulsed Boston, Buffalo, Cincinnati, New Haven, Providence, Wilmington, Cambridge, Maryland, and a hundred other cities. North and South, from coast to coast, authorities reported unprecedented numbers of blacks throwing

Molotov cocktails, looting and burning stores, and firing upon police.

No riot was more expected than Newark's; none was more bloody. With the nation's highest rates of black joblessness, condemned housing, crime, new cases of tuberculosis, and maternal mortality, Newark verged on the brink of a race war between its despairing majority black population and a callous, corrupt, almost all-white city administration. The arrest of a black taxidriver and rumors that he had been beaten to death triggered the bloodbath on July 12. Looting began immediately. Then the arsonists took over. On the second night, the police began using live ammunition. They killed five blacks. Although the rioting seemed on the wane the third day, the Governor of New Jersey described the situation as "a city in open rebellion" and ordered in the National Guard. Over the weekend, the Guardsmen and police fired over thirteen thousand rounds of ammunition, killing twenty more blacks and wounding some twelve hundred. Over thirteen hundred blacks had been arrested and property losses were put at $10 million.

More unexpectedly, yet just as bloodily, Detroit erupted the next Sunday. In death and destruction it was the worst race riot in half a century. Unlike Newark, the Motor City had a progressive mayor who, backed by black voters, attended energetically to ghetto problems. Many of the city's officeholders were black, and Washington had lavished millions of dollars on Detroit's anti-poverty and urban-renewal programs. The auto industry, the economic mainstay of Detroit blacks, moreover, was booming. Unemployment was low and wages high. As opposed to the large-scale black poverty of Newark, nearly two-thirds of the black families in Detroit owned cars and almost half owned their homes. Yet relations between the police and the Detroit ghetto duplicated those in Newark and Watts and scores of other Northern cities. Recurring instances of unwarranted police brutality had caused massive black resentment toward law-enforcement officers and a constant, unrelenting low level of warfare between black citizens and white cops.

On July 23 the mass arrest of blacks at a nightclub selling liquor after the legal closing time detonated six days and nights of epidemic arson and vandalism, six days and nights of black defiance of a system of law and order which seemed so terribly biased against them. Nearly four thousand fires destroyed thirteen hundred buildings. The devastation left five thousand blacks homeless and an equal number jobless. Observing the smoking ruins from a helicopter, the Governor of Michigan remarked that Detroit looked like "a city that had been bombed." Added to the damage caused by burning, looting by tens of thousands of blacks brought the total of lost property to a quarter of a billion dollars. Worse, frightened and untrained National Guardsmen, firing without discipline, accounted for most of the riot's forty-three dead and over a thousand wounded. All told, the 1967 summer riots resulted in at least ninety deaths, more than four thousand casualties, and nearly seventeen thousand arrests.

Self-serving politicians and pundits of every ideological shade offered explanations to a bewildered nation. Leftist black radicals described the riots as calculated revolutionary violence to overthrow a reactionary, racist society. They compared them to the colonial rebellions in Africa and Asia, and predicted that the urban guerilla warfare and sabotage by the oppressed masses would not cease until the ultimate destruction of white, capitalist rule. Sharing much of this fantasy, white reactionaries also saw the specter of revolution in the riots. However, they blamed the efforts of the mass of blacks to bring down the United States on foreign agitators and black Communists rather than on social conditions. To meet fire with fire, the far right demanded a government vendetta against radical black groups, and the incarceration of all black extremists. They urged patriotic whites to arm themselves to defend the nation against a black insurrection.

Eschewing economic nostrums, black nationalists depicted the riots as a repudiation of the "Uncle Toms" and "handkerchief-head niggers" in the NAACP and SCLC and a rejection of their goal of an integrated society. "The Negro was really in exile in America," they repeatedly quoted Malcolm X, insisting that only separatism could end the violence. Some nationalists stipulated that the government finance the black repatriation to Africa as compensation for slavery. Others clamored for the United States to deed blacks a separate homeland on the continent so that the two races could live apart. Most settled for urging ghetto autonomy and complete black control over black institutions. All agreed that the alternative to separatism would be more widespread black retaliation.

Liberals, white and black, refused to give up on desegregation. They explained the riots as a manifestation of social deprivation, as a consequence of ghetto conditions, as a cry from the lowest classes for the traditional reforms advocated by liberals: job opportunities, better housing, quality integrated education, and more generous welfare benefits. The National Advisory Commission on Civil Disorders blamed the riots on the "explosive mixture" of poverty, unemployment, slum housing and segregated education in the nation's cities. To allay black discontent, the commission recommended the creation of two million new jobs in the ghetto, an attack on de facto segregation, the construction of six million new units of public housing, and the institution of a national system of income supplementation. Although liberals squabbled among themselves over how much should be spent on particular items, and about what could be done to end police brutality and white racism, they unanimously advocated massive federal expenditures to improve the material conditions of the ghetto as the surest way to end the rioting.

Such proposals horrified conservatives as rewarding criminal behavior. Poverty and squalor did not cause the riots, they argued: youth groups did; the hoodlum element did; agitators preying on the idle young did; a permissive society which encouraged blacks to sate their greed and which indulged the anti-social tendencies of blacks was to blame. Accordingly, conservatives preached the gospel of "law and order." Rather than shackle the police with civilian review boards, they wanted to strengthen law-enforcement agencies with additional manpower and riot control weapons, and to encourage the police to get yet tougher with the lawless, even "to shoot to kill" looters. Instead of letting the media disseminate the advocacy of violence by black demagogues, they urged the government to repress radical black organizations. In place of ameliorating the horrors of ghetto life, conservatives exhorted the government to punish rioters.

Most of these commonly accepted interpretations of the racial turbulence had little basis in fact. Although no single set of generalizations can encompass all the unique and varying conditions in some two hundred cities and towns, in different years, or the individual motivations and behavior of hundreds of thousands of participants in the riots, certain inferences can be drawn from the vast data collected during and immediately after the riots. Outside agitators played virtually no part in the disturbances. Most riots showed no evidence of planning. Yet, for all their apparent randomness, the vast majority of rioters acted purposefully. They looted and put the torch to white businesses, especially those reputed to exploit black customers, and spared those of blacks who scrawled "soul brother" on their windows. They sought to avoid damaging the institutions that served them, such as churches, libraries, and schools. In some instances, nearly half the adult population of the ghetto joined the riot. In almost all others, those who participated constituted a cross section of the black community. Neither criminals nor teenagers predominated. Only a minority came from the ranks of the unemployed or most deprived. Men and women of the black working class in the main, the majority supported the goals of the civil-rights movement and accepted the leadership of Martin Luther King, Jr. Most sought neither to separate from nor to destroy American society.

Ghetto blacks rioted to enter the mainstream of that society, to be treated as outsiders no longer. They rioted to protest the pervasiveness and depth of white racism in the supposedly racially egalitarian North. They rioted to draw attention to the squalor of the slums and the savagely oppressive behavior of the police in the ghetto. They rioted to make the needs of the ghetto visible, to smash the narrow view of the race problem as just a Southern phenomenon, to force whites to pay heed to the plight of urban blacks. They rioted to assert their unrequited plea for all the decencies and dignities possessed by other Americans. Most of all, they rioted to raise the economic questions which the civil-rights movement had ignored; and, nationwide, a huge preponderance of blacks who had never burned or looted expressed approval for the protest articulated by those who had.

Urban blacks chose to protest by rioting in the second half of the sixties because they had no other viable strategy of change and because the struggle for equality in the South had changed the psychology of the Nothern ghetto. The battle for civil rights gave the blacks of Watts in 1965, of Cleveland in 1966, of Detroit in 1967, a far different sense of themselves than they had had in 1950. The movement shook the ghettos out of their lethargy. It proved that protest could succeed and it raised black consciousness. It stimulated expectations for a better life. It aroused black wrath by focusing media attention on the vicious savagery of white racists. For the better part of a decade, Northern blacks watched their brethren in the South gain concessions by creating disorder. They would have to do no less. Ghetto blacks saw the movement reform Dixie, and they grew hopeful and impatient. Surely, if the massive edifice of Southern racism could be toppled, then a solution to the urban problems of race could be expected. Television's transmission of the civil-rights story especially encouraged anticipations of speedy success. Simultaneously, the dwelling on Klan violence by television helped transform Northern black grievances into deep loathing and bitterness. The vivid depiction of white brutality in Alabama, Georgia, and Mississippi, observed by blacks throughout the nation, generated an obsessive hatred of the white police in the ghetto, who seemed to behave no differently from "Bull" Connor or Jim Clark.

The success of the struggle for racial equality in the South accelerated aspirations but did nothing to improve the day-to-day lot of ghetto blacks. The panoply of court decisions, congressional acts, and executive orders failed to affect the subordinate status of blacks in the North. None of the marches, pickets, rallies, or other forms of peaceful protest abolished filthy dope-ridden streets or inferior segregated schools. No lawful strategy of social change dented the hostility of police departments or the discrimination of labor unions. All the tactics that had worked in the South miscarried against greedy slumlords and their intransigent political allies. Steadily the gap widened between what blacks desired and what they obtained, between what they expected and what they attained. In addition, the more urban blacks sought change, the more apprehensive and resentful Northern whites became. Many of the same whites who praised the actions of the civil-rights movement in Birmingham and Selma exhibited anti-black prejudice comparable to the worst in the South when they felt their neighborhood school or lily-white union threatened by the presence of blacks. The white backlash grew harsh. Resistance to open housing flared in every Northern city, as did opposition to funding the War on Poverty, to ending de facto school segregation, and to establishing civilian review boards for the police. The adamant refusal of whites to correct the abuses that had been legally and peaceably protested forced blacks ultimately to desperate and destructive acts.

Within the movement, the emergence of Black Power paralleled the rage expressed by Northern blacks in the urban riots.

The reaction against nonviolence as a tactic and integration as a goal similarly grew out of frustration over the limited pace and scope of racial change and out of bitterness toward unceasing brutal white opposition to the most minimal black advances. Black Power, like the riots, brought important psychological gains for blacks at the terrible cost of further disintegrating the movement, polarizing the races, sanctioning the cult of violence, and fueling the white backlash.

On June 5, 1966, James Meredith, who had integrated the University of Mississippi in 1962, set out to march the 225 miles from Memphis to Jackson. He believed that by demonstrating his bravery he could instill in Mississippi blacks the courage to exercise their right to vote. On the second day of his pilgrimage, when Meredith was barely ten miles into his native state, a white man jumped out of the bushes beside Highway 51 and emptied the birdshot in his shotgun into the black veteran, wounding Meredith in the legs, back, and neck. The major civil-rights organizations, which had initially derided Meredith's march, rushed their leaders to Memphis to confer on how best to capitalize on the shooting. In addition to Martin Luther King, Jr., Roy Wilkins, and Whitney Young, two newcomers joined the circle: Floyd McKissick of CORE and SNCC's Stokely Carmichael. Both symbolized the radically new direction their groups had embarked on.

After the Selma campaign, the leading organizations of the movement had floundered in their search for new programs. Everyone agreed on the need to move beyond the traditional civil-rights agenda. But none developed a viable strategy for solving the complex problems of inadequate housing, dead-end jobs, no jobs, and inferior schooling. A sense of irrelevancy particularly rankled the dedicated activists in CORE and SNCC. They considered themselves the cutting edge of the movement, yet they now stood still. They yearned to lead the struggle to improve the living conditions of poor rural and ghetto blacks, but did not know how. They had paid too high a price in suffering and bloodshed to confess futility, so their impotence festered and turned bitter.

In the midst of this malaise, the young militants abandoned their former beliefs and ideals. Continued school and residential segregation convinced the disenchanted blacks that King's goal of an integrated society was an impossible dream. Embittered, they took the growth of the white backlash as proof of the hopeless position of blacks in America. SNCC and CORE began to believe they had to transform the struggle for desegregation into a battle for self-determination. They would have to engage in grass-roots organizing that built the power of black communities and enabled blacks to control their own destinies. Whites could not help in this endeavor. Indeed, the militants concluded that the participation of white liberals had harmed the movement. It had led to the militants' humiliations at the March on Washington and the 1964 Democratic convention. White volunteers had undermined the initiative of Mississippi blacks and reinforced their feelings of inferiority during the Freedom Summer. White liberals had continually forced the black leaders to compromise and temporize to suit the needs of the Kennedy and Johnson Administrations. Clearly, to the militants, the new liberation struggle required a restricted and subordinate role for whites, if not their total exclusion.

The movement radicals also adopted McKissick's description of nonviolence as "a dying philosophy" that had "outlived its usefulness." They had turned the other cheek too often, with too little to show for it. Traumatized by years of pain and fear, by too many vicious beatings and jailings at the hands of the Klan and sadistic sheriffs, by too many funerals for close friends killed by white racists, the militants in CORE and SNCC eagerly trumpeted their new inalienable right of self-defense. After the Watts riot, that concept rapidly metamorphized into the doctrine of retaliatory violence. Ultimately, it would blossom into the advocacy of violence as a legitimate tactic wherever feasible.

In charting this new course, the young militants borrowed much from the New Left and even more from Malcolm X. The rhetoric of CORE and SNCC often seemed indistinguishable from that of the Students for a Democratic Society in its condemnation of the Vietnam War, criticism of capitalism, rejection of bourgeois values, and attack on liberalism as the problem rather than the answer. Mostly, SNCC and CORE's new thrust resembled that of Malcolm X. On February 20, 1965, as Malcolm approached the lectern in Harlem's Audubon Ballroom to address a meeting of his Organization for Afro-American Unity, three men affiliated with Elijah Muhammed's Black Muslims had suddenly risen from their seats in the first row and, like a firing squad, felled Malcolm X with their shotgun and revolvers. Several months later, his autobiography appeared. An extraordinary account of his life and exposition of his beliefs, *The Autobiography of Malcolm X* immediately swept Black America and profoundly influenced the young in the ghetto and in the movement. In death, Malcolm X achieved an eminence and a devoted following that he had never had in his lifetime.

Malcolm's separatism articulated the mood of blacks whose hopes had been dashed. "The Negro was really in exile in America," he had repeatedly insisted. "No, I'm not an American. I'm one of the 22 million black people who are the victims of Americanism," he had lashed his critics. "And I see America through the eyes of the victim. I don't see any American dream; I see an American nightmare." Malcolm's black nationalism crystallized the feelings of those whose expectations had been frustrated. Over and over he had emphasized how racism had brainwashed the blacks. "We must revamp our entire thinking and redirect our learning trends so that we can put forth a confident identity and wipe out the false image built up by an oppressive society." Pride in blackness, pride in the Afro-Americans' roots in Africa, and pride in the blacks' capacity to control their own destinies had been his primary teachings.

Malcolm's increasingly socialistic bent, moreover, spoke to the needs of the majority of blacks who remained impoverished. In the last year of his life, Malcolm X conjectured frequently that black freedom necessitated a class uprising; and he often urged that "the revolt of the American Negro" become part of "a global rebellion of the oppressed against the oppressor, the exploited against the exploiter."

SNCC and CORE eagerly noted the extent to which the rioters in Watts, and ghetto youths throughout the nation, acknowledged the slain prince of black nationalism as their standard-bearer. It meshed with their own transformation, and the two movement groups acted accordingly. They took up his plea for black pride. They acted on his exhortation to raise racial consciousness rather than eradicate it. They embraced his vision of the black struggle, not as an isolated phenomenon but as part of the broader worldwide struggle of all oppressed, non-white, colonial peoples.

By the time of Meredith's shooting, SNCC and CORE had turned decisively against integration, interracialism, and non-violence. "Too much love/Too much love/Nothing kills a nigger like/Too much love," their fieldworkers sang. In a series of votes, a growing majority within CORE rejected the organization's traditional goals and tactics at its mid-1965 and 1966 national conventions. SNCC did the same in a series of staff meetings beginning in late 1965 and ending in May 1966. The election of Carmichael over John Lewis as the new head of SNCC, and CORE's selection of McKissick to replace James Farmer as national director, confirmed the changed temper. The two organizations which had done so much to impress the ideals of the movement on the nation discarded Farmer and Lewis as relics of the past. Now Carmichael and McKissick craved an opportunity to put their views into practice. The Meredith March gave them their chance.

Although all five civil-rights leaders wanted to resume the Memphis-to-Jackson march, Carmichael and McKissick angrily differed with Wilkins and Young over the nature and objectives of the protest. The Urban League and NAACP wanted another Selma. They proposed a nationwide call to whites to join the movement in a nonviolent demonstration to garner support for the 1966 civil-rights bill. SNCC and CORE countered with demands that the marching blacks denounce the pending legislation and insist that the civil-rights bill be thoroughly revised, condemn the Johnson Administration for its lax enforcement of existing civil-rights acts, highlight the urgency of developing independent black political power, deemphasize the role of whites, and invite the Deacons for Defense, an armed black group in Louisiana, to provide protection for the marchers. Reluctantly, King cast his lot with Carmichael and McKissick. He wished to preserve the façade of unity in the movement and believed his presence would constrain the excesses of the militants. But Wilkins and Young desired no part in such a march and quickly left Memphis.

King's effort to be a moderating influence failed. SNCC and CORE dominated the processions. On the first day of the Meredith March Against Fear, Carmichael shouted to a rally: "The Negro is going to take what he deserves from the white man." Thereafter, the rhetoric of the militants grew ever more bellicose and incendiary. When King preached nonviolence, the young blacks shouted: "White blood will flow." If King spoke of Christian love, the militants clamored: "Seize power." Each attempt of King's followers to sing "We Shall Overcome" was drowned out by the new SNCC version, "We Shall Overrun." Along the march route, Mississippi blacks taking their cue from Carmichael, chanted: "Hey! Hey! Whattaya know? White folks must go—must go!" And each evening, as the marchers pitched their camps, Carmichael's aides proclaimed loudly to the amazed Mississippians looking on: "If anybody touches one of our workers, we're going to tear this place up!"

Following the arrest of Carmichael in Greenwood for erecting a sleeping tent on the grounds of a black high school contrary to the orders of state troopers, the CORE-SNCC contingent of the Meredith March Against Fear scheduled a special protest rally. Word of Carmichael's jailing brought out a large and angry crowd, as well as numerous correspondents of the national news media. The fiery young head of SNCC grabbed his chance for the limelight. Straight from the jail, he leaped on a flatbed truck to stir the Greenwood rally with a raised-arm and clenched-fist salute. "This is the twenty-seventh time I have been arrested —and I ain't going to jail no more!" he hurled defiance. "The only way we gonna stop them white men from whippin' us is to take over. We been saying freedom for six years and we ain't got nothin'. What we gonna start saying now is Black Power!" Mesmerizing his audience, Carmichael repeated rhythmically: "We . . . want . . . Black . . . Power!" Soon the crowd roared back in unison. "That's right," Carmichael shouted, "that's what we want. Now, from now on, when they ask you what you want, you know what to tell them. What do you want?" "Black Power!" "What do you want?" "BLACK POWER!" "What do you want? Say it again!" "BLACK POWER! BLACK POWER! BLACK POWER!" It made headlines across the nation the next day.

King tried to mute the threat implied in the slogan. "We must never seek power exclusively for the Negro," he insisted, "but the sharing of power with white people." But Carmichael and McKissick would have no part of any effort to dilute the impact of the electrifying phrase which began to spread like a firestorm through the black ghettos. Every time SCLC representatives chanted "Freedom Now!" the followers of SNCC and CORE bellowed "Black Power!" With intensifying bravado, Carmichael kept challenging blacks to "stop begging and take power—black power." He insisted: "Power is the only thing respected in this world, and we must get it at any cost." He made the keynote of his insurgency: "It's time we stand up and take over. Take over. Move on over, or we'll move on over you." When the fifteen thousand marchers reached the Mississippi capital on

June 26, most roared, with neither coaxing nor coaching: "Black Power! Black Power! Black Power!" Few of the many whites who had long marched with King stood beside him in Jackson. McKissick closed the final rally with the declaration: "1966 shall be remembered as the year we left our imposed status as Negroes and became *Black Men* . . . 1966 is the year of the concept of Black Power."

But Black Power remained more an angry slogan than a clear program. Carmichael kept altering its meaning, defining and redefining it to suit the needs of different audiences. Although a few civil-rights leaders completely repudiated the expression (Wilkins castigated Black Power as "the father of hatred and the mother of violence"), most black spokesmen sought to hitch the popularity of the phrase with blacks to their own wagon. Each gave it a congenial connotation. Each elaborated on it in line with its own ideology. Revolutionaries used it to preach guerrilla warfare, liberals to demand reform, and conservatives to emphasize self-help. Both separatists and integrationists employed it, as did proponents of love and of hostility, of violence and of nonviolence. Politicians saw it as an instrument to win black votes, businessmen as a means to preserve and expand black markets, and artists as a basis for developing a black aesthetic. Black capitalists claimed it, and so did black socialists and publicists for black cooperatives. To some, it meant coalition politics; to others, withdrawal from the system. Assertions of cultural autonomy vied with strategies for economic advancements; emphases on black identity competed with calls to "pick up the gun." Black Power became a goal and a means, something permanent and a temporary stage, a legal tool and a lawless one, a tactic and an end in itself.

Despite the confusion, Black Power generated valuable changes. It galvanized many whom the movement had never touched to mobilize for concerted action. It spawned an array of new associations, caucuses, and community organizations. It spurred self-reliance and a phalanx of assertive local leaders.

Unlike the civil-rights movement, which had largely focused on the aspirations of the burgeoning black middle class, Black Power drew attention to the needs of the lower classes, and to the root of their plight: powerlessness. It called attention to the exigency of restructuring the nation's economic and political institutions. It pinpointed the urgency of transforming the culture's value structure.

Fundamentally, Black Power made blacks proud to be blacks, a psychological precondition for equality. It revolutionized the black perspective, confining to the dustbin of the black past the belief born out of centuries of oppression that what was white was good and what was black was inferior. Black became beautiful. Throwing away skin bleaches and hair straighteners, blacks emphasized their racial characteristics and joyously affirmed their skin color and life-styles, music and food, dialect and culture. "Say it loud—I'm black and I'm proud," sang James Brown, and a generation of blacks agreed. Wearing Afros and dashikis, self-assured blacks awakened interest in the neglected heritage of Africa and stimulated the writing and study of black history. They made "soul" the rage, preached a black theology, took Arabic surnames, established black-studies programs at universities, and wore their color, in Langston Hughes's words, "like a banner for the proud." In whatever form it took, pride in being black proved invaluable in aiding blacks to discard the disabling self-hatred inculcated by white culture.

But, as Carmichael observed, "to most whites, Black Power seems to mean that the Mau Mau are coming to the suburbs at night." His leadership did much to make that seem inevitable. Under Carmichael, SNCC abandoned all pretense of working within the movement, expelled its white staff members, and denounced its white supporters and financial backers. By 1967, SNCC was bankrupt and reduced to some twoscore shrill nihilists. Carmichael talked incessantly to the media about blacks becoming "the executioners of our executioners," about "offing the pigs" and "killing the honkies." "When you talk of

Black Power," he announced, "you talk of building a movement that will smash everything Western civilization has created." Identifying himself with the Black Panthers, Carmichael snarled: "If we don't get justice we're going to tear this country apart." In his last act as SNCC's chairman, Carmichael toured the black colleges of the South in the spring of 1967 to urge students to "fight for liberation by any means necessary" and to stand up "to say 'To hell with the laws of the United States.' " Rioting followed his speeches at Fisk and Texas Southern Universities, and at Jackson State and Tougaloo College. Then Carmichael left to tour Cuba and North Vietnam.

His successor as head of SNCC, twenty-three-year-old H. Rap Brown of Louisiana, quickly made Carmichael sound like a moderate. He told reporters after his election: "The white man won't get off our backs, so we're going to knock him off. . . . America won't come around, so we're going to burn America down." He delighted in calling President Johnson a "mad wild dog" and a "hunky cracker," and in exclaiming: "If you give me a gun I might just shoot Lady Bird." "Violence is as American as cherry pie" became Brown's catchphrase. Just a month after taking office, he addressed a black rally in Cambridge, Maryland, during the week that the Detroit riot raged. Brown urged his audience to "get you some guns."

> You'd better get you some guns. The man's moving to kill you. The only thing the honky respects is force. . . . I mean, don't be trying to love that honky to death. Shoot him to death. Shoot him to death, brother, cause that's what he's out to do to you. Like I said in the beginning, if this town don't come around, this town should be burned down. It should be burned down, brother.

"Don't you see what your brothers in Detroit are doing?" Brown implored. "It's time for Cambridge to explode." It did. Several hours after Brown's speech, flames destroyed the center of the black ghetto. Two days later, Brown was arrested for incitement to riot, beginning a series of jailings and bailings which did nothing to dampen the incendiary preachments of the head of SNCC.

The prominence of CORE and SNCC, and especially King, in the anti-war movement further eroded the legitimacy of the black struggle in the eyes of most whites. At a time when an overwhelming majority of Americans considered opposition to the government's Vietnam policy to be disloyal, King demanded in 1965: "The long night of war must be stopped." His call for a negotiated Indochina settlement infuriated President Johnson and lost SCLC the support of influential and wealthy white liberals. Moderates in the movement stipulated to King that civil rights remain divorced from foreign policy, and the minister backed down, assured by the White House of the war's imminent end. But the promised peace did not come.

Early in 1966, Johnson admitted: "Because of Vietnam, we cannot do all that we should, or all that we would like to do." Drastic cuts in the domestic budget followed. The war against poverty and the government's efforts to achieve racial equality ground to a halt. CORE angrily insisted that the United States withdraw its forces from Indochina. Declaring its sympathy with "the men in this country who are unwilling to respond to a military draft," SNCC officially resolved: "Vietnamese are being murdered because the United States is pursuing an aggressive policy in violation of international law." Six SNCC staffers in Atlanta then invaded an induction center, provoking parallel anti-war maneuvers by militant, educated young blacks throughout the country, who chanted: "Hell, no! We won't go!" A hero of black youth, Muhammad Ali, capsulated their alienation in his adamant refusal to serve in a "white man's war." Nikki Giovanni delineated their anger in her poetry: "We kill in Vietnam/for them/We kill for UN & NATO & SEATO & US/ And everywhere for all alphabet but BLACK."

King broke his silence. He knew it would be neither popular nor politic. But to say nothing about the heinous killing and destruction in Vietnam made a mockery of his life's work to teach love and nonviolence. King also believed his leadership could channel constructively the inchoate anti-war protests of young militants. The SCLC head deemed the war and racial injustice "inextricably bound together." Blacks could no longer concern themselves with just civil rights. "It is very nice to drink milk at an unsegregated lunch counter—but not when there is strontium 90 in it." As King sought to forge an inter-racial alliance of the poor and oppressed, moreover, he increasingly considered the unjust, immoral war ten thousand miles away to be robbing the nation of the resources necessary to create new jobs and to eradicate the slums. "The bombs in Vietnam explode at home," the black minister preached. "They destroy the hopes and possibilities of a decent America." Despite great pressure from the White House, King kept reiterating that the United States spent $500,000 to kill each enemy soldier but only $35 a year to assist each American in poverty. "The promises of the Great Society," he intoned, "have been shot down on the battlefield of Vietnam."

Disregarding the consequences, King made opposition to the war his top priority in 1967. While his lieutenants conspicuously organized anti-war demonstrations, King assumed the leadership of the unprecedented Spring Mobilization Against the War, completely burning his bridges to the Administration, to the Congress, and to most of his erstwhile allies. Rustin, Wilkins, and Young loudly disagreed with his denunciation of the United States as "the greatest purveyor of violence in the world today." Senator Edward Brooke, Ralph Bunche, and Jackie Robinson openly lambasted King for urging Americans to become conscientious objectors. The media repeatedly described King's criticism of the war as destructive to his people and his cause, and Lyndon Johnson did all he could covertly to destroy the minister's influence. Deserted by the liberals for going too far in his remonstrance, derided by the more vitriolic radicals for not going far enough, King lost power and status. The intensification of black violence and white backlash in 1967 underlined his ineffectuality. King sank into despondency.

Looking to 1968 to recoup, King began planning a Poor People's March on Washington. To bestir the nation's apathy toward economic injustice, he envisaged an interracial coalition of the dispossessed descending on Washington in far greater numbers, and engaging in far more disruptive tactics, than in any of his previous demonstrations against racial injustice. "Timid supplication for justice will not solve the problem," King announced. "We have got to confront the power structure massively. We can't live with another summer like the last. This is a desperate plea. I want to give the nation the opportunity to respond."

In March 1968, King interrupted his efforts to organize the Poor People's Campaign to go to Memphis to rally support for the mostly black sanitation workers of the city striking for union recognition and a living wage. The protest march he attempted to lead quickly degenerated into violence as a black youth gang went on a looting and burning rampage and the police responded with tear gas and bullets. Shaken, King vowed to stay in Memphis to prove it was still possible "to hold a nonviolent march."

On April 3, King addressed his last church rally. He rambled softly about the progress that had been made since 1955, and of the gains yet to be made. Quietly he told of recent threats on his life. "But it doesn't matter with me now. Because I've been to the mountaintop." He turned to face his aides on the platform behind him. "I don't mind. Like anybody, I would like to live a long life. Longevity has its place. But I'm not concerned about that now." His voice began to rise. "I just want to do God's will. And He's allowed me to go up to the mountain!" He faced the hushed audience. Some wept openly. "And I've looked over and I've seen the promised land!" King shouted emotionally: "I may not get there with you, but I want you to know tonight" —he paused—"that we as a people will get to the promised land." "King, King, King, King," the crowd chanted jubilantly, as the minister looked at length at his brother A.D. standing near the podium. "And I am happy tonight!" King roared. "I'm not worried about anything! I'm not fearing any man! Mine eyes have seen the glory . . . of the coming of the Lord!"

The next evening, while the thirty-nine-year-old minister conversed with his friends on the balcony at the Lorraine Motel, a rifle shot rang out and Martin Luther King, Jr., fell, murdered by a white assassin.

Within hours after the announcement of King's death, black uprisings flared in the ghettos of nearly a hundred and thirty cities. Twenty blocks of the Chicago West Side went up in flames before Mayor Richard Daley ordered his police to "shoot to kill." In Washington, D.C., over seven hundred fires set by arsonists lit up the night as army units in full combat gear took battle positions around the Capitol and on the grounds of the White House. By the end of the week, twenty-one thousand federal troops and thirty-four thousand National Guardsmen had been called out to quell the upheavals in over a hundred cities that had left forty-six dead, more than three thousand injured, some twenty-seven thousand arrested, and $45 million of property lost.

The hopes of the movement died with King. More than any individual, Martin Luther King, Jr., epitomized the quest for racial brotherhood and equality by nonviolent means. Simultaneously he had been able to inspire blacks to struggle against racism and to encourage whites to acknowledge their responsibility for the plight of blacks without turning them against the movement. His death meant the abandonment of the middle ground that had been rapidly disintegrating since the passage of the voting-rights act in 1965. No other black leader would succeed in convincing large numbers of both races to share his dreams; no other would galvanize the movement to heroic exertions. In countless ways, individual blacks would continue to battle for a better existence, but the grand passion of the organized struggle was moribund. Ralph Abernathy's effort to continue the Poor People's March on Washington proved a fiasco. The nation barely noticed the passing mule train, or the erected shantytown called Resurrection City, which rapidly sank in the mire of its own disunity and criminality. The arrest of the SCLC leaders and the brutal dispersement of the poor encamped in Washington aroused no significant howls of protest. King's crusade already appeared to be a relic of a bygone era.

White backlash ruled the roost. The fiery riots had rationalized expressions of hostility toward blacks. The prominence of movement leaders in anti-war activities, associated by many with the counterculture and student rebellions, had reinforced old prejudices and justified new antagonisms. The anti-white connotations of Black Power had cooled the ardor of white liberals for the struggle. And the movement's work in the North had fired the anxiety of the white working class that racial equality would come at the expense of the safety of its neighborhoods and schools, the security of its jobs and homes. Northern politicians adapted to the white urge to end racial reform with alacrity. In California, Ronald Reagan came to power in 1966 on the strength of his tough stance toward the rioters of Watts. In Boston, the adamant refusal of Louise Day Hicks to correct racial imbalance in the schools made her the most potent new political force in that city in 1967. "Law and order" and "Get tough with blacks" candidates triumphed in almost every city that had experienced a riot, and even in some that had not suffered racial turmoil.

For the first time in a decade, Congress rejected a proposed civil-rights bill in 1966. The House of Representatives in 1967 refused to seat Harlem Congressman Adam Clayton Powell, Jr., for illegal payroll practices that whites in Congress went unpunished for, and defeated a minor appropriation for the control of rats in the slums, laughingly deriding it as a "civil-rats bill." Following King's assassination in 1968, Congress did enact civil-rights legislation—a fair-housing bill seen by many as an act of atonement for his murder. It sought to quiet the cries of angry blacks by outlawing racial discrimination in the sale and rental of housing. But the measure appeased, even pleased, the white majority by making incitement to riot a serious federal offense. Still other manifestations of the backlash included the landslide defeats of referenda for civilian boards to review police actions, the deluge of support for teachers' strikes against black community control of schools, and the emergence of huge white mobs jeering, "Nigger, nigger, nigger!" and stoning black protesters in the North.

The Presidential election of 1968 further substantiated the shift in momentum to the opponents of racial equality. Appealing to those weary of protest, Richard Nixon rode the backlash into the White House. He campaigned against open housing and busing for racial balance. He promised to slow federal efforts at school integration and to appoint only conservative justices to the federal courts. Nixon particularly solicited the support of traditional Democratic voters disgruntled with the excesses of the black struggle. Many responded to the appeal. The Democratic nominee, Hubert Humphrey, long associated in the public mind with the civil-rights movement, won just one out of every three white votes. The ethnic working class that deserted Humphrey largely rallied to the banner of George Wallace, whose American Independent Party made the fear and resentment of blacks the central thrust of its campaign. "On November 5," Wallace had predicted, "they're going to find out there are a lot of rednecks in this country." He was right. Despite all the difficulties of mounting an independent run for the Presidency, Wallace amassed 9.9 million votes, just under 14 percent of the turnout. The anti-black crusader polled almost as many votes in the North as he did in the South in this best showing of a third-party candidate since 1924.

Immediately after entering the White House, President Nixon began wooing the Wallace constituency to insure his reelection in 1972. He deliberately pursued a "Southern strategy," conceding the votes of blacks and those committed to liberalism and going after those of white Southerners, suburbanites, and ethnic workers troubled by the specter of racial equality. Rather than follow the course counseled by his domestic advisor, the sociologist Daniel Patrick Moynihan, to behave with "benign neglect" on the race issue, the President intentionally focused public attention on the matter, and in a manner hardly benign to blacks.

The Nixon Administration took every opportunity to exploit the emotions of race. It urged Congress to impose a moratorium on court-ordered school busing, nominated conservative "strict constructionists" to the Supreme Court, and pleaded before the high tribunal for a postponement in the desegregation of Mississippi's schools. It lobbied in Congress to defeat the fair-housing enforcement program and the extension of the Voting Rights Act of 1965. While Vice-President Spiro Agnew played on the racial anxieties of Americans with his rhetoric, Nixon emasculated the Offices for Civil Rights in the Justice and Health, Education and Welfare Departments. To outflank Wallace, the President vetoed bills and impounded funds designed to assist blacks, and he fired government officials who sought to implement integration guidelines. In dismay, the chairmen of the Equal Employment Opportunity Commission and the United States Commission on Civil Rights resigned in protest, as did the head of the Small Business Administration's program for minorities. The president of the NAACP lamented: "For the first time since Woodrow Wilson we have a national administration that can rightly be characterized as anti-Negro." But Nixon had accurately gauged the national mood. In a resounding victory, the President swept every state save Massachusetts and the largely black District of Columbia in his 1972 reelection.

The continued deterioration of the public perception of the black struggle contributed immeasurably in President Nixon's success. During his years in office the media highlighted the activities of only the most vengeful blacks. The residue of flickering TV images of armed black students seizing college buildings, of Black Panther shoot-outs with police and the FBI, of the Revolutionary Action Movement conspiring to murder Roy Wilkins and Whitney Young, and of bank robberies and kidnappings by the Symbionese Liberation Army diminished the already nearly exhausted sympathy for the movement. With SNCC no longer in existence, CORE reduced to one of many impotent black nationalist sects, SCLC ripped apart by dissension among King's associates, and the NAACP confining itself once again almost exclusively to the courtroom struggle, Angela Davis and Eldridge Cleaver dominated the airwaves with their exaltation of violent revolution. Disgusted by the mayhem and invective, the vast majority of whites fully approved of Nixon's racial policies.

After Watergate, Gerald Ford appealed to the same backlash emotions as had his predecessor. With less rancor, President Ford maintained Nixon's budgetary freezes and rigorous opposition to school busing. He did nothing to implement the legislative agenda, "Priorities for the Future," submitted by the congressional black caucus, and welcomed the Democratic denunciation of him as "the most veto-prone Republican President in the twentieth century." Ford shelved virtually every bill Congress passed that would have assisted the black poor. The President, in addition, earned the rebuke of the U.S. Civil Rights Commission for accelerating the trend toward resegregation by his resistance to open housing and school desegregation.

Not surprisingly, an estimated 6.6 million blacks gave Jimmy Carter 94 percent of their vote in 1976. The former Governor of Georgia promised to alleviate the plight of the economically and socially disadvantaged, but his performance in office earned him the sobriquet "a second-hand Ford." Blacks were hardly recompensed for their massive support of President Carter. More black judges and more blacks were appointed to significant federal posts than in any previous Administration. And Carter did not seek to inflame racial antagonisms as had Nixon and Ford. But, like his immediate predecessors, the President never sought to make the perpetuation of racial inequality a central concern of Americans, and he proved as ready to beef up defense spending and balance the budget at the expense of school-lunch programs, financial assistance to black students, and health care for the poor as the Republicans had been. Carter would not expend his moral or political capital in the national debates raging over affirmative action and busing; and he selected as head of the Civil Rights Division of the Justice Department a man who hoped publicly that in the fight against segregation "the courts would not overreach." Blacks, moreover, became the chief victims of Carter's unsuccessful battles against inflation and recession. His economic failures resulted in the highest black jobless rate in over a decade, a deterioration of life for the black poor, and a weakening of the tenuous hold on middle-class status that a slim majority of blacks had recently achieved. "It is easy to see why many have concluded," Julian Bond commented, that "we voted for a man who knew the words to our hymns, but not the numbers on our paychecks."

Blacks faced a sorry choice in the 1980 Presidential election. Jimmy Carter asked for their support on the basis of his many black federal appointments, but avoided committing his Administration to alleviating the economic plight of depressed blacks or to pressing for an end to residential or school segregation. The Independent candidacy of John Anderson barely acknowledged the afflictions of Afro-Americans. And the Republican nominee, their old nemesis Ronald Reagan, made clear his continued opposition to busing to achieve racial integration in the schools, to affirmative action, and to the varied government programs designed to aid the poor and the unemployed. The vast majority of blacks voted Democratic, although in fewer numbers and with less unanimity than in 1976. But more than two out of every three white voters opted for the GOP alternative. Again, blacks faced a new Administration hostile to the needs of millions of the jobless and the impoverished, and a threat to the hopes of millions of middle-class blacks who looked to the White House for assistance in their quest for full inclusion in the American mainstream.

Nor could blacks look confidently to the Supreme Court any longer. The Court had boldly declared in 1969 that every school district was obligated to end dual school systems "at once" and "now and hereafter" to operate only unitary desegregated schools. It followed that with a decision in 1971 which granted broad authority to the district courts to order the desegregation of school systems by busing if necessary. But then the Nixon appointees to the high court signaled a halt, abandoning the familiar yellow school bus as a vehicle of racial reform. Because the suburbs had not themselves caused Detroit's segregation, the Court stated in 1974, that they need not be part of the solution. A five-to-four majority held that the equal-protection clause required racial busing only within school districts and not interdistrict busing. The Supreme Court then further restricted busing in cases involving Pasadena in 1976, Dayton in 1977, and Atlanta in 1980. Despite the near universality of racial apartheid in the housing patterns of metropolitan America, with the consequence that more than a majority of black students in the nation's cities attended schools at least 90 percent black, the Supreme Court rejected busing as the means for integrating the schools and offered no alternative procedure for achieving desegregation, further depressing the hopes that *Brown* had initially raised.

An even more crushing blow to black expectations came from the Supreme Court's 1978 *Bakke* decision declaring unconstitutional the fixed admissions quota for racial minorities of the medical school at the University of California at Davis. Attracting sixty-one *amicus curiae* briefs, more than had ever before been submitted in the history of the Court, the issue of preferential, or compensatory, or affirmative action split the Supreme Court down the middle and resulted in a muddle of six different opinions totaling 154 pages. The single clear point that emerged was that a majority of Justices explicitly rejected the use of racial quotas as a means of overcoming the accumulated handicaps that past racism had imposed on blacks. The Court retreated a bit in subsequent rulings on racial quotas in 1979 and 1980, approving special help to minorities "narrowly tailored" to remedy proven discrimination. But the impact of *Bakke* reinforced the resurgent white opposition to "reverse discrimination" and weakened the commitment of private and public agencies to assist blacks in achieving equality by considering race in their policies. In 1965 President Johnson had stated: "You do not wipe away the scars of centuries by saying, now you are free to go where you want, do as you desire and choose the leaders you please. You do not take a person who, for years, has been hobbled by chains and liberate him, bring him up to the starting line of a race and then say, 'You are free to compete with all the others,' and still justly believe that you have been completely fair." Yet that is all that most whites in 1980 would permit. They still wished to avoid the responsibility defined by Johnson fifteen years earlier: "It is not enough just to open the gates of opportunity. All our citizens must have the ability to walk through those gates."

In a gloomy, troubled mood, Afro-Americans thus entered the next to last decade of the twentieth century. A quarter of a century after *Brown*, the United States remained a deeply divided and unequal society. The black struggle had brought significant changes. It achieved substantial progress. Black America in 1980 was radically different from what it had been in 1954. Yet the full promise of the civil-rights revolution was unrealized. Prejudice, discrimination, and segregation, both subtle and blatant, continued to poison social relations. Neither the franchise nor the demolition of legal racism had resulted in equality or justice. The ghetto was still a time bomb, its people social dynamite. Despite all that the movement had accomplished, the hardest and most paramount tasks lay ahead.

"Anyone looking for the civil-rights movement in the streets is fooling himself. Politics is the civil-rights movement of the 1970s," said the black mayor of Atlanta. "Politics is our first hurrah. It's where things are today." Indeed, the right to vote and the opportunity to hold public office has been one of the most visible changes in Afro-American life since *Brown*; more than a symbol of first-class citizenship, political participation has also produced important, tangible gains for blacks. Fewer than one in four adult blacks in the South could register to vote in 1954; over two-thirds were on the voting lists in 1970. Because of that turnabout, white officials found their traditional race-baiting rhetoric and practices no longer politically profitable. A onetime militant segregationist, Senator Strom Thurmond of South Carolina quickly realized the political wisdom of sending his child to a desegregated school. Even George Wallace saw the light. The former leader of Alabama's white supremacist forces appointed blacks to high state positions, crowned a black homecoming queen at the very university he had once sworn to deny to black students, and in 1979 sat on the podium applauding the inaugural remarks of Birmingham's first black mayor. By 1980, Mississippi, the state that had most violently and thoroughly resisted the civil-rights movement, claimed more black officeholders than any other state.

The number of black elected public officials in the South rose from fewer than a hundred in the year of the Voting Rights Act to some 500 in 1970, 1,600 in 1975, and nearly 2,500 in 1980. Equally impressive, the national total jumped from 300 in 1965, to 1,400 in 1970, 3,000 in 1975, and 4,700 in 1980. The number of black mayors of towns and cities leaped from none in 1965 to eighty in 1970 and to 120 in 1980, including Atlanta, Dayton, Gary, Detroit, Los Angeles, New Orleans, Newark, Richmond, and Washington, D.C. In the main, cities with black mayors spent more per capita for education and social services, and directed a higher proportion of their budgets toward the needs of the disadvantaged, than those headed by whites. Black mayors, overall, also did more than their white counterparts to establish affirmative-action programs in municipal agencies and to enforce a less biased, less brutal, law-enforcement system. The slightly over one thousand blacks who served on city councils and in the state legislatures in 1980 had a similarly incremental yet important effect on policies and priorities.

At the national level, blacks held eighteen seats in Congress in the late 1970s. They had held none between 1901 and 1928, only one in the following fifteen years, and just two between the end of the Second World War and *Brown*. In 1970, the congressional black caucus was established. Augmenting its presence were scores of blacks in sub-Cabinet-level leadership positions and in highly visible offices filled by the President. By the end of the decade, Carter had appointed two black Cabinet officers, two black ambassadors to the UN, a half dozen black ambassadors to foreign countries, a black Solicitor General, a black Secretary of the Army, a host of black United States attorneys and United States marshals, and numerous black justices to the federal district courts and the United States courts of appeals.

"You don't have to demonstrate when you can pick up a phone and call someone," claimed Andrew Young. Yet politics has not proved a panacea. It has not changed the basic inequalities between blacks and whites. Excessive black loyalty to one political party has been fatal. The Democrats take black votes for granted and do not adequately reward them. Yet, given the steady rightward drift of the Republicans, few blacks conceive the GOP to be a viable alternative. Blacks, moreover, remain on the fringe of national politics. Despite impressive gains, blacks held fewer than one percent of the nation's half a million elective offices in 1980, and just three percent of them in the South, where they constituted 20 percent of the population. Over half the hundred counties in the South with majority black populations still had no elected black officials. Whites in power there used all manner of subtle disenfranchising devices to sap black political strength.

Blacks, nationwide, participated in politics more infrequently than whites. Some explained this as a consequence of poverty; the poor, regardless of color, vote less than the middle and upper classes. Others thought it was due to black alienation from the political system. Still others considered it a legacy of past exclusion, when blacks became conditioned not to vote or join political organizations. Whatever the reasons, blacks in the 1970s engaged in less political activity than whites. Just one half of the 14 million blacks who could have voted bothered to register in 1972. Two years later, only a third of those eligible voted in the congressional elections. Barely 42 percent of voting-age blacks went to the polls in 1976, compared to a national turnout of 55 percent of eligible voters, and even fewer sought to exercise their franchise in 1980. Most important, black politics has not provided jobs for the jobless, adequate housing and health care for the poor, or quality integrated schooling. In Greene County, Alabama, where blacks control the entire political structure, the average black family income is about $2,500. Seventy percent of black homes in rural Alabama have no indoor flush toilet. Despite a black mayor and a phalanx of black officials, Newark in 1980 remains as spiritually and physically dilapidated as it was in 1967. Although the blacks in South Carolina constitute a quarter of the population—and are well represented politically—over half are in the most menial and lowest-paying jobs, and fewer than 5 percent are in managerial or professional positions. Atlanta and Detroit, with its official posts heavily black, have few jobs for their black youth and the highest unemployment rate for adult blacks in the country.

More black students attended segregated schools in 1980 than at the time of *Brown*. Only in the South has there been some progress. The passage of the Civil Rights Act of 1964 and the

Elementary and Secondary Education Act of 1965, combined with an increasingly tougher stance by the federal courts and government officials responsible for implementing desegregation guidelines, brought significant results below the Mason–Dixon line. The proportion of Southern blacks in desegregated schools rose from 2 percent in 1964 to 14 percent in 1966, 16 percent in 1967, 20 percent in 1968, and 58 percent in 1970. The following year, President Nixon warned federal officials to stop pressing for desegregation or find other jobs. Two years later, the Supreme Court began its about-face by barring the busing of Virginia schoolchildren across city-suburban lines. Resegregation commenced. White flight to the suburbs, tracking, segregated private academies, and segregated church schools resulted once again in fewer than half the black students in the South attending desegregated schools in 1980. Significantly, much of the South's integration is rural. In Southern cities, where the population is growing, the late 1970s witnessed rapidly decreasing desegregation. The urban South appeared more and more similar to its Northern counterpart, where over two-thirds of the blacks went to schools at least 90 percent black. The absence of any considerable move toward residential desegregation, the refusal of the courts to order busing to eliminate de facto segregation, and the rejection by virtually every white suburb of suggestions to redraw attendance zones across school districts in order to foster integration, insured the continuance of the trend toward greater racial isolation in education.

Striking changes did come in the educational levels of blacks. Although sometimes of questionable quality, black schooling has steadily increased in quantity since *Brown*. Then, about 75 percent of blacks aged five to nineteen were enrolled in school. Over 95 percent were in 1980. The median school years completed by blacks aged twenty-five to twenty-nine rose from 8.6 in 1954 (3.5 years fewer than whites), to 10.8 in 1960 (about 2.5 years fewer than whites), to 12.7 in 1972 (only .4 of one year less than whites). In 1980, about 75 percent of black students were finishing high school, compared to 85 percent for whites. Two decades earlier, only some 40 percent of young blacks finished high school. In addition, 20 percent of blacks aged eighteen to twenty-four enrolled in college in 1980, compared to 26 percent for whites. The percentage of black high-school graduates going to college (31.5 percent) had nearly caught up with that of whites (32.2 percent). In 1954, 75,000 blacks attended college; 234,000 did so in 1963; about a half million, 7 percent of the total college population, attended in 1970; and over a million blacks did so in 1977, constituting 10 percent of the total college enrollment. This substantial progress was due largely to the increased availability of financial aid, the growth of community colleges, and greater access to predominantly white universities. Where 82 percent of black college students in the South enrolled in all-black institutions in 1965, 43 percent did in 1976. Still, at the end of the 1970s, blacks lagged considerably behind whites in graduating from college and being awarded baccalaureate degrees. Nearly six of ten black college students went to two-year rather than four-year institutions of higher education in 1980.

Perhaps the least change of all since *Brown* came in residential segregation. Despite court rulings and legislation outlawing racial discrimination in housing, such discrimination persisted. The index of residential segregation rose in nearly every American city between 1960 and 1980. Whites of every class continued to resist housing integration if it involved anything other than token numbers of blacks. Twelve percent of the population, blacks in 1980 accounted for less than 6 percent of the suburban population, barely an increase of 2 percent in more than twenty years. And most black suburbanites lived in all-black suburbs, usually the older, run-down industrial suburbs deserted by whites. The majority of America's 25 million blacks in 1980 had been confined to the inner cities of a score of metropolitan areas, mainly Atlanta, Baltimore, Chicago, Cleveland, Detroit, Los Angeles, Newark, New Orleans, New York,

Philadelphia, St. Louis, and Washington, D.C., fulfilling the prophesy, and not heeding the warning, of the National Advisory Commission on Civil Disorders in 1968: "Our nation is moving toward two societies, one black, one white—separate and unequal."

Two unequal societies also developed within the black cities: a black middle class struggling to move upward or to maintain a tenuous grip on their precarious new status, and a sinking, permanent black underclass mired in poverty and despair. Those who justified a diminution of public and private efforts to end racial inequality overemphasized the extent of progress made by the black middle class and obscured the magnitude of the predicament of those left behind. They trumpeted the news of the absolute gains in the number of jobs for blacks, of the decline of the percentage of black families below the poverty line, and of the narrowing of the income gap between black and white workers, especially female wage earners. They made much of the proliferation of blacks in well-paying positions and in occupations never before open to them.

A far different picture, and a more accurate gauge of black economic progress, emerges from the statistics on median family income. In 1954, black families earned approximately 53 percent of what white families did. It gradually inched up to 60 percent in 1969, then to 62 percent in 1975. But it plummeted to 57 percent in 1979. Blacks had gained four percentage points in a quarter of a century. At that rate, racial equality in family income would come in 250 years. Median income in 1979 stood at $9,242 for black families and $16,740 for white families. Undeterred by this dismal prognosis, critics of plans for programs by the federal government to correct the imbalance argued the need to factor out of these all-inclusive national averages anomalies based on age, geography, and sex. They preferred to stress the fact that stable black families in the North earned incomes nearly equal to those of whites. That was true. But such families constituted a minority of black families, and a dwindling minority at that.

Blacks did earn less in the South, both absolutely and relative to whites, than in the North. In 1975, when the national median income for all black families was $8,779, 62 percent of that for whites, the same amount in the South was $7,696, 59 percent of that earned by Southern white families. But half the blacks in the country lived in the South in 1980, and that percentage is not slackening. "Freedomland" lost its luster in the 1970s, and for the first time in the twentieth century blacks reversed the pattern of migration from South to North. The Northern states experienced a net loss of 64,000 blacks between 1970 and 1975, and 104,000 between 1975 and 1977. Similarly, the black working population is proportionately younger than the white, and younger workers earn less than older ones, thus further depressing the overall median earning of blacks; and there is little likelihood of that trend changing in the near future. In 1970, the median age for white Americans was twenty-eight years and 21.2 for blacks, and the greater fertility rate for blacks in the seventies promises a still greater differential. Add to that the fact that lower family income necessitates more blacks entering the job market at an earlier age than whites, and the probability of blacks narrowing the income gap dims appreciably.

The dramatic increase in one-parent black families affected the relative economic decline of blacks more than any other factor. While the proportion of white families with more than one wage earner rose steadily in the seventies, the proportion of such black families decreased from 57 percent in 1969 to 46 percent in 1979. While the proportion of white families headed by a woman has hovered at about 10 percent since 1965, the comparable figures for blacks jumped from 23.7 percent that year to 34 percent in 1974, 37 percent in 1976, and 40 percent in 1980. A devastating half of all one-parent black families lived below the poverty line in 1978, compared to fewer than a third of such white families. Most important, nearly two-thirds of all black families living in poverty were headed by women, and the number of those families continues to soar, as does the number of children in such families. One in three blacks lived in poverty in 1980, compared to one in ten whites, and in all likelihood the number of black poor, both absolute and relative to whites, will mushroom in the decade ahead.

The prospects for the black middle class are less certain. Great gains had been made since the civil-rights movement began. Although a third of all blacks lived in poverty, and another 15 percent eked out a bare existence just above the official poverty line, a majority of black families in 1980 earned over $10,000, including nearly 13 percent with incomes over $25,000. But those blacks climbing the social ladder could slip easily. Many are heavily dependent on public-sector jobs, and government at all levels is being forced to retrench. Conservatism is in the saddle, driving hard to cut government spending and balance budgets. The rightward trend also threatens the continuation of affirmative-action programs responsible for the middle-class status of many blacks.

Overall, black improvement came because of an expanding economy. Black progress did not come at the expense of whites. The United States made a bigger economic pie, but it did not slice it differently than it had in previous decades. As the eighties began, however, the forecast was for years of scarcity, a dwindling of resources to be shared by yet more people. That did not bode well for blacks aspiring for more, or even aspiring to maintain past gains. By 1980, in fact, double-digit inflation and recession had already significantly eroded part of the moderate advancement made by blacks in the early 1970s. Blacks had good reason to be troubled as they faced the future.

What appeared most certain is that any future progress would require persistent organized struggle, as it had in the past. The attainment of civil rights by the movement resulted from the blacks themselves taking up the fight and making the ultimate commitment. A renewed battle would be needed to hold prior gains and to expand them so that the mass of blacks who have not yet shared the fruits of the struggle can do so someday. A Third Reconstruction, aiming for economic justice, is imperative if civil rights are to be meaningful to the poor and unemployed, to all those still in despair. Just as the First Reconstruction foundered on the failure of the federal government to establish a viable economic base for the freed slaves, so the Second did not result in equality because of the lack of a thorough economic transformation in the status of Afro-America. Despite the end of Jim Crow, the black struggle did not result in racial equality.

The mighty triumphs over legally enforced segregation and disenfranchisement proved the capacity of blacks to compel change. They augmented black self-respect, power, and understanding of what remains to be done. Because of the movement, blacks today are far closer to equality than they had been in 1954. As a consequence of the struggle, blacks are now in an immensely better position to launch a Third Reconstruction. However dark the moment seems, a new day will surely dawn. The struggle to complete the unfinished business of American democracy will endure until its fulfillment.

BIBLIOGRAPHICAL
ESSAY

The literature on the modern black struggle is voluminous, and mostly of an ephemeral nature. To date, few significant historical monographs analyze racial events since 1954. The student of history must, accordingly, make judicious use of journalistic and participants' accounts, and works by social scientists. What follows is a selective sample of the books, and a few indispensable articles, I found most helpful in preparing this volume. Many of the specialized studies include comprehensive bibliographies, and these need to be consulted for the full range of materials on a given subject.

For detailed overviews of the movement, see Thomas R. Brooks, *Walls Come Tumbling Down: A History of the Civil Rights Movement, 1940–1970* (1974); Anthony Lewis, *Portrait of a Decade: The Second American Revolution* (1964); and Benjamin Muse, *Ten Years of Prelude: The Story of Integration Since the Supreme Court's 1954 Decision* (1964) and *The American Negro Revolution: From Nonviolence to Black Power, 1963–1967* (1968). Howell Raines's *My Soul Is Rested: Movement Days in the Deep South*

Remembered (1977) is best for the words of those who participated in the struggle. Much vital information is also contained in Lerone Bennett, Jr., *Confrontation: Black and White* (1965); Robert H. Brisbane, *Black Activism: Racial Revolution in the United States, 1954–1970* (1974); Louis E. Lomax, *The Negro Revolt* (1962); and Edward Peeks, *The Long Struggle for Black Power* (1971).

Overall analyses of particular insight are Lerone Bennett, Jr., *The Negro Mood* (1965); Debbie Lewis, *And We Are Not Saved: A History of the Movement as People* (1970); and Pat Watters, *Down to Now: Reflections on the Southern Civil Rights Movement* (1971). Also useful: W. Heywood Burns, *The Voices of Negro Protest in America* (1963); Joseph S. Himes, *Racial Conflict in American Society* (1973); and James W. Vander Zanden, *Race Relations in Transition: The Segregation Crises within the South* (1965). Nat Hentoff's *The New Equality* (1964) and Charles E. Silberman's *Crisis in Black and White* (1964) brilliantly illuminate the difficulties of the struggle in Northern ghettos. Ruth P. Morgan's *The President and Civil Rights—Policy Making by Executive Order* (1970) and Allan Wolk's *The Presidency and Black Civil Rights: Eisenhower to Nixon* (1971) analyze executive decision-making. Important analytical articles are Kenneth B. Clark, "The Civil Rights Movement: Momentum and Organization," *Daedalus* XCV (Winter 1966); James A. Geschwender, "Social Structure and the Negro Revolt: An Examination of Some Hypotheses," *Social Forces* XLIII (Dec. 1964); and James H. Laue, "Power, Conflict and Social Change," in Louis Masotti and Don Bowen, eds., *Riots and Rebellion: Civil Violence in the Urban Community* (1968). The most helpful attitudinal studies are Angus Campbell, *White Attitudes toward Black People* (1971); Peter Goldman, *Report from Black America* (1970); Samuel Lubell, *White and Black: Test of a Nation* (1964); Richard Lemon, *The Troubled Americans* (1970); Gary Marx, *Protest and Prejudice: A Study of Belief in the Black Community* (rev. ed., 1969); and two compilations of poll data by William Brink and Louis Harris, *The Negro Revolution in America* (1964) and *Black and White* (1967).

The indispensable documents of the struggle can be found in Richard A. Bardolph, ed., *The Civil Rights Record: Black Americans and the Law, 1849–1970* (1970); Albert P. Blanstein and

Robert L. Zangrando, eds., *Civil Rights and the American Negro: A Documentary History* (1968); Leon Friedman, ed., *The Civil Rights Reader: Basic Documents of the Civil Rights Movement* (1967); Joanne Grant, ed., *Black Protest: History, Documents and Analyses, 1619 to the Present* (1968); August Meier, Elliott Rudwick, and Francis L. Broderick, eds., *Black Protest Thought in the Twentieth Century* (rev. ed., 1971); and Lester A. Sobel, ed., *Civil Rights, 1960–66* (1967).

The best collections of articles on the struggle are John H. Bracey, Jr., August Meier, and Elliott Rudwick, eds., *Conflict and Competition: Studies in the Recent Black Protest Movement* (1971); Kenneth B. Clark, ed., *The Negro Protest* (1963); John Hope Franklin and Isidore Starr, eds., *The Negro in Twentieth Century America: A Reader on the Struggle for Civil Rights* (1967); August Meier and Elliott Rudwick, eds., *Black Protest in the Sixties* (1970); and Alan F. Westin, ed., *Freedom Now! The Civil Rights Struggle in America* (1964). The two most useful journals are *Freedomways* and *New South,* a publication of the Southern Regional Council. Much can also be gleaned from *Race Relations Law Reporter* and *The Civil Rights Digest,* a quarterly of the U.S. Commission on Civil Rights.

Germinal developments leading to the emergence of the modern black struggle have been studied by numerous historians. For analyses focusing on three different decades, see Raymond Wolters, *The New Negro on Campus: Black College Rebellions of the 1920s* (1975); Harvard Sitkoff, *A New Deal for Blacks: The Emergence of Civil Rights as a National Issue,* Vol. I: *Depression Decade* (1978); and Richard M. Dalfiume, *Desegregation of the U.S. Armed Forces: Fighting on Two Fronts, 1939–1953* (1969). Civil-rights organizations in the second quarter of the twentieth century are the subject of Langston Hughes, *Fight for Freedom: The Story of the NAACP* (1962); Herbert Garfinkel, *When Negroes March: The March on Washington Movement in the Organizations's Politics for FEPC* (1959); Louis C. Kesselman, *The Social Politics of FEPC: A Study in Reform Movements* (1948); Thomas A. Krueger, *And Promises to Keep: The Southern Conference for Human Welfare, 1938–1948* (1968); B. Joyce Ross, *J. E. Spingarn and the Rise of the N.A.A.C.P.* (1972); and Nancy Weiss, *The National Urban*

League, 1910–1940 (1974). Charles Abrams, *Forbidden Neighbors* (1955); E. Franklin Frazier, *Black Bourgeoisie: The Rise of a New Middle Class in the United States* (1957); Eli Ginzberg, *The Negro Potential* (1956); Spencer Logan, *A Negro's Faith in America* (1946); and Ray Sprigle, *In the Land of Jim Crow* (1949) reveal much about black attitudes and problems at mid-century.

No civil-rights topic has been more written about than the school-desegregation decision. In a class by itself, Richard Kluger's *Simple Justice: The History of Brown v. Board of Education: Black America's Struggle for Equality* (1976) is magisterial. Not to be over-looked are Daniel M. Berman, *It Is So Ordered: The Supreme Court Rules on School Segregation* (1966); Albert P. Blaustein and Clarence C. Ferguson, Jr., *Desegregation and the Law: The Meaning and Effect of the School Segregation Cases* (rev. ed., 1962); and Robert V. Harris, *The Quest for Equality: The Constitution, Congress and the Supreme Court* (1960). For a dissenting view, see Lino S. Graglia, *Disaster by Decree: The Supreme Court Decision on Race and the Schools* (1976). NAACP strategy is treated in Randall W. Bland, *Private Pressure and Public Law: The Legal Career of Justice Thurgood Marshall* (1973), and Jack Greenberg, *Race Relations and American Law* (1959).

Post-*Brown* developments are the subject of Numan V. Bartley, *The Rise of Massive Resistance: Race and Politics in the South During the 1950's* (1969); Earl Black, *Southern Governors and Civil Rights: Racial Segregation as a Campaign Issue in the Second Reconstruction* (1976); Neil R. McMillen, *The Citizens' Council: Organized Resistance to the Second Reconstruction, 1954–64* (1971); and Francis M. Wilhoit, *The Politics of Massive Resistance* (1973). Contemporary conservative opposition to the Court is expressed in Tom Brady, *Black Monday* (1955); James J. Kilpatrick, *The Southern Case for School Segregation* (1962); and William D. Workman, *The Case for the South* (1960). Liberal rejoinders are Harry Ashmore, *The Negro and the Schools* (1954) and *Epitaph for Dixie* (1958), and John B. Martin, *The Deep South Says "Never"* (1957). Additional information on Little Rock is in Virgil T. Blossom, *It Has Happened Here* (1959); Brooks Hays, *A Southern Moderate Speaks* (1959); and Wilson and Jane C. Record, eds., *Little Rock U.S.A.: Materials for Analysis* (1960).

The politics of civil rights during the Eisenhower years is covered by J. W. Anderson, *Eisenhower, Brownell and the Congress: The Tangled Origins of the Civil Rights Bill of 1956–1957* (1964); Daniel M. Berman, *A Bill Becomes a Law: The Civil Rights Act of 1960* (1962); and Foster Rhea Dulles, *The Civil Rights Commission: 1957–1965* (1968). Excellent analyses of this Administration and the two subsequent ones are Steven F. Lawson, *Black Ballots: Voting Rights in the South, 1944–1969* (1976), and James L. Sundquist, *Politics and Policy: The Eisenhower, Kennedy, and Johnson Years* (1968). A negative "insider" account is E. Frederic Morrow's *Black Man in the White House* (1963).

Numerous biographies of King, treating his major campaigns, have been published. The one with the greatest insight is David Lewis, *King: A Critical Biography* (1970). Also of value are Lerone Bennett, Jr., *What Manner of Man* (rev. ed., 1968); William Robert Miller, *Martin Luther King, Jr.* (1968); and Lawrence D. Reddick, Jr., *Crusader Without Violence* (1959). August Meier's "On the Role of Martin Luther King," *New Politics* IV (Winter 1965), is particularly enlightening. Further details on the bus boycott are provided by Martin Luther King, Jr., *Stride Toward Freedom* (1958). Also see Preston Valien, "The Montgomery Bus Protest as a Social Movement," in Jitsuichi Masouka and Preston Valien, eds., *Race Relations: Problems and Theory* (1961). Unfortunately, no adequate history of the Southern Christian Leadership Conference has yet been published.

The Student Non-Violent Coordinating Committee is the subject of several penetrating analyses, especially Howard Zinn, *SNCC: The New Abolitionists* (1964); Jack Newfield, *A Prophetic Minority* (1966); Cleveland Sellers, *River of No Return: The Autobiography of a Black Militant and the Life and Death of SNCC* (1973); and Clayborne Carson, *In Struggle: A History of SNCC* (forthcoming from Harvard University Press). William H. Chafe's *Civilities and Civil Rights: Greensboro, North Carolina and the Black Struggle for Freedom* (1980) is the best case study of a sit-in and description of the evolving nature of the movement in a single city. Also see Merrill Proudfoot, *Diary of a Sit-in* (1962); Jack L. Walker, *Sit-ins in Atlanta: A Study in the Negro Revolt* (1964); and Donald R. Matthews and James W. Prothro, *Negroes and the New Southern*

Politics (1966), particularly chapter 14. Of special value are J. Allen Williams, "Negro College Students Participation in Sit-ins," *Social Forces* XL (March 1962), and Emily Stoper, "The Student Non-violent Coordinating Committee: Rise and Fall of a Redemptive Organization," *Journal of Black Studies* VIII (Sept. 1977).

The history of the Congress of Racial Equality is comprehensively and judiciously treated by August Meier and Elliott Rudwick, *CORE: A Study in the Civil Rights Movement, 1942–1968* (1973). Also see Inge Powell Bell, *CORE and the Strategy of Nonviolence* (1968), and a case study of CORE in Chapel Hill, John Ehle, *The Free Men* (1965). Two personal views of the Freedom Rides are James Farmer, *Freedom—When?* (1965), and James Peck, *Freedom Ride* (1962). Indispensable for the voter-registration campaigns and the meaning of Albany are Pat Watters and Reese Cleghorn, *Climbing Jacob's Ladder: The Arrival of Negroes in Southern Politics* (1967), and Howard Zinn, *The Southern Mystique* (1964). Also essential for an understanding of the movement is Gerald McWorter and Robert Crain, "Subcommunity Gladiatorial Competition: Civil Rights Leadership as a Competitive Process," *Social Forces* XLVI (Sept. 1967); James W. Vander Zanden, "The Non-Violent Movement Against Segregation," *American Journal of Sociology* LXVIII (March 1963); and Archie E. Ellen, "John Lewis—Keeper of the Dream," *New South* XXVI (Spring 1971).

Events in Birmingham are described by Michael Dorman, *We Shall Overcome* (1964); Marshall Frady, *Wallace* (1970); Martin Luther King, Jr., *Why We Can't Wait* (1964); and Charles Morgan, Jr., *A Time to Speak* (1964). Vincent Harding's "A Beginning in Birmingham," *The Reporter* (June 6, 1963), and Bayard Rustin's "The Meaning of Birmingham," *Liberation* VIII (June 1963), are perceptive statements by advisors to King. President Kennedy's response to the black struggle is favorably evaluated in Carl M. Brauer, *John F. Kennedy and the Second Reconstruction* (1977). More critical is Victor S. Navasky, *Kennedy Justice* (1971). Also see James C. Harvey, *Civil Rights during the Kennedy Administration* (1971) and Doris E. Saunders, ed., *The Kennedy Years and the Negro* (1964). On the March on Washington, see Anna Arnold Hedgeman, *The Trumpet Sounds: A Memoir of Negro Leadership* (1964), chapter 9, and the photographic survey by Doris E.

Saunders, *The Day They Marched* (1963). Clifford M. Lytle's "The History of the Civil Rights Bill of 1964," *Journal of Negro History* LI (Oct. 1966), records the legislative battle.

Participants in the struggle in Mississippi best convey the critical events of 1964. See Sally Belfrage, *Freedom Summer* (1965); Len Holt, *The Summer That Didn't End* (1968); Ann Moody, *Coming of Age in Mississippi* (1968); Tracy Sugerman, *Stranger at the Gates* (1966); Elizabeth Sutherland, ed., *Letters from Mississippi* (1965); and Nicholas Von Hoffman, *Mississippi Notebook* (1964). Further analysis is provided by Paul Good, *The Trouble I've Seen* (1975), and William McCord, *Mississippi: The Long Hot Summer* (1965). William Bradford Huie's *Three Lives for Mississippi* (1965) graphically depicts the murder of the civil-rights workers. Also see Walter Lord, *The Past That Would Not Die* (1965); James Meredith, *Three Years in Mississippi* (1966); and Frank Smith, *Congressmen from Mississippi* (1964). James Silver's *Mississippi: The Closed Society* (1964) is uniquely compelling.

The Selma campaign is analyzed in David J. Garrow, *Protest at Selma, Martin Luther King, Jr., and the Voting Rights Act of 1965* (1978). Conflicting interpretations are presented by James G. Clark, Jr., *The Jim Clark Story—"I Saw Selma Raped"* (1966), and Charles E. Fager, *Selma 1965* (1974). The President's view is best stated in Lyndon B. Johnson, *The Vantage Point: Perspectives of The Presidency, 1963–1969* (1971). Further documentary and statistical material can be found in James C. Harvey, *Black Civil Rights during the Johnson Administration* (1973). The consequences of the laws passed in the Johnson years are described by Frances R. Cousens, *Public Civil Rights Agencies and Fair Employment: Promise vs. Performance* (1969); William R. Keech, *The Impact of Negro Voting: The Role of the Vote in the Quest for Equality* (1968); Gary Orfield, *The Reconstruction of Southern Education: The Schools and the 1964 Civil Rights Act* (1969); Harrell R. Rodgers and Charles S. Bullock III, *Law and Social Change: Civil Rights Laws and Their Consequences* (1972); and Frederick W. Wirt, *Politics of Southern Equality: Law and Change in a Mississippi County* (1970).

The transformation and demise of the movement is best told by Vincent Harding, "Black Radicalism: The Road from Montgomery," in Alfred Young, ed., *Dissent: Explorations in the History of American Radicalism* (1968); John Herbers, *The Lost Priority: What Happened to the Civil Rights Movement in America* (1970); Allen J. Matusow, "From Civil Rights to Black Power: The Case of SNCC, 1960–1966," in Barton J. Bernstein and Matusow, eds., *Twentieth Century America: Recent Interpretations* (1969); and Pat Watters, *Down to Now, Reflections on the Southern Civil Rights Movement* (1971). C. Vann Woodward's "What Happened to the Civil Rights Movement?" *Harper's* CCXXIV (Jan. 1967), should be read in conjunction with *The Strange Career of Jim Crow* (rev. ed., 1966), chapter 5.

Most manifestations of racial violence in the 1960s were extensively reported and analyzed. The best studies of single riots are Robert Conot, *Rivers of Blood, Years of Darkness* (1968); Tom Hayden, *Rebellion in Newark: Official Violence and Ghetto Response* (1967); and John Hersey, *The Algiers Motel Incident* (1968). Joe R. Feagin and Harlan Hahn's *Ghetto Revolts: The Politics of Violence in American Cities* (1973) and Robert Fogelson's *Violence as Protest: A Study of Riots and Ghettos* (1971) are especially discerning. Martin Oppenheimer's *The Urban Guerilla* (1969) and Garry Wills's *The Second Civil War: Arming for Armageddon* (1968) are chilling speculations. The most useful anthologies are David Boesal and Peter H. Rossi, eds., *Cities under Siege: An Anatomy of the Ghetto Riots, 1964–1968* (1971); Robert H. Connery, ed., *Urban Riots: Violence and Social Change* (1968); and Louis H. Masotti and Don R. Bowen, eds., *Riots and Rebellion: Civil Violence in the Urban Community* (1968).

Also essential to an understanding of the riots are Kenneth B. Clark, *Dark Ghetto: Dilemmas of Social Power* (1965); Charles Grier and Price M. Cobbs, *Black Rage* (1968); James A. Geschwender, "Civil Rights Protest and Riots: A Disappearing Distinction," *Social Science Quarterly* XLIX (Dec. 1968); and T. M. Tomlinson, "Determinants of Black Politics: Riots and the Growth of Militancy," *Psychiatry* XXXIII (May 1970).

The starting point for understanding Black Power is Stokely Carmichael and Charles V. Hamilton, *Black Power: The Politics of Liberation in America* (1967). Two prominent interpretations are Julius Lester, *Look Out Whitey! Black Power's Gon' Get Your*

Mama (1968), and Nathan Wright, Jr., *Black Power and Urban Unrest* (1967). Its diversity is best sampled in Floyd Barbour, ed., *The Black Power Revolt* (1968), and LeRoi Jones and Larry Neal, eds., *Black Fire: An Anthology of Afro-American Writing* (1968). King's critique is stated in Martin Luther King, Jr., *Where Do We Go from Here: Chaos or Community* (1967). Perceptive explanations for the emergence of the slogan are contained in Thomas L. Blair, *Retreat to the Ghetto* (1977), and Lewis Killian, *The Impossible Revolution: Black Power and the American Dream* (1968). Also worth consulting are the views of Harold Cruse, *The Crisis of the Negro Intellectual* (1967) and *Rebellion or Revolution* (1968).

A personal account of radicalization within the movement is James Forman, *Sammy Younge, Jr.* (1968) and *The Making of Black Revolutionaries* (1972). H. Rap Brown's *Die Nigger Die* (1969); Stokely Carmichael's *Stokely Speaks* (1971); Eldridge Cleaver, *Soul on Ice* (1968); and Floyd McKissick's *Genocide USA: A Blueprint for Black Survival* (1967) express the changed mood. The influence of Malcolm X is the subject of Archie Epps, *Malcolm X and the American Negro Revolution* (1969). Also see George Breitman, ed., *Malcolm X Speaks* (1965); Peter Goldman, *The Death and Life of Malcolm X* (1973); and Malcolm X, with Alex Haley, *The Autobiography of Malcolm X* (1965). James Baldwin's *The Fire Next Time* (1963) is prophetic on the appeal of Malcolm X and the transformation of the black struggle.

Leon E. Panetta and Peter Gall's *Bring Us Together—The Nixon Team and the Civil Rights Retreat* (1971) pinpoints the direction of the politics of civil rights in the 1970s. Also see Milton D. Morris, *The Politics of Black America* (1975). Changing attitudes on the high court are explained in J. Harvie Wilkinson III, *From Brown to Bakke: The Supreme Court and School Integration, 1954–1978* (1979). Continuing instances of white racism are documented by Michael N. Danielson, *The Politics of Exclusion* (1976), and Orlando Patterson, *Ethnic Chauvinism: The Reactionary Impulse* (1977). Indispensable for understanding the current status of blacks are Leonard Broom and Norval Glenn, *Transformation of the Negro American* (1965); Sar Levitan, William B. Johnson and Robert Taggart, *Still a Dream: The Changing Status of Blacks Since 1960* (1978); Mabel M. Smythe, ed., *The Black American Reference*

Book (1976); and William J. Wilson, *The Declining Significance of Race: Blacks and Changing American Institutions* (1978). Also see Reynolds Farley, "Trends in Racial Inequalities: Have the Gains of the 1960s Disappeared in the 1970s?" *American Sociological Review* XLII (April 1977), and Elliot Zashin, "The Progress of Black Americans in Civil Rights: The Past Two Decades Assessed," *Daedalus* CVII (Winter 1978).

INDEX